This is the first major study in English for over half a century of one of Portugal's most important historical figures, Sebastião José de Carvalho e Melo, marquês de Pombal (1699–1782), who is best known today as the key figure in the reconstruction of Lisbon after the devastating earthquake of 1755.

Pombal's achievements, however, went far beyond the reconstruction of the capital. An unusually single-minded and ruthless first minister, he was also one of the eighteenth century's most successful "enlightened despots": for example, he reformed the Portuguese system of education, expelled the Jesuits from Portugal, thereby beginning the process leading to their suppression by the pope in 1773, and mounted a formidable challenge to British commercial hegemony in Portugal.

Recent renewed interest in the theory of enlightened absolutism has tended to ignore developments in the Iberian peninsula. This book is therefore essential to a full understanding of the complexities and paradoxes of enlightened rulership in a southern European context.

KENNETH MAXWELL is a Senior Fellow at the Council on Foreign Relations, New York, and is the founder of the Camões Center at Columbia University. Educated at St John's College, Cambridge, and Princeton University, Professor Maxwell is a former member of the Institute for Advanced Study, Princeton, and an Honorary Fellow of the Romance Institute, University of London. His publications include *Conflicts and Conspiracies: Brazil and Portugal 1750–1808* (1973). His account of Portugal in the 1970s, *The Making of Portuguese Democracy*, is scheduled for publication in 1995.

This is the first major study in English for over half a century of one of Portugal's most important historical figures, Sebastião José de Carvalho e Melo, marquês de Pombal (1699–1782), who is best known today as the key figure in the reconstruction of Lisbon after the devastating earthquake of 1755.

Pombal's achievements, however, went far beyond the reconstruction of the capital. An unusually single-minded and ruthless first minister, he was also one of the eighteenth century's most successful "enlightened despots": for example, he reformed the Portuguese system of education, expelled the Jesuits from Portugal, beginning the process whereby the Jesuits were suppressed by the pope in 1773, and mounted a formidable challenge to British commercial hegemony in Portugal.

Recent renewed interest in the theory of enlightened absolutism has tended to ignore developments in the Iberian peninsula. This book is therefore essential to a full understanding of the complexities and paradoxes of enlightened rulership in a southern European context.

POMBAL, PARADOX OF THE ENLIGHTENMENT

Frontispiece
Sebastião José de Carvalho e Melo, marquês de Pombal.
Painting by Louis Michael Van Loo, 1766 (Câmara Municipal de Oeiras)

POMBAL

Paradox of the Enlightenment

Kenneth Maxwell

CAMBRIDGE
UNIVERSITY PRESS

Published by the Press Syndicate of the University of Cambridge
The Pitt Building, Trumpington Street, Cambridge CB2 1RP
40 West 20th Street, New York, NY 10011–4211, USA
10 Stamford Road, Oakleigh, Melbourne 3166, Australia

First published 1995

Printed in Great Britain at the University Press, Cambridge

A catalogue record for this book is available from the British Library

Library of Congress cataloguing in publication data
Maxwell, Kenneth, 1941–
Pombal, paradox of the Enlightenment / Kenneth Maxwell.
p.   cm.
Includes bibliographical references and index.
ISBN 0 521 45044 6
1. Pombal, Sebastião José de Carvalho e Melo, Marquês de,
1699–1782. 2. Portugal – Politics and government – 1750–1777.
3. Enlightenment. 4. Statesmen – Portugal – Biography. I. Title.
DP641.M39 1995
946.9'03'092 – dc20   [B]   94–10650   CIP

ISBN 0 521 45044 6 hardback

WD

To John Funt

Contents

Color plates

Text illustrations

A note on Portuguese orthography

In direct transcription I have preserved the original spellings and punctuation, hence scribal inconsistencies in footnotes of this type. Elsewhere, I have attempted to follow modern forms, i.e. Correia for Corrêa, Meneses for Menezes, Melo e Castro for Mello e Castro, though Portuguese and Brazilian sources often differ in their usage despite several international conventions to standardize usage between Portugal and Brazil.

Acknowledgements

I owe a great debt to Professor Sir Harry Hinsley, who at Cambridge first encouraged me to look south; to Professor Stanley J. Stein in whose memorable seminar on eighteenth-century Iberia at Princeton I first tried to deal with Pombal in a systematic manner; to the late Professor Felix Gilbert at the Institute for Advanced Study, who was a valued friend and mentor in all matters historical; to Professor Ragnhild Hatton of the London School of Economics who first persuaded me to write a book on Pombal; to Professor Jaime Reis of the New University of Lisbon, Dr. Hamish Scott of St. Andrews, Professor Angela Delaforce of the Anglo-Portuguese Foundation, and Dr. Robert Oresko of the Institute for Historical Research in London, who in different ways all put me back on track at critical moments.

Without the support, encouragement, and patience of the Gulbenkian Foundation of Lisbon, and in particular of Dr. José Blanco, little would have been accomplished. António Barreto, José Barreto, José Freire Antunes, Bernardo Futscher Pereira, and Rudy Bauss, all provided important assistance with sources; and Audrey McInerney and Allison C. de Cerreño, with their enviable skills with computers, helped in the preparation of the final manuscript. William Davies, with his own deep affection and knowledge of Portugal, encouraged me to return to Cambridge University Press with *Pombal*, where I am delighted to be. I am grateful to Dr. Blanco, to Dr. Simonetta Luz Afonso of the Portuguese National Institute of Museums and to the Institute's excellent national photographic archive, as well as to Jay Levinson of the National Gallery of Art in Washington, DC, for permission to use the illustrations contained in this book.

Abbreviations

AAP	*Anais da Academia Portuguesa da História*, Lisbon
ABNRJ	*Anais da Biblioteca Nacional*, Rio de Janeiro
ACC	*Anais do Congresso Comemorativo do Bicentenário da Transferência da Sede do Governo do Brasil da Cidade do Salvador para o Rio de Janeiro*, 3 vols., Instituto Histórico e Geográfico Brasileiro, Rio de Janeiro, 1967
AHN	Archivo Histórico Nacional, Madrid
AHR	*American Historical Review*
AHU	Arquivo Histórico Ultramarino, Lisbon
AMHN	*Anais do Museu Histórico Nacional*, Rio de Janeiro
AMI	*Anuário do Museu da Inconfidência*, Ouro Prêto, Minas Gerais
ANRJ	Arquivo Nacional, Rio de Janeiro
ANTT	Arquivo Nacional da Torre do Tombo, Lisbon
APM	Arquivo Público Mineiro, Belo Horizonte, Minas Gerais
BEP	*Bulletin des Etudes Portugaises*
BL	British Library, London
BMP	Biblioteca Municipal do Porto [Oporto]
BNL	Biblioteca Nacional, Lisbon, fundo geral
BNLCP	Biblioteca Nacional, Lisbon, Pombal Collection
CCANRJ	Mathias, Herculano Gomes, *A coleção da casa dos contos de Ouro Prêto*, Arquivo Nacional, Rio de Janeiro, 1966
CCBNRJ	Casa dos Contos Collection, Biblioteca Nacional, Rio de Janeiro
CHLA	*The Cambridge History of Latin America*, 8 vols., ed. Leslie Bethell, Cambridge, 1984–1994
Correspondência inédita	Marcos Carneiro de Mendonça, *A Amazônia na era pombalina. Correspondência inédita do Governador e Capitão-General do estado do Grão-Pará e Maranhão, Francisco Xavier de Mendonça Furtado 1751–1759*, Instituto

	Histórico e Geográfico Brasileiro, 3 vols., Rio de Janeiro, 1963
DH	*Documentos históricos*, Biblioteca Nacional, Rio de Janeiro, 1928–
DISP	*Documentos interessantes para a história e costumes de S. Paulo*, São Paulo
EcHR	*Economic History Review*
EHR	*English Historical Review*
HAHR	*Hispanic American Historical Review*
IHGB	Instituto Histórico e Geográfico Brasileiro, Arquivo, Rio de Janeiro
IHGB/AUC	The Arquivo Ultramarino collection of transcripts in the Instituto Histórico e Geográfico Brasileiro
JAPS	*Journal of the American Portuguese Society*
JSH	*Journal of Social History*
MHPB	Col. Inácio Accioli de Cerqueira e Silva, *Memórias históricas e políticas da província da Bahia*, 6 vols., annotated by Brás do Amaral, Bahia, 1940
Min Just	Ministry of Justice
PRO	Public Record Office London (FO = Foreign Office, BT = Board of Trade, SP = State Papers)
RAPM	*Revista do Arquivo Público Mineiro*
RHDI/M de P	*Revista de história das ideias: o marquês de Pombal e o seu tempo*, 2 vols., Coimbra, 1982
RHES	*Revista de História Económica e Social*, Lisbon
RHSP	*Revista de História* (São Paulo)
RIHGB	*Revista do Instituto Histórico e Geográfico Brasileiro*, Rio de Janeiro
TRHS	*Transactions of the Royal Historical Society*

I

Ideas and images

> . . . a little genius who has a mind to be a great one in a little country is a
> very uneasy animal.
>
> Sir Benjamin Keene (1745)

> The Pasha has obtained his objective, such are the ways of the world! It is
> the people who will suffer for it, and the tidings will go down to future
> generations who will admire the effects of his expansive ideas in everything
> that pertains to his own department, if he does not interfere in the others.
>
> Alexandre de Gusmão to Martinho Velho Oldemberg (1750)

Eighteenth-century Portugal is almost inseparable from the dominating figure of the
marquês de Pombal (1699–1782). To some Pombal, who to all intents and purposes
ruled Portugal between 1750 and 1777, is a great figure of enlightened absolutism,
comparable to Catherine II in Russia, Frederick II in Prussia and Joseph II in the
Austrian monarchy; to others he is no more than a half-baked philosopher and a
full-blown tyrant. Even before he took power, Pombal's contemporaries were divided
in their views about him. The political testament of Dom Luís da Cunha, one of
eighteenth-century Portugal's most eminent diplomats and political thinkers,
recommended Pombal for his "patient and speculative temperament."[1] Others were
not so complimentary. Sir Benjamin Keene, who had been the British envoy in
Lisbon from 1745 to 1749, wrote of him, "it is a poor Coimbran pate as ever I met
with, to be as stubborn, as dull, is the true asinine quality . . . I shall only say that a
little genius who has a mind to be a great one in a little country, is a very uneasy
animal."[2] One of Pombal's closest collaborators in the area of educational and

---

[1] "Maximas sobre a reforma . . . dirigidas ao . . . Sr. D. José . . . por D. Luís da Cunha . . . ," BNLCP,
codex 51, f. 178v. For a detailed discussion of the intellectual sources of Pombal's ideas, Francisco José
Calazans Falcon, *A época pombalina: política econômica e monarquia ilustrada* (São Paulo, 1982).

[2] Benjamin Keene to Abraham Castres, October 1745, in Sir Richard Lodge, ed. *The Private
Correspondence of Sir Benjamin Keene*, K.B. (Cambridge, 1933), p. 72. Keene had been in Lisbon from
1745 to 1749 before his appointment as envoy in Spain. Abraham Castres was (from 1746) British
consul in Lisbon. Both men died in 1757.

ecclesiastical reform, António Ribeiro dos Santos, during a period of self-criticism following Pombal's demise, summarized the paradox of Pombal's authoritarianism and his enlightenment as follows: "[Pombal] wanted to civilize the nation and at the same time to enslave it. He wanted to spread the light of philosophical sciences and at the same time elevate the royal power of despotism."[3] This paradox, one not uncommon among the eighteenth-century European absolutists, but which finds perhaps its most extreme example in Portugal, is the theme of this book.[4]

Sebastião José de Carvalho e Melo, born in Lisbon, came from a family of modest gentry who had served as soldiers, priests, and state functionaries within Portugal and occasionally in Portugal's still extensive overseas empire. His father, Manuel de Carvalho e Ataíde (1668–1720), served in the navy and the army, and was appointed in 1708 to the prestigious position of officer of the court cavalry. His uncle, a priest, Paulo de Carvalho e Ataíde, was the proprietor of an entailed estate in Lisbon, comprising the property where Pombal was born and an estate in Oeiras, a small town overlooking the Tagus estuary close to Lisbon. He became a professor at the University of Coimbra and was later an archpriest of the Lisbon patriarchy. Pombal inherited the Lisbon house and the Oeiras property and it was at Oeiras, after his return from diplomatic service in Vienna in 1750, that he built an impressive country house, an elaborate pleasure garden and accumulated a vast landed estate with vineyard, mulberry bushes and extensive and expensive aqueducts.[5]

The powerful minister's ancestry was, therefore, neither as grand as his title might imply, nor as modest as his enemies claimed. In fact, Pombal's background was much like that of many of the ministers the absolutist monarchs chose to strengthen their power and enhance that of the state. His honors had been awarded late in life. He was granted the title of marquês de Pombal in 1769 when he was 71 years of age, and had been made count of Oeiras in 1759. Since he is known to history as Pombal this practice is followed here; but it is important to remember that this noble status was not that confirmed by inheritance but was obtained as a reward for service to the monarch and to the Portuguese state.

Pombal was the eldest of twelve children, four of whom died young. His youngest brother, José Joaquim, was killed in Portuguese India in combat while in military

[3] Cited by C. R. Boxer in *The Portuguese Seaborne Empire, 1415–1825* (Oxford, 1963), p. 191.
[4] See the stimulating discussion of the recent historiography of enlightened absolutism in Derek Beales, *Joseph II in the Shadow of Maria Theresa, 1741–1780* (Cambridge, 1987), pp. 1–16.
[5] Very little research has been done on the extraordinary estate Pombal accumulated at Oeiras which, together with the virtual reconstruction of the Oeiras Palace itself during his rule, also involved the development of a series of massive Baroque pleasure gardens and an agricultural and industrial estate with plantings of vineyards, mulberry bushes and associated aqueducts, fish ponds, and silk manufactories. Most of these buildings and rural properties were alienated in the twentieth century and fell into great disrepair. For a pioneering series of articles on this now largely destroyed eighteenth-century marvel, see José Meco, "O palácio e a quinta do marquês em Oeiras: algumas notas sobre a arte no tempo de Pombal," in *Pombal revisitado*, 2 vols. (Lisbon, 1983), II, pp. 158–171; and his "Azulejos pombalinos," in the catalogue *Exposição Lisboa e o marquês de Pombal*, 3 vols. (Lisbon: Museu da Cidade, 1982), III, pp. 49–66.

service and his sisters took religious orders.[6] Two of his brothers, Paulo de Carvalho e Mendonça (1702–1770) and Francisco Xavier de Mendonça Furtado (1700–1769), became very close collaborators in his administration, and a third brother, Frei Diogo de Carvalho, lived in Italy, where he taught philosophy at Ascoli Piceno.[7] Paulo de Carvalho, a priest, elevated to cardinal by Pope Clement XIV, became Inquisitor General and president of the municipal council of Lisbon (a position to which Pombal appointed his eldest son, Henrique, following the death of his brother). Mendonça Furtado served as governor and captain general of the Brazilian provinces of Grão Pará and Maranhão (an area which covered essentially, at the time, the vast Amazon river valley), and later in Lisbon he worked closely with Pombal as secretary of state for the overseas dominions. The family was a very close one. Neither Mendonça Furtado nor Paulo de Carvalho married and they pooled their financial resources and property in his interest. There is a remarkable ceiling portrait of the three with linked arms at the Oeiras mansion entitled *Concordia Fratrum* (color plate 1).

Following the death of his father, with the family facing severe financial difficulties, and dependent on his uncle, the archpriest, Pombal left the capital city and spent seven years managing the rural property belonging to his family in Gramela, north of the town of Pombal in central Portugal.[8] The cause for Pombal's rural exile is unclear, but in private correspondence with his children towards the end of his life he attributed it to a family squabble.[9] During this period (1723) he eloped with a widowed niece of the count of Arcos, Dona Teresa de Noronha e Bourbon Mendonça e Almada, an arrangement which related him to the high nobility, but his marriage was opposed by the Noronha family which did not consider the future marquês de Pombal a suitable match. It was a childless union, and following his wife's death Pombal married again (1746) while he was Portuguese envoy in Vienna. His second wife, by whom he had five children, was Maria Leonor Ernestina Daun (fig. 1). The Countess Daun was a niece of the Marschall Heinrich Richard Graf von Daun, a leading figure in the war of Austrian succession, and in the aftermath of the Seven Years War, as commander-in-chief of the Austrian monarchy's armed forces, was the minister of state responsible for a radical program of army reform. Pombal's second marriage also brought the personal blessing of the Empress Maria Theresa.[10] Maria Theresa in fact took a more than usual interest in the connection, telling Pombal's new wife in private

---

[6] For Pombal's family connections, see Joaquim Veríssimo Serrão, *O marquês de Pombal: o homem, o diplomata, e o estadista* (Lisbon, 1982). Also, the genealogical discussion by J. T. Montalvão Machado, *Quem livrou Pombal da pena de morte* (Lisbon: Academia Portuguesa da História, 1979), pp. 70, 390.

[7] José Barreto's introductory notes to Sebastião José de Carvalho e Melo, *Escritos económicos de Londres (1741–1742): seleção, leitura, introdução e notas de José Barreto* (Lisbon: Biblioteca Nacional, 1986), p. lxvii, n. 65.

[8] Ercília Pinto, *O marquês de Pombal: lavrador e autodidacta em Souré* (Coimbra, 1967), pp. 12, 29, 34.

[9] See discussion by Joaquim Veríssimo Serrão, *O marquês de Pombal*, pp. 18–19. Also, Marcus Cheke, *Dictator of Portugal: A Life of the Marquis of Pombal* (London, 1938), pp. 18–19, and João Lúcio d'Azevedo, *O marquês de Pombal e a sua época*, 2nd edition (Lisbon, 1922), p. 61.

[10] On Daun, see Derek Beales, *Joseph II*, II, pp. 92, 140, 163–184.

correspondence that she "owed the preservation of the monarchy" to the Daun family.[11] Pombal's marriage was also well received in Lisbon by the Austrian wife of Dom João V (1707–1750), Maria Anna of Austria. The Portuguese envoy in Rome sourly observed that it was the marriage to the Countess Daun which guaranteed Pombal a position as secretary of state in Lisbon. It was Maria Anna of Austria, in fact, the queen regent of Portugal during the final illness of her husband, who recalled Pombal from Vienna in 1749 to join the ministry in Lisbon. Pombal was 50 years of age at the time.[12] His preeminence and power were to coincide exactly with the reign of Dom José I (1750–1777), a monarch who preferred the opera and hunting to government. Following the Lisbon earthquake of 1755, he placed virtually complete authority in his minister's hands.

Pombal's considerable diplomatic experience had come about through the intervention of his relatives. On his return to Lisbon from his self-imposed exile in Gramela his uncle, the archpriest, had arranged a position with the new Academia Real da História Portuguesa and also presented his nephew to João da Mota e Silva, the Cardinal da Mota, who was Dom João V's *de facto* prime minister. The Academy of Portuguese History had been established by Dom João V in 1720 with the intention of fortifying the dynastic and absolutist claims of the Bragança family. Pombal's role here was to some degree a rehabilitation for the Carvalho family since Pombal's father had fallen into disgrace over the falsification of his own progenitors. In 1738 Dom João V reorganized his government into a system of secretaries of state, and Marco António de Azevedo Coutinho, who had been ambassador to France (1721–1728) and to England (1735–1738), was recalled from London to fill the position of secretary of state for foreign affairs and war. Pombal and Azevedo Coutinho were cousins, although Pombal referred always to his distinguished relative as "uncle," and Azevedo Coutinho, in turn, sent Pombal to London to replace him.[13]

Thus, from 1739 until 1743 Pombal had represented the Portuguese king at the court of St. James. The period was crucial to the crystallization of expansionist and imperial ideas and mythology in Britain. These were critical years – the era of the War of Jenkins' Ear and Vernon's attack on Cartagena, the great bastion of Spanish strategic control over the trade routes from Spanish South America. For Pombal the threat the British posed to Portugal's vast and rich dominions in South America became a major preoccupation. The "envy of our Brazil so strong in British hearts," as he put it, "would eventually lead them to an attack on Portuguese

[11] Correspondence of Maria Theresa and the Countess of Oeiras, printed in the appendix to John Athelstone Smith, *The Marquis of Pombal*, 2 vols. (London, 1843) II, pp. 376–377.
[12] A. Castres, British consul in Lisbon, informing London of the sudden death of the secretary of state, Azevedo Coutinho, on May 25, 1750, reported that Pombal "was powerfully supported by the queen." See PRO SP 89/47, f. 109. Later, on August 3, 1750, Castres, writing to N. Aldword, claimed the Pombal promotion to the post of secretary of state was due to the influence of his Austrian wife and the queen's support. See PRO, SP 89/47, f. 145.
[13] Montalvão Machado, *Quem livrou Pombal*, pp. 72–73.

1 Maria Leonor Ernestina, countess of Daun, marquesa de Pombal. Painting by Pierre Jouffroy, 1770 (private collection, Évora)

America."[14] He was convinced the British had designs on the Rio de la Plata and believed a scheme was afoot in 1739 to set up a British colony in Uruguay financed by Jewish capital based on an idea of João da Costa.[15]

The British government in 1739, in fact, had proposed an Anglo-Portuguese convention which would have provided a naval squadron to help relieve the siege of Colônia do Sacramento, a Portuguese outpost on the northern side of the Rio de la Plata estuary, but on the condition that British merchant vessels and warships be given free access to Brazilian ports as long as war with Spain continued. This the Portuguese would not accept and Pombal saw this proposed convention as linked to the scheme of João da Costa. Dom Luís da Cunha, who commented on Pombal's dispatches, observed that the Spanish who had established Montevideo as a counterweight to Colônia were preferable to the possibility of a British colony in Uruguay: "neighbor for neighbor," he wrote, "the less powerful the least bad."[16]

Pombal was offended by the casual way in which the British took the Anglo-Portuguese relationship for granted. He became convinced it was essential to understand the origins of Britain's commercial and military superiority and of Portugal's economic and political weakness and military dependency. Pombal's sponsors in Portugal during the reign of Dom João V had been deeply involved in discussions over theories of government and strategies for economic development. Cardinal da Mota, for example, had patronized the establishment of the Royal Silk Factory of the Rato in Lisbon in the 1730s.[17] In justifying this intervention by the state, the cardinal had identified in some detail one of the central problems facing the old regimes in Europe, that is, the choice between the state's long-term interest in mercantilist development and its short-term interest as tax gatherer. The more immediate necessity to finance the operations of the government almost always risked in da Mota's view the more important questions of encouraging and sustaining economic development.[18]

In London, Pombal, who moved in the circle of the Royal Society, set out to investigate the causes, techniques and mechanisms of British commercial and naval power. In the process he succeeded in obtaining a remarkably sophisticated and detailed appreciation of the British position.[19] The books he accumulated in his London library (mainly French editions since he did not master English) included such classic mercantilist texts as those of Thomas Mun, William Petty, Charles Davenant,

---

14 "Ofício . . . [Carvalho e Melo]" London July 8, 1741, *RIHGB* IV, 2nd edition (Rio de Janeiro, 1863), pp. 504–514; Richard Koebner, *Empire*, 2nd edition (New York, 1961), p. 82; Vincent T. Harlow, *The Founding of the Second British Empire 1763–1793*, 2 vols. (London, 1952, 1964) II, pp. 626–630; and the classic study by Richard Pares, *War and Trade in the West Indies 1739–1763* (London, 1936).

15 See David Francis, *Portugal, 1715–1808* (London, 1985), pp. 90–91. Also, Calazans Falcon, *A época pombalina*, p. 289.

16 See excellent discussion of the affair by José Barreto in his introductory notes, in Sebastião José de Carvalho e Melo, *Escritos económicos*, pp. xvii, xviii, xix, and lxvi.

17 See discussion by Calazans Falcon, *A época pombalina*, pp. 234–239.

18 See Jorge Borges de Macedo, "O pensamento económico do Cardinal da Mota," *Revista da Faculdade de Letras de Lisboa*, 3rd series, no. 4 (Lisbon, 1960).

19 For Pombal in London also see David Francis, *Portugal, 1715–1808*, p. 89.

Charles King, Joshua Gee, and Joshua Child; select reports on colonies, trade, mines, woolen manufactories; specialized tracts on sugar, tobacco, fisheries; parliamentary acts on tonnage and poundage; shipping and navigation; fraud in customs houses; the book of rates; ordinances of the British marine; and, above all, a heavy concentration of works on the British trading companies.[20] Pombal wrote in 1742 that "all the nations of Europe are today augmenting themselves by reciprocal imitation, each carefully watching over the actions of the others."[21] Such careful watching was his "most interesting duty in London," he told Cardinal da Mota.[22] He used his extensive reading to formulate his famous critical account of the unfair advantages the British enjoyed in Lisbon and Oporto, advantages for which, Pombal claimed, Portuguese merchants in Britain had gained no reciprocal privileges.[23] Pombal also concluded that the commercial advantages to Britain arose not only from the "pernicious transfer of gold" to pay for manufactured goods but also from the almost total remittance of commercial profits as well as the interest earned on commercial credit, freight charges, insurance, arising not only from the reciprocal commerce but also on a large part of Portuguese colonial trade.[24] He also believed it essential that the state become active in attracting skilled foreigners to Portugal who could assist the Portuguese in obtaining the commercial skills they lacked and that private Portuguese capitalists be encouraged to invest in commercial companies engaged in the colonial trade, where the state guaranteed exclusive privileges and assistance from the royal treasury.[25]

The affairs of the Portuguese territories in India were also a major preoccupation during Pombal's London posting. The Marathas had seized the island of Salsete and Goa was under siege. Pombal had sought the assistance of the government in London, but the East India Company had opposed any assistance to the Portuguese and were not averse to the idea of the total expulsion of the Portuguese from their remaining enclaves in India. Eventually, Dom João V sent a Portuguese squadron though it arrived too late to prevent the loss of Salsete and other Portuguese outposts in the Bombay region. Pombal's younger brother, José Joaquim de Carvalho, was killed at this time (1740) in the defense of Goa; "a brother I raised and who I loved also as a son," was how the envoy described his reaction to Marco António de Azevedo Coutinho.[26]

He also, with a Mr. Cleland, proposed to Lisbon the idea of establishing an East India Company on the English model.[27] John Cleland, who later became notorious as the author of *Fanny Hill* or *Memoirs of a Woman of Pleasure* (1748–1749), had spent

[20] Based on the catalogue of Pombal's books in London, BNLCP codices 165, 167, 342, 343.
[21] Cited by J. Lúcio d'Azevedo, *O marquês de Pombal*, p. 40.
[22] Cited by Marcus Cheke, *Dictator of Portugal*, p. 33.
[23] For an excellent collection of Pombal's writings from this period, see Sebastião José de Carvalho e Melo, *Escritos económicos*. Also analyzed by Calazans Falcon, *A época pombalina*, pp. 286–289.
[24] See introduction and notes by José Barreto in Sebastião José de Carvalho e Melo, *Escritos económicos*, pp. lii, liv, lxxii.
[25] Ibid., p. 41.
[26] Ibid., pp. lii, liv, lxxii.
[27] Calazans Falcon, *A época pombalina*, pp. 290–291.

many years in Bombay and was a high official of the East India Company. He had
offered the Portuguese detailed intelligence on the plans and operations of the
company.[28] This plan for a Portuguese East India company was blocked by Pombal's
enemies in Lisbon, but once Pombal had been sent to Vienna a similar scheme was
put forward by the circle around Alexandre de Gusmão. Pombal believed his
appointment to central Europe had been intended to keep him away from
commercial questions and his thankless engagement in the affairs of the Austrian papal
mediation had been deliberately intended to saddle him with a task which could well
ruin his reputation.[29]

In fact, Pombal's Austrian posting provided him with a critical boost to his career.
He arrived in Vienna via London in 1745. His activity in the Austrian capital met with
considerable success despite his complaints. In Vienna, the Portuguese envoy's "skill,
uprightness, amiability, and especially his great patience" won the praise of all at court,
according to the French minister.[30] In terms of contacts in Vienna, Pombal also found
a well-placed ally when he became the very intimate friend of Manuel Teles da Silva,
a Portuguese émigré of aristocratic lineage who had risen high within the Austrian
state. Manuel Teles da Silva had as a boy absconded from Portugal on a merchant
vessel together with Prince Manuel, Dom João V's brother. Reaching The Hague,
where the count of Tarouca, Manuel Teles da Silva's father, was Portuguese
ambassador, the young men had refused to be dissuaded from their adventures and
continued on to Vienna where Prince Manuel had joined Prince Eugene in his
Turkish campaigns. The prince stayed on in Austria some twenty years, only
returning to Portugal in 1735.[31] Manuel Teles da Silva remained in Austria for the rest
of his life. He had been created Duke Silva-Tarouca by Austrian Emperor Charles VI
in 1732 and he served in the high position of president of the council of the
Netherlands and of Italy and was a confidant of Empress Maria Theresa. He served as
a principal sponsor at the marriage of Pombal to the Countess Daun in 1746.[32] "For
eight years Your Excellency observed with a vision more secure than that of corporal
eyes the constitution of Great Britain, of her forces and accidental riches," Duke
Silva-Tarouca wrote to Pombal in 1757, "and for another period of five years in
Vienna of Austria Your Excellency with equal judgement and perspicacity observed
the non-accidental riches and forces of these most fertile states."[33]

---

[28] William H. Epstein, *John Cleland, Images of a Life* (New York, 1974).
[29] Barreto, in introduction to Sebastião José de Carvalho e Melo, *Escritos económicos*, pp. xii, xiii, lxiv.
[30] Smith, *Pombal*, part I, pp. 55–56.
[31] Francis, *Portugal, 1715–1808*, pp. 14–15.
[32] "Certidão de casamento de Sebastião José de Carvalho e Melo," Vienna, June 3, 1748, BNLCP, codex
640, fos. 20–23.
[33] [Silva-Tarouca] to [Pombal], Schönbrunn, July 25, 1757, "Correspondência entre o duque Manuel
Teles da Silva e Sebastião José de Carvalho e Melo," edited by Carlos da Silva Tarouca, S.J., *AAP*, 2nd
series, 6 (1955), p. 379. This remarkable private correspondence between Pombal and a close friend
and admirer provided a very intimate view of his thinking during the first decade of his preeminence.
For a discussion of Maria Theresa's use of public servants of diverse backgrounds, see Beales, *Joseph II*
I, p. 55.

The importance of Pombal's Austrian connections in his reforms has been insufficiently appreciated. The impact was clearest, of course, in the relationship with Silva-Tarouca. But the influence of the Austrian sojourn is shown even in domestic architecture. Pombal's palace at Oeiras (fig. 2), with its Germanic double-hipped roof, was influenced by the Hungarian Carlos Mardel, who collaborated with Pombal in the rebuilding of Lisbon. The extensive remodeling and expansion of the mansion dates from 1750 following Pombal's return from Vienna, and bears a striking resemblance to Duke Silva-Tarouca's country estate in Moravia (color plate III). Silva-Tarouca had been superintendent of the architectural remodeling of the summer palace of the Habsburgs at Schönbrunn.[34] As can be seen from the visiting book of the Portuguese mission to Vienna, which has survived, Pombal received a very wide range of visitors while he was Portuguese envoy to Maria Theresa's court, including the great reformer and Roman Catholic Dutchman, Gerhard van Swieten, who was his personal doctor as well as being that of the empress and her family.[35] Maria Theresa's measures to reform the censorship system and the University of Vienna, both directed against the virtual monopoly of the Jesuits, were begun under the aegis of van Swieten. In Vienna Pombal had also been in contact with the enlightened Portuguese "New Christian" physician, António Nunes Ribeiro Sanches. (The "New Christians" were the descendants of Portuguese Jews compelled to embrace Christianity in 1497 rather than face expulsion.) Van Swieten and Ribeiro Sanches were friends and correspondents, both having worked under the great Dutch doctor Boerhaave.[36]

Following the death of Dom João V in late July 1750, news of Pombal's ascendancy in the government reached Vienna that September. Duke Silva-Tarouca wrote at once to Lisbon. "We are not slaves of fashion and foreign practices," he told his old friend, "we conserve unalterably the names and external practices and national establishments, but still less are we slaves of ancient habits and preoccupations. If there is puerility in fashions, there is a folly in the obstinacy of old ways." He recalled their "intimate conversations" and recommended that "when great new dispositions are necessary they should always be put forward by ancient names and in ancient clothing."[37] "Great new dispositions" Pombal clearly had in mind, and Duke Silva-Tarouca's recommendation of the need for subterfuge is in many ways a succinct description of the methods Pombal was to make his own. It was a policy of reform, disguised, when prudence dictated, by traditional institutions and language.

---

[34] See Ludwig Scheidl, "Breves apontamentos sobre as reformas públicas na Austria no período da missão diplomática de Sebastião José Carvalho e Melo em Viena (1744–1749)," *RHDI/M de P*, I, p. 22.

[35] Beales, *Joseph II*, I, p. 44. For the visitors see Maria Alcina R. C. Afonso dos Santos, "A vida pública de Sebastião José de Carvalho e Melo em Viena de Austria (1744–1749)," *RHDI/M de P* I, pp. 29–39, especially pp. 36–37. Also Robert C. Smith, *The Art of Portugal* (New York, 1968) pp. 104–106.

[36] See David Willemse, "António Ribeiro Sanches, élève de Boerhaave et son importance pour la Russie," *Janus: Revue internationale de l'histoire des sciences* . . . VI (Leiden, 1966).

[37] [Silva-Tarouca] to [Pombal], Vienna, September 25, 1750, *AAP*, pp. 277–422, citations from pp. 313–315.

Thus, Pombal entered office with much diplomatic experience and a well formulated set of ideas and circle of friends and acquaintances which included some of the leading figures in the sciences, especially among the community of Portuguese expatriates, many of whom had been forced to leave Portugal because of the Inquisition. Pombal's preoccupations also reflected those of a generation of Portuguese officials and diplomats who had given much thought to imperial organization and the mercantilist techniques which they believed had brought about the startling and growing power and wealth of France and Great Britain and built on two distinct but interrelated aspects of the intellectual environment in eighteenth-century Portugal.[38] First, there was the immediate background of intense debate over fundamental questions concerning philosophy and education. Second, there was a considerable body of thought about various aspects of Portugal's political economy and the old conundrum which had presented Portugal's rulers since the fourteenth century with a particularly cruel dilemma: the need to protect its national interests in the face of military challenges from land-based enemies, yet at the same time always being faced by the need to contain the commercial challenges of maritime allies whose support rarely came cost free.

As elsewhere in Europe, the stimulus to new thinking in Portugal was provided by the intellectual achievements of Descartes, Newton, and Locke who, during the seventeenth century, promoted a bold break with the tradition of authority, whether biblical or Aristotelian, and promoted the merits of reason, experience, and utility. Newton, using the powers of reason, the data provided by observation, and the mathematical system of his invention (calculus), charted the basic laws governing motion both on earth and in space. Newtonian physics created a confidence in the potentialities of research and reason. Locke sought to demonstrate that the functioning of human nature also could be explained and, therefore, improved. Descartes' contribution was to insist that ideas must be analyzed without preconceptions, and be free of dependence or guidance by accepted authority.[39]

The most important works to emerge from this intellectual school in Portugal included those of Martinho de Mendonça de Pina e Proença (1693–1743), who attempted to adapt to Portugal some of Locke's theories; the writings of the "new Christian" Dr. Jacob de Castro Sarmento (1692–1762), who introduced Newtonian ideas in Portugal, and the works of Dr. António Nunes Ribeiro Sanches (1699–1783), also a "New Christian" and Pombal's acquaintance from Vienna.

Martinho de Mendonça de Pina e Proença (1693–1743) had traveled extensively in Europe, meeting Christian Wolff in Saxony and W. 's Gravesande in Holland, studying with them the ideas of Leibniz and Newton. He had, like Pombal, been an

---

[38] Manuel Nunes Dias, "Fomento ultramarino e mercantilismo: a Companhia Geral do Grão Pará e Maranhão 1755–1778," *RHSP* 66 (São Paulo, April–June 1966), p. 426; Moses Bensabat Amzalak, *Do estudo e da evolução das doutrinas económicas em Portugal* (Lisbon, 1928), pp. 88–98; [Teles da Silva] to [Pombal], Vienna, November 3, 1755, *AAP*, pp. 346–348.

[39] For an excellent discussion of popular and published literature available at mid-century in Portugal, see António Alberto Banha de Andrade, *Vernei e a cultura do seu tempo* (Coimbra, 1966), pp. 119–125.

2 The palace of the marquês de Pombal, Oeiras, viewed from the garden side

associate of the Academia Real da História Portuguesa and later served as acting governor of Minas Gerais in Brazil and the mining district of Cuiabá in the far west.[40] Proença also served as librarian to the royal library and custodian of the national archives. He was the author of *Apontamentos para a educação de um menino nobre* (1734) which was much influenced by John Locke, as well as Fénelon and Rollin. Proença recommended that teachers should instil not only Latin but geography, history, mathematics, and public law. Ribeiro Sanches had developed plans for the reform of medical teaching in Portugal as early as 1730. He had left Portugal in 1726 to escape the Inquisition, working thereafter in England, Holland, Russia, and finally in France, where, from 1747 until his death in 1783, he was a collaborator of the encyclopedists, and wrote on medicine, pedagogy, and economics.[41] Ribeiro Sanches also wrote on educational reform in his *Cartas sobre a educação da mocidade* (Paris, 1759).[42] Castro Sarmento sought to develop relationships between the Royal Academy of History in Lisbon and the Royal Society in London. While Pombal was away in London, he had intervened to protect Castro Sarmento from the British revenue authorities (Castro

[40] Francis, *Portugal, 1715–1808*, p. 83. For activities of Castro Sarmento and Ribeiro Sanches in London, see *The Portuguese Jewish Community in London (1656–1830)* (London, 1992), pp. 10–11.
[41] Rómulo de Carvalho, *A física experimental em Portugal no século XVIII* (Lisbon, 1982).
[42] See discussion by Banha de Andrade, *Contributos*, pp. 654–656.

Sarmento dedicated a work to Pombal published in London in 1742).[43] Castro Sarmento began the translation of Francis Bacon's *Novum Organon* and wanted to see a botanical garden established at the University of Coimbra. He had dedicated his *Cronologia Newtoniana epitomizada* (1737), the translation of a historical essay by Newton written for the instruction of the prince of Wales, to Prince Dom José, future king of Portugal. His *Matéria médica-física-histórica-mecánica, Reino Mineral* (London, 1735) was dedicated to Marco António de Azevedo Coutinho, Pombal's uncle. Castro Sarmento also translated Newton's theory on tides under the title *Teórica verdadeira das marés conforme à filosofia do incomparável cavalheiro Isaac Newton* (London, 1737). These works comprised the "first serious attempt," according to Professor Banha de Andrade, "to implant practical studies in place of abstract theories," in Portugal.[44]

Most influential of all in this process of pedagogical innovation was the Oratorian, Luís António Vernei (1713–1792), the author of *O verdadeiro método de estudar* (The True Method of Education), first published in Naples in 1746.[45] *O verdadeiro método de estudar* was an eclectic manual in logic, a method of grammar, a book about orthography, and treatise in metaphysics and dozens of letters on all types of subject. Luís António Vernei, born in Lisbon of a French father and Portuguese mother, lived most of his adult life in Italy (he arrived in Rome in 1736), where he was a friend of the leading Italian encyclopedist, Ludovico Antonio Muratori (1672–1750), and was a member of the Roman Arcadia.[46] Vernei served for a time as secretary to the Portuguese envoy to the Vatican, Francisco de Almada e Mendonça, who was Pombal's cousin. Paraphrasing Newton, Vernei wrote that "philosophy is to know things by their causes, or to know the true cause of things."[47] Vernei believed grammar should be taught in Portuguese, not Latin, and he was a staunch partisan of experimental methods, and opposed to a system of argumentation based on authority.

The most immediate consequence of this philosophical debate in Portugal was to call into question the influence of the Society of Jesus. This was because the Jesuits held a near-monopoly of higher education and were, in the view of their opponents, the principal upholders of a dead and sterile scholastic tradition, ill suited to the age of reason. The Jesuits were, in fact, much less closed to modern ideas than their enemies claimed. The inventory of the books from the University of Évora contained the works of Bento Feijo, Descartes, Locke, and Wolff. The College of Jesuits at Coim-

[43] See José Barreto's notes in *Escritos económicos*, p. lxvii.

[44] Banha de Andrade, *Vernei*, pp. 126–127.

[45] See Joaquim de Carvalho, *Jacob de Castro Sarmento et l'introduction des conceptions de Newton au Portugal* (Lisbon, 1935).

[46] For Muratori see Beales, *Joseph II*, p. 47, especially note; Franco Venturi, *Settecento riformatore*, I, *Da Muratori a Beccaria (1730–1764)* (Turin, 1969).

[47] For a brief introduction see A. A. Banha de Andrade, *Vernei e a projecção da sua obra*, which contains in an appendix extracts from Vernei's correspondence with Muratori (Lisbon, 1980). Also valuable is the broad overview by J. S. da Silva Dias, "Portugal e a cultura européia, séculos XVI a XVIII," *Biblio* 28 (1953) and Calazans Falcon, *A época pombalina*, pp. 208–210.

bra listed Vernei's *Verdadeiro método*.[48] In Portugal the Jesuits held the exclusive right to teach Latin and philosophy at the College of Arts, the obligatory preparatory school for entrance into the faculties of theology, canon law, civil law, and medicine at the University of Coimbra. The only other university in Portugal, at Évora, was a Jesuit institution. In Brazil the Jesuit *colégios* were the principal sources of secondary education. And in what remained of Portugal's empire in Asia the Jesuits had been a dominating force from the early years of Portuguese expansion in the Orient.

As elsewhere in Europe, however, much substantive discussion took place in private debating or philosophical societies. One major circle of critics of the status quo in Portugal had, since the turn of the century, centered around the Ericeiras, a family made famous by the third count, Dom Luís de Meneses (1632–1690), a proponent of mercantilist development and Colbertian economic policies in Portugal during the late seventeenth century. Dom Francisco Xavier de Meneses, fourth count of Ericeira (1674–1743), maintained close contact with scientists outside Portugal. In fact, he was responsible for the communications between Dom João V and Dr. Sarmento which led to the consultation with Sarmento over the reform of medical studies at Coimbra.[49] Ericeira had been nominated a member of the Royal Society of London in 1738. Writing to Dom Luís da Cunha in 1741 he said: "as a new member of the Academy of London I abjure Cartesianism for Newtonianism" and confessed he read widely in "Mr. Voltaire."[50] Several short-lived conclaves of individuals, organized to discuss scientific and philosophical questions, had developed under the Ericeiras' protection. One of them, the Academia dos Ilustrados, met during 1717 at the Lisbon house of Pombal's uncle.[51] The fourth count of Ericeira was one of the most distinguished members of the Academia dos Ilustrados, and a director of the Academia Real da História Portuguesa, founded in 1720. He had sponsored Pombal's election to the Academy on October 24, 1733. Pombal was the author of a eulogy of the fifth count of Ericeira, which appears to have been first published in London.[52]

Priests also played an important role in the introduction of new ideas. Unlike northern Europe, where proponents of "modern" rationalistic philosophy and scientific experimentation became harsh critics of the church and religion, in Portugal some of the most outspoken advocates (as well as practitioners) of educational reform came from within the religious establishment. The activity of the Oratorians, who arrived in Portugal after the restoration of independence in 1640 and to which Vernei belonged, was notable. The congregation of the Saint Felipe de Néri, a

---

[48] "Inventário dos livros que se acharam em a livraria grande do colégio desta cidade de Évora," ANTT, Min Just, M22; ANTT, "Registro das ordens ministerio do reino," vol. 417, files 76 and 52 v; Min Just M22; "Orden régio de sequestro inventário," 19.1, 1759, ANTT, Min Just bundle 20, ANTT, Min Just bundle 17.

[49] Banha de Andrade, *Vernei*, pp. 136–139.

[50] Ibid., p. 139.

[51] Rómulo de Carvalho, *A física experimental em Portugal*, p. 64.

[52] "Declaração que fez o conde da Ericeira sendo director da Academia Real da História Portugueza na conferencia de 24 de outubro de 1733," BNL, fundo geral no. 875.

society of secular priests, had taken the lead in Portugal, as they had elsewhere in Catholic Europe, in the introduction of scientific experimentation. They were leading opponents of the Jesuits in the debate over pedagogical models. The Oratorians were strong promoters of the natural sciences, introducing the ideas of Francis Bacon, Descartes, Gassendi, Locke, and Antonio Genovesi in Portugal. They also stressed the importance of the Portuguese language, grammar, and orthography, which they believed should be studied directly and not via Latin.[53] Their library at the Necessidades convent contained over 30,000 volumes and a small experimental laboratory with a collection of scientific instruments for their course on physics. Members of the royal family occasionally attended sessions of this course of study and Pombal was to send his two sons, Henrique José (b. 1748) and José Francisco (b. 1753), to study with the Oratorians at the Necessidades.[54] The Chevalier des Courtils, who visited the convent of Necessidades in 1755, found

a prodigious quantity of books in all languages and very rare manuscripts, mathematical instruments, and a telescope. The oratorians are of all the monks of the kingdom the most amiable and the most wise . . . these good fathers almost all speak French.[55]

Vernei was an Oratorian of course and his *Verdadeiro método* produced a furious polemic conducted mainly between the Oratorians and the Jesuits. Between its publication and 1757 over forty books appeared in response to Vernei. The dispute with the Jesuits was aggravated by the fact that the Jesuit scholars discerned a large dose of Jansenism in Vernei's arguments, especially his positions over the papacy and the jurisdiction of the Roman Catholic Church.[56]

In addition to the philosophical debate which was characteristic of Catholic Europe in this period, there existed an important current of thinking specific to Portugal. This was a body of ideas and discussion about governance, economy, and diplomacy, which emerged in the first half of the eighteenth century among a small but influential group of Portugal's overseas representatives and government ministers. Sometimes members of this group were pejoratively called the "foreignizers" (*estrangeirados*) because of their supposed infatuation with foreign models.[57] Yet their preoccupations were in fact intimately a product of a Portuguese milieu. Dom Luís da Cunha, successively Portuguese ambassador to England, the Dutch Republic, Spain and France, and Portuguese representative at the Peace Congresses of Utrecht and Cambrai, was the

---

[53] Dom João V had granted the convent of Nossa Senhora das Necessidades to the Oratorians in 1744 with the obligation to conduct classes in Christian doctrine, rhetoric and grammar, moral philosophy, and theology. See Manuel H. Côrte-Real, *O palácio das Necessidades* (Lisbon: Ministério dos Negócios Estrangeiros, 1983), pp. 14–19.

[54] Banha de Andrade, *Contributos*, p. 421; also, the discussion by Tarcisio Beal, "Os jesuítas, a universidade de Coimbra e a igreja brasileira: subsídios para a história do regalismo no Brasil, 1750–1850" (unpublished Ph.D. dissertation, Catholic University of America, 1969), pp. 7–8.

[55] "Extraits du journal de la campagne des vaisseaux du roy en 1755 par le Chevalier des Courtils," *BEP* 26 (1965), p. 18.

[56] Banha de Andrada, *Vernei*, pp. 233–334.

[57] See J. Borges de Macedo for discussion of *estrangeirados*, in *Dicionário de história de Portugal*, ed. Joel Serrão, 6 vols. (Lisbon, 1979) II, pp. 466–473.

3 Dom Luís da Cunha (Biblioteca Nacional, Lisbon)

most formidable of these thinkers and author of a comprehensive analysis of Portugal's weaknesses and the means to remedy them (fig. 3).

These discussions, unlike the disputations of the philosophers and pedagogues, in the main took place in private and were built on the longer tradition of Portuguese economic and diplomatic thinking that had emerged from the experience in the decades following the reestablishment of Portugal's independence from Spain in 1640. Less concerned with the specific impact of the discovery of Brazilian gold on Portugal, this debate focused on the broader parameters of Portugal's location in the international system, and confronted directly both the constraints and the options with which a small country like Portugal, part of Iberia but independent of Spain, had to live. Central to these discussions was the problem of retaining and exploiting the considerable overseas assets that Portugal controlled in Asia, Africa, and America and developing a mechanism to challenge British economic domination without weakening the political and military alliance which was needed to contain Spain.

Dom Luís da Cunha's sophisticated critique of Portugal's international relations and social and mental condition was contained both in his "instructions" for Pombal's uncle and sponsor, Marco António de Azevedo Coutinho (1738), and in his political testament (1748).[58] Dom Luís da Cunha placed Portugal's problems in the context of its relationship with Spain, its dependence on and economic exploitation by Britain, and on what he believed were Portugal's self-inflicted weaknesses in terms of lack of population and spirit of enterprise. This sad mental and economic condition he attributed to the excess number of priests, the activity of the Inquisition, and the expulsion and persecution of the Jews. The Treaty of Methuen (1703) had been, in his view, an arrangement beneficial only to Britain. He praised Ericeira's short-lived attempt to introduce manufacturing industry in Portugal during the late seventeenth century. He proposed the creation of monopolistic commercial companies on the Dutch and British models. As to the purpose and impact of these commercial enterprises he had no illusions. "There is no doubt," he wrote, "that such companies are at base no more than monopolies defended by the state, because they take from the people the liberty to engage in certain commercial activities. But states should take such action when they see that although such intervention prejudices some subjects, in other areas it produces a greater utility."[59]

So acute had Portugal's reliance on Brazil become during the early eighteenth century that Dom Luís da Cunha foresaw the eventual transfer of the Portuguese court to Rio de Janeiro. The king would take the title "Emperor of the West" and appoint a viceroy to rule in Lisbon. In his 1738 "instructions" for Marco António de Azevedo Coutinho, Dom Luís da Cunha envisioned a Portuguese empire in America extending from the Rio de la Plata and Paraguay to north of the Amazon estuary. "It is safer and more convenient to be where one has everything in abundance," he wrote, "than where one has to wait for what one wants."[60] Pombal, who also demonstrated a special concern for Brazil's importance and potential, believed that the state had a central role in promoting economic well-being and drew models from his interpretation of the experience of the more developed European countries. The diminished European stature of the Iberian nations in the eighteenth century together with their continuing role as overlords of vast overseas territories, generated among both Spanish and Portuguese statesmen of Pombal's generation the acute consciousness that

---

[58] For an excellent discussion of Dom Luís da Cunha's ideas, see Calazans Falcon, *A época pombalina*, pp. 247–258.

[59] Academia das Ciências de Lisboa, *Instrucções inéditas de D. Luís da Cunha a Marco António de Azevedo Coutinho*, ed. Pedro de Azevedo with a preface by António Baião (Coimbra, 1929), pp. 139, 211, 214, 215.

[60] Cited also by C. R. Boxer, *The Golden Age of Brazil 1695–1750* (Berkeley and Los Angeles, 1962), pp. 323–324.

governmental efficiency and imperial consolidation were essential if either country was to regain its influence and power in an increasingly competitive and jealous world.

Despite these intellectual stirrings, however, the country Pombal was to rule for almost three decades had a sorry image in the rest of Europe at mid-century. The eighteenth-century rationalist writer who needed a stereotype of superstition and backwardness almost invariably turned to Portugal. Voltaire summed up the attitude well. Writing about the gold-rich Portuguese monarch Dom João V, he observed: "When he wanted a festival, he ordered a religious parade. When he wanted a new building, he built a convent, when he wanted a mistress, he took a nun."[61] There was, of course, a kernel of truth in these prejudices. Dom João V had long affairs with several nuns (fig. 4). The king had several children by Mother Paula (Teresa da Silva), including Dom José, who became the Inquisitor General. Another son, Dom António, was born of a French woman, and Dom Gaspar, who became bishop of Braga, was son of the king by Dona Magdalena de Miranda, a lady-in-waiting at the court. These three sons the king acknowledged.[62] It is also a fact that Dom João V did indeed spend vast sums of Brazilian gold to build his great palace monastery at Mafra (fig. 5). And in 1750 Portugal, with a population of less than 3 million people, had a veritable army of clergy, numbering 200,000 according to some estimates.[63] The number of convents and monasteries had reached 538 by 1780.[64] Charles Boxer called eighteenth-century Portugal "more priest ridden than any other country in the world with the possible exception of Tibet."[65] It is also true that the Portuguese burned people at the stake in public ceremonies as late as 1761. The torture and public destruction in 1759 of members of two of Portugal's most distinguished families, accused of attempting to assassinate King Dom José I in the infamous Távora case particularly shocked foreigners – although their consternation, it should be noted, was caused less by the torture and breaking of limbs and burning than by the fact that the victims were aristocrats, not commoners, nor the Jews and heretics for whom such treatment had been commonplace in the Iberian peninsula for centuries (fig. 6).

The contrast between the views of foreigners and the image of the eighteenth century within Portugal, however, is striking. The period, especially after the 1750s, is seen in Portugal as being the very embodiment of the Enlightenment. Among the developments singled out is the legislative activity which left few aspects of Portuguese life untouched. This included the establishment of the first system of public state-supported education, the root and branch reform of the University of Coimbra, the

---

[61] Cited by Susan Schneider in *O marquês de Pombal e o vinho do Porto; dependência e subdesenvolvimento em Portugal no século XVIII* (Lisbon, 1980), p. 8.
[62] Francis, *Portugal, 1715–1808*, p. 20.
[63] See Carl A. Hansen, "D. Luís da Cunha and Portuguese Mercantilist Thought," *JAPS* 15 (1981), pp. 15–23. Also, Hansen's excellent book, *Economy and Society in Baroque Portugal 1668–1703* (Minneapolis: University of Minnesota Press, 1981).
[64] Fortunato de Almeida, *História da igreja em Portugal*, 4 vols. (Coimbra, 1910–1922) III, pp. 521–522.
[65] Boxer, *The Portuguese Seaborne Empire*, p. 189.

4 Dom João V, from a contemporary portrait

reduction of the Inquisition's power, the abolition of slavery in Portugal (but not in the colonies), and the modernization of the army. A royal treasury with centralized accounting systems and uniform fiscal powers was established and its first head was designated, following British practice, the king's chief minister. Above all, the reconstruction of Lisbon after the devastating earthquake of 1755 is held up as a model

5 The palace-convent at Mafra, from a photograph of 1892 (Arquivo Nacional de Fotografia)

of Enlightenment town planning. In the colonies, Brazil most especially, the reform of the whole administrative structure can be claimed – the creation of joint stock companies, the outlawing of discrimination against Amerindians in Portuguese America and Asians in Portuguese India, and the ending of the distinction between so-called "Old" and "New Christians." Portuguese historians will agree that eighteenth-century Portugal was governed by an authoritarian and absolutist regime. It was, however, a regime inspired by an absolutism of reason, and its authoritarianism was essential to the process of reestablishing national control over the economy and revitalizing the state.[66]

There are several special reasons for the contrast of views from inside and outside, and it is well to enumerate some of them at the outset because it is important to be aware of what they are and how they originated.

One important cause of the partisan nature of the discussion about enlightened absolutism in Portugal was a result of Pombal's formidable promotion of state propaganda. The most striking example of this activity was the concerted assault on the Jesuits. The Pombaline administration stimulated and subsidized throughout Europe a virulent campaign against the order. Pombal himself was intimately involved in the writing and formulation of the remarkable piece of propaganda known as the *Dedução cronológica e analítica*. The "Chronological and Analytical Deduction" divided the history of Portugal between the useful and the disastrous, inversely linked to the rise of the influence of the Jesuits. It upheld a rigorous regalist view concerning the church in Portugal. Professor Samuel Miller describes the work, not unjustifiably, as

[66] See a good summary by J. Borges de Macedo in *Dicionário de história de Portugal*, v, pp. 113–121.

"a monotonous repetition of all the accusations ever leveled at the Jesuits by anyone at any time."[67]

The history of the assault by the Portuguese and Spanish crowns on the Jesuit missions along the Uruguay river in South America during the late 1750s was also encapsulated, and was, for many, defined by another piece of state-supported and financed propaganda, the *Relação abreviada*. Published in Portuguese, Italian, French, German, and English, the *Relação abreviada* was an account of the joint Portuguese and Spanish military campaign against the Jesuit missions in what is now the southern borderlands of Brazil. Some 20,000 copies are estimated to have been distributed.[68] It was a major weapon in the Europe-wide battle which led to the suppression of the Jesuits by Pope Clement XIV in 1773. The success of the Portuguese propaganda offensive had much to do with the receptivity Pombal's ideas found among other Catholic reformers in southern Europe. Bernard Tanucci, for example, the powerful minister of Charles of Bourbon, king of Naples (later Charles III of Spain) regretted the ferocity and pure *raison d'état* of Pombal, but approved his objectives.[69] As Franco Venturi has shown, Venice and Rome in particular specialized in printing and reprinting *cose del Portogallo*.[70] The *Relação abreviada* and the *Dedução cronológica e analítica*, therefore, represented an official historiography, which the Jesuits were and remain dedicated to the task of refuting. And if anyone should think that this struggle for historical memory is over, they need only read the comments in the Jesuit magazine *Brotéria* (Lisbon) published in 1982 to mark the bicentenary of Pombal's death. "Pombal's methods owed nothing to our own contemporaries," the lead article asserted. "His methods were in effect an anticipation and mixture of the methods of Goebbels and Stalin."[71]

A second area of public controversy, also involving surreptitious use of subsidized propaganda to influence public opinion, grew from the disputes between the Portuguese and the British over trade, the Port wine sector, and the Portuguese government's attempts to stimulate manufacturing in Portugal. Both sides had recourse to pamphleteering, industrial spying and even industrial sabotage.[72] This had a large impact on the image of Portugal in Britain, and by extension has influenced British historiography. The Anglo-Portuguese commercial relationship, it should also

---

[67] Samuel J. Miller, *Portugal and Rome c. 1748–1830: An Aspect of the Catholic Enlightenment* (Rome, 1978), p. 187; *Dedução cronológica e analítica . . . dada a luz pelo Doutor Joseph de Seabra da Silva . . . em Lisboa anno de 1767*, 3 vols., original manuscript with annotations and additions in handwriting of Pombal, BNLCP, codices 444–446. For discussion of the *Dedução cronológica*, see J. Lúcio d'Azevedo, *O marquês de Pombal*, pp. 290–291.

[68] First published in late 1756 and written mainly by Pombal, the full title is *Relação abreviada da república que os religiosos das províncias de Portugal e Espanha estabeleceram nos domínios ultramarinos das duas monarquias e da guerra que neles tem movido e sustentado contra os exércitos espanhóis e portugueses* (1758), Biblioteca Nacional, Lisbon, Reservados 4.394.

[69] Miller, *Portugal and Rome*, p. 53.

[70] Franco Venturi, *Settecento riformatore: la chiesa a la republica dentro i loro limiti (1758–1774)* (Turin, 1976) II, pp. 3–29.

[71] *Brotéria, no bicentenário do marquês de Pombal* no. 115 (2 vols.) II, p. 127.

[72] Calazans Falcon, *A época pombalina*, pp. 296–297.

6 *Auto da fé* in the Terreiro do Paço. Engraving, *c.* 1741 (Biblioteca Nacional, Lisbon)

be remembered, was a touchstone in the arguments of the eighteenth-century economists, including David Ricardo and Adam Smith.[73]

A further cause of the fractured image of eighteenth-century Portugal was undoubtedly the impact of the Lisbon earthquake of 1755 (figs. 7 and 8), the literary and public reaction to which T. C. Kendrick devoted a whole volume some years ago.[74] The great earthquake of All Saints' Day 1755 reduced one of the richest and most opulent cities of the epoch to ashes and provoked an extraordinary philosophical debate about optimism, God, and natural phenomena (fig. 9).

The British consul Edward Hay, writing to London two weeks after the earthquake, provides a concise eye-witness account of the event.

The first shock began about a quarter before 10 o'clock in the morning, and as far as I could judge, lasted six or seven minutes, so that in a quarter of an hour, this great city was laid in ruins. Soon after, several fires broke out, which burned for five or six days. The force of the earthquake seemed to be immediately under the city . . . It is thought to have vented itself at

---

[73] H. E. S. Fisher, *The Portugal Trade* (London, 1971), p. 133.
[74] T. D. Kendrick, *The Lisbon Earthquake of 1755* (London, 1956).

7 The Lisbon earthquake

8 The Lisbon earthquake

9 The ruins of the Patriarchal church and square after the earthquake, from a colored etching by Jacques Philippe le Bas, 1757 (Museu da Cidade, Lisbon)

the quay which runs from the Customs House towards the king's palace, which is entirely carried away, and has totally disappeared [figs. 10 and 11]. At the time of the earthquake, the waters of the river rose twenty or thirty feet . . . [75]

About one third of the city was totally destroyed by the quake and flood (fig. 8).

Hay wrote on December 13:

the part of the town towards the water where was the Royal Palace, the public tribunals, the Customs House, India House, and where most of the merchants dealt for the convenience of transacting their business, is so totally destroyed by the earthquake and by the fire, that it is nothing but a heap of rubbish, in many places several stories high, incredible to those who are not eye-witnesses of it.[76]

---

[75] Cited in C. R. Boxer, *Some Contemporary Reactions to the Lisbon Earthquake of 1755* (Lisbon, 1956). Also, *The Lisbon Earthquake of 1755: British Accounts*, introduction, translation, and notes by Judith Nozel (Lisbon, 1990).

[76] Cited by Charles Boxer in "Pombal's Dictatorship and the Great Earthquake of 1755," *History Today* (1955).

Estimates of casualties ranged from 10,000 to 40,000 – at the time the latter estimate was widely believed, though the true figure was probably closer to 15,000. The royal family, who were at Belém, outside of the city, escaped what would have been certain death in their collapsed palace in Lisbon (figs. 10 and 11). The bewildered and frightened king placed full authority in the hands of his only minister who showed any capacity to deal with the catastrophe – Pombal.

The scope of the destruction was colossal. The Royal Opera House, completed only a month before, was in ruins. Of Lisbon's forty parish churches, thirty-five had collapsed, many onto parishioners who had been at mass when the earthquake struck, crushing them to death within the ruins. Only 3,000 of Lisbon's 20,000 houses were inhabitable. The palace of the Inquisition on the Rossio had crumbled (fig. 12) and many townhouses and palaces of the aristocracy were destroyed (fig. 13). At one mansion alone 200 paintings were lost, including a Titian and Rubens and a library of 18,000 books and 1,000 manuscripts; 70,000 books in the king's library perished. It was the earthquake that propelled Pombal to virtual absolute power which he was to retain for another twenty-two years until the king's death in 1777. He took quick, effective, and ruthless action to stabilize the situation. Looters were unceremoniously hanged, bodies of the earthquake victims were quickly gathered and with the permission of the Lisbon patriarch, taken out to sea, weighted and thrown into the ocean. Rents, food prices, and the cost of building materials were fixed at pre-earthquake levels. No temporary rebuilding was permitted until the land was cleared and plans for new construction drawn up (fig. 18).

Military engineers and surveyors, headed by General Manuel de Maia (1672–1768) (fig. 14), the 80-year-old chief engineer, Colonel Carlos Mardel (1695–1763), and Captain Eugénio dos Santos (1711–1760), were charged with making inventories of property rights and claims, and implementing the myriad of practical decisions to assure that sanitary and leveling operations were carried out safely. They were also charged with drawing up plans for the new city (fig. 15).[77]

It was these practical-minded engineer officers who, under the closest scrutiny from Pombal, developed the economical Pombaline architecture and grid of streets and the great waterfront square which make Lisbon to this day a classic example of eighteenth-century town planning (figs. 16–18). The waterfront area and the zone back from the river to the Rossio square were leveled and the grading of the steep western slopes reduced. The streets were fixed at 60 feet in width (50 for the roadway and 10 for the sidewalk), the street crossings were set at right angles, and the cross streets were 40 feet in width. To speed up the reconstruction and simultaneously encourage national enterprises, an innovative effort at pre-fabrication was promoted; ironwork, wood joints, tiles, ceramics, for instance, were all standardized, as was the overall design of the façades for the new buildings (figs. 15, 16, 17). The ingenious wooden *gaiola* was designed and used in all buildings – a structure of wood which, by its elasticity, was

---

[77] The classic work on the rebuilding of Lisbon remains José-Augusto França, *Lisboa pombalina e o iluminismo*, 2nd edition (Lisbon, 1977).

10 The royal palace before the earthquake

11 The royal palace after the earthquake

12 The Rossio and castle before the earthquake

intended to adapt to the movement of the earth in the event of future earthquakes (fig. 13). Ribeiro Sanches contributed a long practical treatise on public health, to be used as a primer by those charged with the restoration of Lisbon. Ribeiro Sanches urged that the new buildings be sanitary and well aired. He also reviewed the theories on earthquakes to make clear that they were natural events.[78]

The lessons gained from the reconstruction of Lisbon were to be applied by Pombal elsewhere, during the planning of the new buildings at the University of Coimbra in the 1770s, for instance, and in the construction of an entirely new town, Vila Real de Santo António, situated in the Algarve on the frontier with Spain, and intended to be a focal point for an effort to recover Portuguese control of the Algarve fisheries.[79] In Oporto extensive urban reconstruction and new buildings in neoclassical style were undertaken by Pombal's energetic cousin, João Almada e Melo, installed by the all-powerful minister as military governor, president of the municipal senate, and head of public works, much as Pombal had installed his brother Paulo de Carvalho as president of the municipal council and director of public works in Lisbon.[80]

The idea to set a great square on the waterfront as the central focal point of the Lisbon scheme came from Eugénio dos Santos. It was also highly significant that

[78] *Tratado de conservação da saude dos povos: obra util, e igualmente necessaria a magistrados, capitaens generais, capitaens da mar e terra, prelados, abbadessas, medicos e pays de famlia; com hum appendix. Consideraciones sobre os terremotos* (Paris, e se vende em Lisboa 1756).

[79] Alberta Iria, "Vila Real de Santo António reedificada pelo marquês de Pombal (1773–1776)," *Ethnos* 3 (Lisbon, 1948), pp. 5–76; and José Eduardo Horta Correia, "Vila Real de Santo António levantada em cinco meses pelo marquês de Pombal," in *Pombal revisitado* 2, pp. 79–88.

[80] Flavio Gonçalves, "A arte no Porto na época do marquês de Pombal," *Pombal revisitado* 2, pp. 101–119. The influence of British palladian style was important in the north.

13 The *gaiola*, the Lisbon earthquake-proof frame required for buildings constructed after the 1750s

the new square, placed on the old Royal plaza, was to be called, as it remains, the Praça do Comércio – the place of commerce (figs. 19–20). The new Lisbon was thus intended to be a preeminently mercantile and administrative center. As the rest of Europe debated the meaning of the earthquake for the philosophy of optimism, engaging Voltaire, Goethe, Rousseau, and John Wesley among others, the reaction in Portugal was more prosaic. Pombal's architectural and city planning was intended to celebrate national economic independence and a modern, well-regulated, and utilitarian state (figs. 21–22). As such, they epitomized what Pombal hoped to achieve for Portugal at large (color plates VI–VII).

Even Pombal's most bitter enemies agreed that the public squares of the new Lisbon were "*belíssimas*," as the Jesuit Padre Anselmo Eckart observed on seeing them after being released from prison in 1777.[81] The *philosophes*, however, remained more interested in the disaster of the earthquake than they did in Pombal's remarkable reconstruction of the city. About the new Lisbon they were largely ignorant; so that

[81] Anselmo Eckart, *Memórias de um Jesuíta: prisioneiro de Pombal* (Lisbon, 1987), p. 230.

14 Manuel de Maia

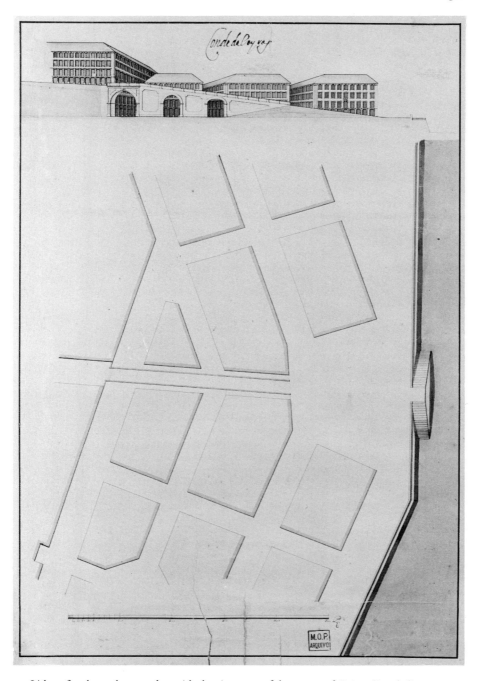

15 Lisbon façades and street plan with the signature of the count of Oeiras (Pombal)

16 The reconstruction of Lisbon

(a) the façade for the Misericórdia

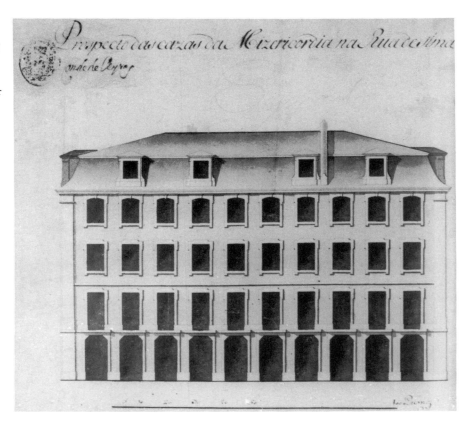

(b) houses belonging to the marquês de Pombal

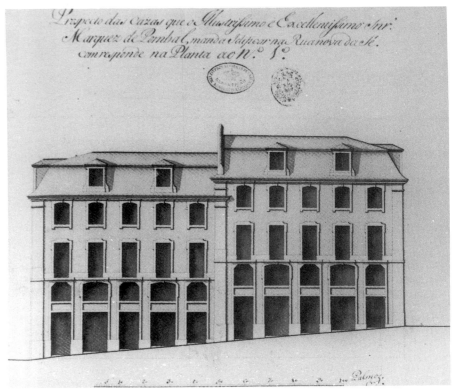

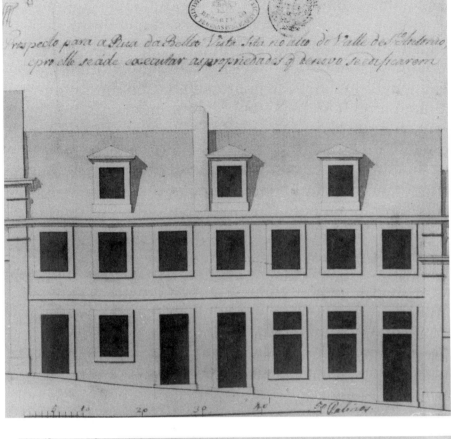

(c) façades

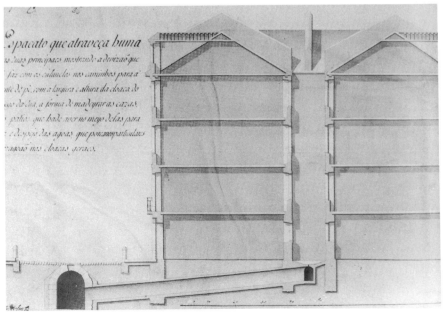

(d) new houses
for the Baixa,
with street
elevation and
sanitation
arrangements

17 The reconstruction of Lisbon: Carlos Mardel's first project for the Rossio with the
signature of the count of Oeiras (Pombal)

the image of Portugal remained fixed, as with Voltaire, as a land of unreasonable
catastrophe mired in irrational superstition. Ironically, the article on the new Lisbon
commissioned for the 1781 edition of the *Encyclopédie méthodique* arrived too late in
Paris for inclusion, and the volume was published without it.[82] So it was Voltaire's
Poème sur le désastre de Lisbonne, and above all Voltaire's *Candide* that set the tone: "The
Portuguese pundits could not think of any better way of preventing total ruin than to
treat the people to a splendid *auto-da-fé*."[83] This was, in fact, precisely the opposite of
what Pombal believed and practiced in the earthquake's aftermath.

[82] "Notice inédite sur Lisbonne en 1781," *BEP*, 35–36 (1974–1975), pp. 93–120.
[83] See the discussion of Voltaire and Lisbon in Kendrick, *Lisbon Earthquake*, pp. 198–212. The quotation
from *Candide* is on p. 206.

18 Topographic plan of Lisbon by Eugénio dos Santos and Carlos Mardel (Instituto Geográfico e Cadastral, Lisbon)

19 The Pombaline Praça do Comércio and Baixa

20 The Pombaline Baixa and Praça do Comércio from a photograph of 1872 (Arquivo Nacional de Fotografia)

21 Lisbon from the Tagus in the 1950s (photograph by Jean Dieuzaide)

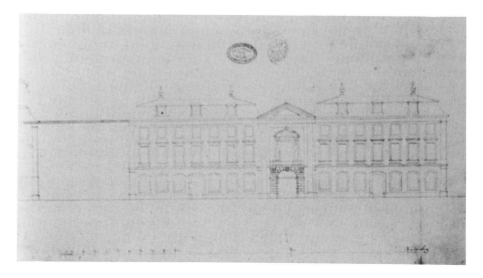

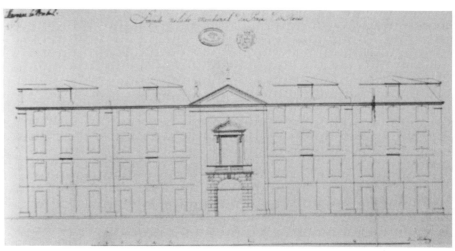

22 Lisbon façades (proposals for southern side of the Rossio)

2

The Golden Age and its consequences

Portugal existed only for England. She was, as it were, entirely absorbed by her. It was for her that the vine flourished at Oporto, that the tree of the Hesperides burdened itself with its golden fruit, that the olive diffused its sweet and unctuous tides; it was for her that the sun of the Brazils hardened the diamond in the bowels of the earth, and it was for her that Portugal rendered her banks and her soil inhospitable to industry.

Europe and America, translated from the French of the Abbé de Pradt
by J. D. Williams, 2 vols. (London, 1822) I, p. 425

But the great Glory of Portugal at present centers in her very extensive and immensely rich Colony of Brazil in South America; from whence she has her vast Treasures of Gold and Diamonds, besides immense Quantities of excellent sugars, hides, drugs, tobacco, fine red-wood, etc.

Adam Anderson, *An Historical and Chronological Deduction of the Origin of
Commerce* I (London, 1740), p. iv

Lisbon's reconstruction after the devastating earthquake of 1755 is something of a paradigm for many of Pombal's activities in government and represented a good example of the role the Portuguese enlightened absolutist wished to see the state perform. It was a role deeply rooted in a pragmatic assessment of options, a mixture of eclectic borrowing and innovation, and the selective intervention by the state in society to promote what was conceived to be the national interest.

Pombal's long preeminence in affairs of state did not, of course, occur in isolation from the rest of the historical experience of the Portuguese eighteenth century. The social, political, and economic context set powerful constraints on what any minister, however powerful, could achieve. For Pombal these constraints emerged out of the special characteristics of the "long" Portuguese eighteenth century which began during the late 1660s and ended in 1807. It was, in fact, Pombal's shrewd assessment of the realities of Portugal's circumstances which provided for him many of the levers he used to consolidate his power and then bring the state's influence to bear in the intents of reform.

Portuguese independence, lost when Philip II of Spain incorporated Portugal into the vast dominions of the Spanish Habsburg dynasty in 1580, had been reestablished in 1640 when Spanish rule had been thrown off. But it was the recognition of Portuguese independence by the major European maritime powers (England in 1654 and 1662, the Netherlands in 1661 and 1667) that was decisive in forcing Spain itself reluctantly to follow suit in 1668. The long Portuguese eighteenth century ended in the climactic winter of 1807/1808 when Napoleon's armies under General Junot seized Lisbon and the Portuguese court fled across the Atlantic to establish its seat in Brazil. Within these broad chronological parameters unfolded the struggles of the eighteenth century: the clash of tradition with the forces of change and innovation, the struggle between the old religion and the new rationalism of the age of reason, the desire to be great again on the basis of the wealth of South America yet the ever-present nostalgia for glories past in the Orient, the conflict between despotic means and enlightened objectives. And it was within this framework also that the events that punctuated the epoch occurred: the exploration of the interior of South America, the discovery of gold in Brazil, the magnificent ceremonials of the new Patriarchate of Lisbon, the cruel spectacles of the Inquisition, the earthquake of 1755, the expulsion of the Jesuits, the reconstruction of Lisbon.

Three monarchs ruled Portugal during the eighteenth century. The long reign of Dom João V covered the first half of the century, during which great wealth flowed into Lisbon from the Brazilian territories, Portugal's "milch cow" as Professor Charles Boxer so graphically described the role of Portuguese America in this period. In 1750 Dom João V was succeeded by his son Dom José I, whose reign was marked by Pombal's long predominance in affairs of state, and by the reign of the pious and later mad Dona Maria I who succeeded her father in 1777. Dona Maria was declared incompetent in 1792, when her portly son Dom João became *de facto* regent. He became the prince regent formally in 1799, and remained so until the death of his mother in 1816, when he was acclaimed in Rio de Janeiro as Dom João VI of the United Kingdom of Portugal, Brazil, and the Algarves.

As elsewhere in Europe, the eighteenth century was, for Portugal, a period of demographic growth. The Portuguese population had been increasing during the first quarter of the century and was in the range of 2 million people in 1732. By 1758 the population reached 2.5 million and increased to 3 million by the 1780s. Lisbon's inhabitants at the time of the 1755 earthquake numbered some 150,000, a figure at which it remained until 1780. Oporto, the second city in the country, by way of contrast, grew rapidly in the eighteenth century, from 20,000 in 1732 to 40,000 in 1787.[1]

In many respects the prosperity of metropolitan Portugal in the mid-eighteenth century depended directly on the fluctuations of its colonial commerce. By Pombal's

---

[1] A. H. de Oliveira Marques, *History of Portugal*, 2 vols. (New York, 1972) I, p. 380. For an analysis of the chronological division of Portuguese history see Vitorino Magalhães Godinho, "A divisão da história de Portugal em período," *Ensaios*, 3 vols. (Lisbon, 1980) II, p. 18.

time, Brazil's population, excluding the Amerindians, had reached 1,500,000, and Portugal's economy throughout the eighteenth century was marked by the pre-eminence of colonial, mainly Brazilian staples in its re-export trades.[2] Since the late seventeenth century the focus of Portugal's imperial interest had shifted decisively westward from the trading-post thalassocracy of the Indian Ocean first established in the early sixteenth century to the plantation-based colonies of the South Atlantic. The trade in African slaves and Brazilian sugar, which had predated the Asian empire and thrived even while overshadowed by the Asian spice trade, came fully into its own. Within the South Atlantic system itself, integrated by the triangular interdependence of Lisbon, the slaving enclaves of the west and central African coast, and the expanding colonies of European and African settlements in Portuguese America, imperial priorities were reordered to favor support of Portugal's territorial empire in Brazil.

For Portugal the most dramatic and decisive consequence of the exploration of the interior of South America was the discovery of gold. The search for precious metals had, of course, brought many of the first Europeans to the western hemisphere. Indeed, the Spaniards had been well rewarded for their early explorations. Within months of Columbus' landfall in 1492, gold had been discovered in Hispaniola. During the 1540s in the barren mountains of the Andes, the Spaniards had discovered a vast mountain of silver at Potosí in present-day Bolivia, and in Mexico along the eastern slope of the Sierra Madre they were no less successful in exploiting silver ore. The Portuguese, on the other hand, were less fortunate. For almost two hundred years after Portugal laid claim to the territory which became known as Brazil, they had to make do with more prosaic products – brazilwood used to produce red dye, sugar, hides, cacao, and tobacco – worthy and valuable products all, but not the precious metals the early settlers had hoped for.

At the end of the seventeenth century, however, half-Indian frontiersmen from the small inland settlement of São Paulo eventually struck it rich. São Paulo was a resource-poor community that made its living by capturing and selling Indian slaves and raiding the prosperous Jesuit missions in Paraguay. The Paulistas were ever on the look-out for booty. In the 1690s, after years of searching, they came across rich deposits of alluvial gold in the streams that flowed from the Mantiqueira mountains. Three hundred and fifty miles inland from the port city of Rio de Janeiro, the Mantiqueira range marked the watershed for the north-flowing São Francisco River as well as for the tributaries that flowed south into the vast La Plata river basin. As word spread, avid speculators used both river systems to reach the goldfield, and within a decade of the Paulistas' discovery, the first gold rush of modern history was in full swing. Gold was found initially in the streams along the flanks of the mountain range, the Espinhaço (the Spine), which runs north–south between the present-day cities of Ouro Prêto and Diamantina in the state of Minas Gerais across the great interior plateau of Brazil. The gold remittances from Brazil increased steadily over the course of the first half of

---

[2] D. Alden, *Royal Government in Colonial Brazil* (Berkeley and Los Angeles, 1968), p. 10.

the eighteenth century, reaching their apogee in the early 1750s. After 1729 diamonds were discovered in the northern area of Minas Gerais and increased the riches flowing to Lisbon and on to Amsterdam from the interior of Portuguese America.[3]

Brazilian gold, sugar, and tobacco formed the basis of the South Atlantic commercial complex, with sugar and tobacco providing profitable re-exports to Spain, and gold balancing the unfavorable trade with the north and paying for the import of wood and grain.[4] "The two cities of Lisbon and Oporto may be justly considered as the two eyes of Portugal," commented the eighteenth-century traveler Arthur Costigan, "for here center the whole riches of the country and all their trade with foreign nations, and their own possessions in the Brazils; upon which last especially depends their whole existence as a people, and the immediate support of the throne."[5] During the decade 1740–1750, in the port of Lisbon alone, the annual movement of shipping surpassed 800 vessels, of which about 300 were Portuguese, and a third of these directly engaged in trade to Brazil (see fig. 23).[6]

Specialization among the Brazilian regions was reflected by a specialization of products carried by the fleets. The Rio fleet brought gold and substantial shipments of hides and silver. From Pernambuco came wood and sugar. The fleets of the north from Grão Pará and Maranhão carried cacao. The riches of Bahia were legendary. A fleet of thirty to forty ships left each year for Lisbon with cargoes of gold, silver, diamonds, jasper, cacao, balsam, cotton, tobacco, and sugar.[7]

Brazilian tobacco had become an important component in the trade between Bahia and Lisbon, and between Brazil and Africa in the late seventeenth century. The tobacco monopoly, composed essentially of duties raised on the trade in tobacco, provided the crown with an important source of revenue throughout the eighteenth century. Brazilian export tobacco was prepared in rolls, coated with molasses, and wrapped in cow hides, which gave it excellent preservative qualities and allowed tobacco to be accumulated as an investment or for speculation. Tobacco snuff was sold

---

[3] Vitorino Magalhães Godinho, "Le Portugal, les flottes du sucre et les flottes de l'or 1670–1770," *Annales* 5, 2 (April–June 1950), pp. 184–197; Virgílio Noya Pinto, *O ouro brasileiro e o comércio anglo-português* (São Paulo, 1979); Kenneth R. Maxwell, *Conflicts and Conspiracies: Brazil and Portugal, 1750–1808* (Cambridge, 1973).

[4] For the Portuguese grain trade, see Vitorino Magalhães Godinho, *Prix et monnaies au Portugal 1750–1850* (Paris, 1955), pp. 147–149; for Spanish–Portuguese trade, see Jean François Bourgoing, *Voyage du ci-devant duc du Châtelet en Portugal . . .* , 2 vols. (Paris, 1778, 1808) I, p 228; comments on the importation of wood from northern Europe, [Francisco Xavier de Mendonça Furtado] to [Sr. Fernando de Lavre], January 26, 1752; and [Mendonça Furtado] to [Pombal], July 15, 1757 in *Correspondência inédita* I, pp. 214–215; III, pp. 1119–1120.

[5] Arthur William Costigan, *Sketches of Society and Manners in Portugal*, 2 vols. (London, 1787) I, p. 285.

[6] Jorge Borges de Macedo, "Portugal e a economia 'pombalina': temas e hipóteses," *RHSP* 19 (July–September, 1954), p. 83.

[7] For background and development of the Atlantic fleet system, see Frédéric Mauro, *Le Portugal et l'Atlantique au XVIIe siècle 1570–1670* (Paris, 1960); on the specialization among the Brazilian regions and their fleets, see Vitorino Magalhães Godinho, "Le Portugal," pp. 184–197; for the Bahia fleet in particular, see Johan Brelim, *De passagem pelo Brasil e Portugal em 1756*, translation from the Swedish by Carlos Perição de Almeida (Lisbon, 1955), p. 106.

23 The launching of the caravel *Lampadoza* with the court in attendance, 1727

to France and tobacco rolls became a vital component in the goods used to purchase slaves in Africa.

The slave trade comprised yet another vital transatlantic component in the Portuguese Atlantic system. In Angola armed raids into the interior from the Portuguese coastal ports helped fuel the system. Africa also remained an important market for Portugal's own commodities and those of its Asian territories of Timor, Goa, and Macau. Angola took wine which was considered unsuitable for the British market and Lisbon merchants were able to shift the burden of risk to their suppliers of slaves in the African ports by selling goods and services rather than buying slaves outright. Credit was at the heart of the system.[8]

A major mechanism linking the Portuguese South Atlantic colonial system to a developing world economy was Anglo–Portuguese commerce. By the Methuen Treaty of 1703 English woolen goods entered Lisbon and Oporto free of duty and, in return, Portuguese wines received advantages on the English market. During the first half of the eighteenth century trade was greatly in Britain's favor and the profits for

---

[8] See discussion by David Birmingham, *A Concise History of Portugal* (Cambridge, 1993), pp. 85–86.

individuals high.[9] Woolen cloth made up two-thirds of total British exports, and from 1756 to 1760 Port wine composed in value 72 percent of the total wine consumption in Britain.[10]

After the early 1730s the great influx of gold and diamonds from Brazil exaggerated the imbalance of Anglo-Portuguese exchange.[11] Deficits could be made up and the purchase of foreign goods facilitated by the outflow of bullion which "Portugal distributes so liberally over Europe," as Henry Fielding observed.[12] Throughout the first half of the eighteenth century only Holland and Germany surpassed Portugal as consumers of English exports. It was only during the most critical moments of the Seven Years War (1759–1762) that British shipping in the port of Lisbon fell below 50 percent of the total.[13] The value of the Portuguese trade to Britain was obvious and well known. "By this treaty we gain a greater balance from Portugal, than from any other country whatsoever," wrote Charles King.[14]

The domestic vineyard owners and wine shippers of northern Portugal were also intimately bound to the Anglo-Portuguese commercial relationship since Portugal's long eighteenth century also saw the rise of viticulture and Port wine production, and by the capture by Port of the English wine market. The English factory in Oporto had initiated the wine trade in 1678 as a substitute for the re-export trade in Brazilian sugar and tobacco the Portuguese had lost to the competition of the West Indian islands which, under the Navigation Acts, received privileged access to the English markets. As a result of pressure on Parliament in London, the English merchants in Portugal obtained a tariff beneficial to them in 1697 and, under the terms of the Methuen Treaty, Portuguese wines paid a rate one-third below those of French wines. Wine exports increased dramatically over the course of the eighteenth century, from a yearly average of 632 barrels (*pipas*) in 1678–87, to 17,692 in 1718–1727, to 19,388 in 1758–1767, to 40,055 in 1788–1789.[15] By the end of the eighteenth century, nine-tenths of all Port wine exported went to Britain where Portuguese wine

---

[9] Background on the Methuen Treaty, A. D. Francis, *The Methuens and Portugal, 1691–1708* (London, 1966); and Alan K. Manchester, *British Preëminence in Brazil* (Chapel Hill, 1933), p. 24. For an account of an individual merchant involved in the Portugal trade, Lucy S. Sutherland, *A London Merchant 1695–1774* (Oxford, 1933).

[10] A. B. Wallis Chapman, "The Commercial Relations of England and Portugal 1487–1807," *TRHS*, 3rd series, 1 (1907), p. 177; Jorge Borges de Macedo, *Problemas de história da indústria portuguesa no século XVIII* (Lisbon, 1963), p. 48.

[11] "Destinations of Exports from England and Wales" (Table v) and "Sources of Imports into England and Wales" (Table vi), in Elizabeth Boody Schumpeter, *English Overseas Trade Statistics* (Oxford, 1960), pp. 17–20; Borges de Macedo, *Problemas*, pp. 46–47, 53; H. E. S. Fisher, "Anglo-Portuguese Trade 1700–1770," *EHR* 16 (1963), p. 229 (republished in W. E. Minchinton, ed., *The Growth of English Overseas Trade in the 17th and 18th Centuries* [London: 1969], pp. 144–160); C. R. Boxer, "Brazilian Gold and British Traders in the First Half of the Eighteenth Century," *HAHR* 49, 3 (August 1969), pp. 455–472. Also overview by José Vicente Serrão in Mattoso, ed. *História*, vol. 4, pp. 71–117.

[12] Henry Fielding, *The Journal of a Voyage to Lisbon*, ed. Austin Dobson (Oxford, 1907), p. 99.

[13] Schumpeter, *Trade Statistics*, p. 17; Borges de Macedo, "Portugal e a economia pombalina," p. 90.

[14] Charles King, *The British Merchant*, 3rd edition, 3 vols. (London, 1748) III, pp. 1–78.

[15] Oliveira Marques, *History of Portugal* I, p. 385.

dominated 70 to 75 percent of the British market.[16] The favorable conditions Portuguese wine enjoyed in the British market, however, led to a speculative expansion of vineyards which adversely affected both the larger merchants and the aristocratic producers of the upper Douro valley.[17]

Portugal remained a chronic grain importer throughout the eighteenth century, from northern Europe at the beginning of the century and later from North America, especially Virginia and the Carolinas. North America also became an importer of Portuguese wines, a factor which helped develop North American taste for Port and Madeira wine, which became as much favored by such founders of the American Republic as George Washington and Thomas Jefferson as they were by the Tory squirearchy in England.[18]

Portugal's own industry suffered from this development of commerce. Portuguese domestic manufacturing had thrived prior to 1700 in part as a result of aggressive mercantilist policies pursued by the count of Ericeira. In the period between 1669 and 1692, moreover, the Portuguese established chartered companies for Cape Verde and Guinea, for Grão Pará and Maranhão in Brazil, and for India. Drawing on the ideas of the Portuguese mercantilist writer, Duarte Ribeiro de Macedo, and his book, *Discourse on the Introduction of the Arts in the Realm* (*Discurso sobre a introducção das artes no reino*), Ericeira attempted to stimulate infant industries on the Colbertian model. Ericeira held the position of superintendent of factories and manufactures of the kingdom, imported skillful artisans from France, England, Spain, and Venice, granted special privileges to them and lent out government funds. In this way, textile industries were established in Lisbon, Covilhã, Fundão, and Tomar, and protectionist legislation was introduced to prohibit the import of luxury clothes and products. But the gold rush in Brazil ended all this. None of the trading companies succeeded and all were dissolved.[19] Ericeira himself committed suicide.[20]

The gold boom had political as well as material consequences. Once Portugal regained its own independence in 1640, and the duke of Bragança had been recognized as king of Portugal, the centrality of Brazil's wealth to Portugal's recuperation of its position in Europe was well recognized. The creation of techniques to capture these riches played a large part in the calculations of the great Jesuit polymath and statesman Padre António Vieira in the immediate post-restoration years. It was, however, the gold from Brazil that allowed the Portuguese monarchs the luxury of avoiding recourse to the nation's ancient representative (and tax granting) institution

[16] Fisher, *The Portugal Trade*, pp. 13–40.
[17] On this aspect of the period see Borges de Macedo, *A situação económica no tempo de Pombal*; Kenneth Maxwell, "Pombal and the Nationalization of the Luso-Brazilian Economy," *HAHR* 47 (1968), pp. 608–631; and Schneider, *Pombal e o Vinho do Porto*.
[18] Albert Silbert, *Do Portugal de antigo regime ao Portugal oitocentista* (Lisbon, 1977) and Magalhães Godinho, *Prix et monnaies*.
[19] Oliveira Marques, *History of Portugal* I, p. 388.
[20] Ibid. I, p. 384. The persecution of "New Christians" by the Inquisition also contributed to the decline of manufacturing. See José Barreto's Sebastião José de Carvalho e Melo, *Escritos económicos*, p. lxxi, n. 117.

and the last Cortes (parliament) met in 1698, and was not to meet again until 1820. The eighteenth century, therefore, saw the apogee of the absolutist state in Portugal.[21]

The prosperity gold brought encouraged many small merchants and speculators to enter the colonial market, which in turn had a profound impact on the entrepreneurial structure of Portuguese society. As far as the colonial trade was concerned, a vast unofficial and illegal commerce developed which, using the fleet system as a cover and means for export and remittance, paralleled and may even at times have surpassed the legitimate traffic.[22]

The great prosperity of colonial commerce and contraband provided a key link in the chain between Brazil, Lisbon, and London and it also created difficulties for the Portuguese merchants in the metropolis and colony. The British and other foreign merchants established in Lisbon, protected by their special privileges, provided the credit and goods which, in the hands of their Portuguese collaborators (itinerant traders known as *comissários volantes*), sustained the contraband connection across the Atlantic and into the interior of Brazil. The *comissários volantes*, who brought goods to the metropolis, sold them personally in America, and returned with the proceeds, were one of the essential elements in the transatlantic commercial connection. They often traveled under false pretenses and carried merchandise in their shipboard accommodations, avoiding outlays for commissions, freight charges, and warehousing.[23]

Within the Portuguese South Atlantic commercial complex the problems of the debtors of the colonial hinterland, the unequal competition facing established merchants, and the high profits of the *comissários volantes* and contrabandists and their foreign supporters were intimately interrelated. The privileged position of the British and foreign merchant corporations in Lisbon and Oporto encouraged the penetration of foreign credit and goods throughout the Luso-Brazilian system, and prejudiced established interests in both metropolis and colony. In effect, the itinerant traders and contrabandists were contributing to the increasing denationalization of Luso-Brazilian commerce. "A sensible Portuguese writer," commented Costigan, "compares, not unaptly, their whole Kingdom to one of that sort of spider which has a large body (the capital) with extremely long, thin, feeble legs, reaching to a great distance, but are of no sort of use to it, and which it is hardly able to move."[24]

The avoidance of freight and other charges by the *comissários volantes* allowed them to undercut the more established merchants of the colonial port cities who received consignments from their correspondents in Lisbon on a regular and legal basis. The goods introduced by the itinerant traders in turn glutted the Brazilian market.

---

[21] For the period between the 1660s and 1700, a good overview is provided by Carl A. Hansen, *Economy and Society in Baroque Portugal*.

[22] Borges de Macedo, *A situação económica no tempo de Pombal*, pp. 61, 68–69. Michel Morineau, *Incroyables garcettes et fabuleux métaux* (Cambridge, 1985).

[23] "Relatório do marquês de Lavradio," *RIHGB* 4 (2nd edition, 1863), p. 459; Lúcio d'Azevedo, *Estudos de história paraense* (Pará, 1893), p. 74.

[24] Costigan, *Sketches* I, p. 285.

Price-cutting in Brazil was of little concern to the foreign suppliers of credit and merchandise in the metropolis. As the British factory in Lisbon pointed out, "It is all one to Great Britain provided the goods are disposed of."[25] The difficulties this caused for the established merchants in Brazil, however, also adversely affected the agricultural producers of the hinterland. The established merchants lacked the ready cash to buy the tobacco, sugar, cattle, and leather of the interior, and their means of exchange in goods had been hopelessly debased. They were often forced to call on their credit and increase interest rates.

The interloping *comissários volantes* did not have the same incentive as the long established merchants to deal leniently with the tobacco and sugar planters who now became their debtors. They were not interested in long-term relationships but in quick profit, preferably in gold. When faced with nonpayments they turned to judicial process and violent foreclosure to obtain their debts and these methods caused severe pressure on farmers and sugar mill owners who, because of the large capital investment in processing machinery and slaves required by the sugar business, needed long credits and tolerant lenders to stay in business.[26] The activities of itinerant traders, who were little more than hired salesmen, and the foreign factors and merchants in Lisbon who supplied and financed them brought serious disruption to regular colonial commerce.

The activities of the interlopers and contrabandists were not confined to the principal trading centers of Bahia, Rio de Janeiro, and Pernambuco. The illicit commerce in Amazon drugs and spices was so profitable, contemporaries claimed, that while bankruptcies were known among other commissaries, they were rare among the traders with Grão Pará and Maranhão.[27] "The foreign merchant houses by means of their great capital had made themselves absolute mistress of the metropolitan and colonial commerce," commented a Portuguese contemporary.

Few or rare were the Portuguese merchants in a condition to do business with their own funds, none with goods that were not foreign. All the commerce of Brazil was made on credit and the greater part by salesmen of the foreign houses and by the *comissários volantes* who received a commission for their work and a bonus for extra service.[28]

---

[25] "Memórias do consul e factória britânica na Corte de Lisboa . . . " (1755–1766), BNLCP, codex 94, fo. 46v.

[26] "Súplica a Rainha . . . " IHGB/AUC, 1-1-8, fo. 43; "Demonstrações da junta [Company of Pernambuco]," April 20, 1780, IHGB/AUC, 1-2-11, fos. 31, 47; "Discurso preliminar, histórico e introductivo, com natureza de discrição da comarca e cidade da Bahia (ca. 1790)," ed. Pinto de Aguiar, *Aspectos de economia colonial* (Bahia, 1957); [Pombal] to [Mendonça Furtado], August 4, 1755, *Correspondência inédita* II, pp. 796–797.

[27] d'Azevedo, *Estudos*, p. 37.

[28] "Súplica a Rainha para que conceda a prorrogação que pede a Companhia do Grão Pará e Maranhão e não a extinga nem a de Pernambuco, com vasta exposição de motivos e alegando que o comércio do Reino para o Brasil se acha quase todo em poder das nações extrangeiras," anon., n.d. (1777?), in "Apontamentos vários sobre a Companhia de Grão Pará e Maranhão," Arquivo Ultramarino collection of transcripts in the Instituto Histórico e Geográfico Brasileiro, Rio de Janeiro, IHGB/AUC, 1-1-8, fo. 43.

The special position of foreign merchants in Portugal was something that had much annoyed the marquês de Pombal during his investigations.

The British merchants in Lisbon and Oporto were not the only foreign merchants in Portugal, to be sure, nor the only foreign merchants enjoying special concessional privileges, but they were the most prominent by far.[29] Peace with Spain in 1688, the treaties with the Dutch in 1661 and 1668, and with the English in 1654 and 1662, had been bought at considerable cost in terms of special privileges granted to foreign merchants and indemnities paid.

The British factories in Lisbon and Oporto were, in effect, privileged commercial communities possessed of a legal status that dated from the seventeenth century. The treaty of 1654 between Portugal and Cromwellian England guaranteed the English not only the "same liberties, privileges, and exemptions as the Portuguese in metropolitan and colonial commerce," but also provided for religious toleration and, by a secret article, prohibited the raising of customs duties on English goods above 23 percent.[30] Parts of the treaty had always remained dead letters, particularly those related to the presence of English merchants in the Portuguese possessions, but the 1654 and subsequent treaties provided a favorable environment for the creation of the state of semicolonial dependency in which mid-eighteenth-century Portugal found herself with relation to her northern ally.

Charles Boxer has compared the Anglo-Portuguese arrangements imposed by the Cromwellian treaty as creating a privileged position legally, financially, and commercially, analogous to those enjoyed by westerners in the treaty ports of China between 1840 and 1940.[31] By 1750 the British factory in Lisbon contained many old established and influential British companies: among them Bristow, Ward and Co., the agents of John Bristow of London; Burrell, Ducket and Hardy, the agents of Burrell and Raymond; and Chase, Wilson and Co., agents of T. Chase.[32] "A great body of His Majesty's subjects reside at Lisbon, rich, opulent, and every day increasing their fortunes and enlarging their dealings," remarked Lord Tyrawly during a special mission to Portugal in 1752.[33] "It is a common observation of the natives," Costigan observed, "that excepting of the lowest conditions of life, you shall not meet anyone on foot some hours of the violent heat every day, but dogs and Englishmen."[34]

[29] On the role of the British factories, see John Delaforce, *The Factory House* (London, 1983).

[30] See discussion of restrictions on worship and burials in Francis, *Portugal, 1715–1808*, p. 42.

[31] See Professor Boxer's introduction to *Descriptive List of the State Papers of Portugal 1661–1780 in the Public Record Office, London*, 3 vols. (Lisbon, 1979).

[32] Sir Richard Lodge, "The English Factory at Lisbon," *TRHS*, 4th series, 16 (1933), pp. 225–226; A. R. Walford, *The British Factory* (Lisbon, 1940), p. 20; Sutherland, *A London Merchant*, p. 25.

[33] Walford, *British Factory*, p. 20. Lord Tyrawly, who had served under Marlborough, was appointed envoy at Lisbon in 1728. He was to remain there for thirteen years, and was considered by Horace Walpole "singularly licentious, even for the courts of Russia and Portugal." When he left Lisbon in July 1741 he had also, according to Walpole, taken with him his third wife and fourteen children. Also see Francis, *Portugal, 1715–1808*, pp. 94–95.

[34] Costigan, *Sketches* II, 29.

Brazilian gold, providing as it did the means to finance Portugal's chronic balance of payments deficit, was not the only link between the British and the South Atlantic colonial complex. A high proportion of the British manufactured goods exported to Brazil via Portugal went straight into the Spanish American colonies as contraband. The functioning of the system at the height of its prosperity thus brought Spanish American silver to Britain via Brazil and Portugal, vital to the commerce with Asia. Bougainville estimated in the 1760s that at least thirty coasting vessels were employed in the contraband trade between Brazil and the Rio de la Plata.[35] The Portuguese outpost at Colônia do Sacramento across the estuary from Buenos Aires had long been a favored port of call for British as well as Portuguese contrabandists.[36] British participation was "very advantageous and profitable" and the silver returning to Europe on the Brazil fleets was almost wholly reshipped to Britain.[37] Nor was it only the officially favored direct contraband with Buenos Aires that brought silver into the system. Extensive fraud throughout the interior mining zones in the returns of the royal fifth (the Quinto Real was a tax of 20 percent on all gold and silver mined) provided the substance for an inter-American contraband of considerable proportions. In fact, according to Alexandre de Gusmão, the Brazilian-born secretary of King Dom João V, most of the gold production escaped official fiscalization.[38]

From the point of view of the British merchants the colonial commission system and the long-term investment it represented (at least a year, usually two or three) was inherent to the Brazil trade. The great advantage the British merchants enjoyed over their Portuguese rivals was the ability to sustain this extension of credit based on their own capital resources. The profits, however, were worth the risks. The Lisbon factory in 1769 estimated an average profit of sales to the Portuguese traders between 12 and 15 percent. The return of goods disposed of in Lisbon was relatively low, from 7 to 10 percent. The profits of the British merchants dealing with agents outside Lisbon was higher, 15 to 17 percent. In the Brazil trade the return was from 25 to 30 percent.[39]

---

[35] *A Voyage Round the World: Performed by Order of His Most Christian Majesty in the Years 1766, 1767, 1768, 1769*, by Lewis de Bougainville, translated from the French by John Reinhold Forster (London, 1772), pp. 82–83.

[36] Olga Pantaleão, *A penetração comercial da Inglaterra na América espanhola, 1713–1783* (São Paulo, 1946); also Luís Ferrand d'Almeida, "Problemas do comércio luso-espanhol nos meados do século XVIII," *RHES* 8 (1981), p. 103.

[37] Allan Christelow, "Great Britain and the Trades from Cadiz and Lisbon to Spanish America and Brazil 1759–1782," *HAHR* 27 (February 1947), p. 12.

[38] "Reparos sobre a disposição da ley de 3 de Dezembro de 1750, a respeito do novo método da cobrança do Quinto; abolindo a da Capitação, Escriptas para ver o Fidelíssimo Senhor Rey Dom José I, por Alexandre Gusmão," Lisbon, December 18, 1750, IHGB/AUC, 1-2-39, fo. 69. Gusmão, educated in Bahia, Coimbra, and at the Sorbonne, became secretary to Dom João V in 1730. For his considerable influence on imperial policy and participation in the negotiation of the Treaty of Madrid see David M. Davidson, "How the Brazilian West Was Won: Freelance and State on the Mato Grosso Frontier, ca. 1737–1752," in *The Colonial Roots of Modern Brazil*, ed. Dauril Alden (Berkeley and Los Angeles, 1973), pp. 61–106.

[39] Details of profitability from H. E. S. Fisher, *The Portugal Trade* (London, 1971), p. 60.

The golden years of the first half of the eighteenth century, however, had not left the British factory unaffected. The prosperity created by the gold boom had wrought changes in the British community in Portugal, not always to the liking of the older merchants. The late 1740s saw the rise of a group of traders who, while taking advantage of the privileged position of the factory, were only tenuously engaged in the traditional pattern of Anglo-Portuguese commerce. Attracted by the spoils of the Portuguese and South American markets, they engaged in a wide variety of commercial exchanges which served to undermine the legitimate sale of higher priced British manufactures.[40] Lord Tyrawly, who had spent thirteen years as the British ambassador to Portugal, noted and lamented the change in the British factory during a visit to Lisbon in 1752. The "traditional, regular, and frugal merchants" had been challenged by "men of a very different character," he told London. These men were "universal traders more than British factors" who dealt "More or at least as Much in French goods, Hamburg linen, Sicilian corn, and other commodities of different countries than in the Produce of their Own." The trade of the factory had ceased to be "Wholly a British trade," that employed "Our own wool, Poor, Handicrafts, and Shops."[41]

The long Portuguese eighteenth century was also framed by the ongoing diplomatic and military struggle between France and Britain for hegemony, especially in so far as this affected the naval, commercial, and colonial affairs of the Atlantic, where Portugal's vital economic and strategic interests now lay. Lisbon tried to accommodate both France and Britain, but because of its Atlantic orientation and the importance of its overseas possessions, Portugal was tied inextricably to Britain, though Portugal always sought to remain neutral and retain, thereby, the prosperous entrepôt function of Lisbon for the re-export of colonial products. This need for external political and military support was, of course, at the core of the commercial concessions Portugal had made to England in the 1650s and 1660s.

The role of Brazil in Portuguese calculations and diplomacy thus held a high priority throughout the eighteenth century. Preoccupation with development of the Portuguese Atlantic empire on the one hand, and with Portugal's diminished stature and apparent backwardness in comparison with France and Britain on the other, permeated the Portuguese political and intellectual milieu of the age. The Chevalier des Courtils, who visited Lisbon in 1755 just before the great earthquake, summed up the dependency of the metropolis on its huge territorial empire in South America with a pithy but accurate analogy.

[Portugal] is more of a province than a kingdom. One might say that the King of Portugal is a potentate of the Indies that lodges in a European land. The vast and rich states under his sovereignty in the new world, with Brazil, Rio de Janeiro, Bahia of all the saints, Goa, Madeira,

[40] Sutherland, *A London Merchant*, pp. 136–138.
[41] "Considerations upon the Affairs of Lisbon," Tyrawly papers, published in Walford, *British Factory*, pp. 34–36.

in Africa, the Azores in Europe, have made him a considerable prince and placed him among the number of powerful maritime powers of Europe if one considered the value of his possessions.[42]

---

[42] "Extraite du journal de la campagne des vaisseaux du roy en 1755 par le Chevalier des Courtils," *BEP* 26 (1965), p. 159.

3

Action in the national interest

Small powers, much more than great powers, need to take carefully considered action, because the first do not have the resources to repair the errors they make, whereas the latter always have the means to recuperate.

Dom Luís da Cunha (1738)

The objective is to hurt them [the British] in such a way they cannot scream.

Frei Mansilla to Pombal

Sporadic warfare with Spain in South America occurred throughout the eighteenth century. The most acute irritant was the Portuguese fortified settlement at Colônia do Sacramento, first established in 1680 across the La Plata estuary from Buenos Aires. Open warfare had broken out here in the period between 1735 and 1737. The accession of Fernando VI in Spain in 1746, however, brought about a *rapprochement* with Portugal. The good offices of the Spanish king's Portuguese wife, Dona Maria Bárbara de Bragança, the daughter of Dom João V, contributed to an overall improvement in relations. It was against this background that negotiations began, led on the Spanish side by Don José de Carvajal y Lencastre, the president of the Council of the Indies, and on the Portuguese side by Alexandre de Gusmão, the Brazilian-born private secretary of Dom João V, to settle the boundary disputes between the two powers in South America, as well as to examine the possibility of a commercial treaty between the two countries.[1]

When Pombal took office as secretary of state for foreign affairs and war in July 1750 the question of the frontier demarcation had been agreed upon and he inherited the Treaty of Madrid approved by both courts in December 1749 and signed in January 1750. The parallel discussions over a possible commercial treaty had been prolonged and complicated. The negotiators decided eventually to treat this question later and

---

[1] Luís Ferrand d'Almeida, "Problemas do comércio Luso-Espanhol nos meados do século XVIII: um parecer de Sebastião José de Carvalho e Melo," *RHES* 8 (1981), pp. 95–131, especially 107–108.

separately so that the boundary disputes could be settled by border commissions and a general agreement over the lines of territorial division in South America. Pombal was adamantly opposed to a commercial treaty with Spain. He believed that Madrid's hegemonic impulses would be such that any treaty granting commercial concessions would become a Trojan Horse for Spanish political and strategic domination. Despite the economic dependencies involved in the old Anglo-Portuguese defensive and commercial alliances he regarded these as being more in Portuguese national interests, provided Portugal took active steps to gain reciprocal advantages. He allowed the discussions with Madrid to go on for a while but put a stop to them in 1751.[2]

Geopolitical concerns in South America, however, dominated the early months of the new administration. Although the Treaty of Madrid had been negotiated by its predecessor, the new Lisbon administration faced the unavoidable task of implementing the Madrid agreement, which was the first negotiated settlement between the Iberian powers to delineate the landward frontiers of their colonial territories in South America in their entirety and superseded the agreements made at Utrecht as well as the vague and long violated line of demarcation established by the Treaty of Tordesillas, some 300 years before. In the period leading up to 1750 the Brazilians, in fact, had pushed the landward frontier far into the continental interior, establishing *de facto* Portuguese sovereignty over vast areas. From the Brazilian perspective, the expansion of the frontier was in the long term the most significant development of these years. In the same period that found British colonists still settled close to the Atlantic tidewater and Spaniards resting their American rule in the highlands and on the backs of the Indian peasantry, the Luso-Brazilians had pushed up the rivers of the interior and crossed vast land areas to claim over half the continent of South America for Portugal.[3]

As the negotiations between Madrid and Lisbon progressed during the 1740s, clear topographical landmarks such as rivers and mountains became generally accepted as the means for delineating frontiers. The Portuguese had two major bargaining chips. In addition to controlling the fortified settlements of Colônia do Sacramento, the westernmost Portuguese mining region, in what is now Mato Grosso, had been integrated administratively and economically with the northern Brazilian coast by means of a fluvial transportation and communications route running along the Guaporé, Mamoré, and Madeira rivers in the western Amazon basin.[4]

In the Treaty of Madrid, the Portuguese agreed, in exchange for Spanish recognition of the western fluvial borders of Brazil, to relinquish control of Colônia

---

[2] See Sebastião José de Carvalho e Melo, "Sobre um projecto de tratado de comércio com a Espanha" (1750), published by Luís Ferrand d'Almeida in *RHES* 8 (1981), pp. 111–131.

[3] The best account of frontier expansion in this period is David Davidson, "Rivers and Empires" (unpublished Ph.D. thesis, Yale University, 1970).

[4] David M. Davidson, "How the Brazilian West Was Won: Freelance and State on the Matto Grosso Frontier, 1737–1752," in *Colonial Roots of Modern Brazil*, ed. Alden, pp. 61–106; and J. R. do Amaral Lapa, *Economia colonial* (São Paulo, 1993), especially pp. 15–138.

do Sacramento and the lands immediately to its north on the La Plata, an objective the Spanish had long sought to achieve by force. The acceptance of fluvial boundaries, however, included the Uruguay river, and placed the Jesuits' Seven Missions and their pasture lands, long part of the Spanish sphere, under Portuguese sovereignty.[5] The treaty envisaged the evacuation of the Jesuits and their Indian converts from the Uruguayan missions (as well as the over a million head of cattle in the missions' *estâncias*) and called for an accurate survey on the ground of the demarcation line between Spanish and Portuguese America by two joint commissions.[6] As Portuguese commissioner for the southern demarcations, Lisbon appointed Gomes Freire de Andrada, who was governor of Rio de Janeiro and the southern captaincies. As commissioner for the north and the Amazon basin, Pombal sent his own brother, Francisco Xavier de Mendonça Furtado, with the added responsibility as governor and captain general of the united captaincies of Grão Pará and Maranhão.

In his "very secret" letter to Governor General Gomes Freire supplementing his formal instructions, Pombal outlined the full extent of his ambitions for Portuguese America and demonstrated how powerful the Austria experience and discussions with Duke Silva-Tarouca in Vienna had been to him. "As the power and wealth of all countries consists principally in the number and multiplication of the people that inhabit it," Pombal wrote to Gomes Freire, "this number and multiplication of people is most indispensable now on the frontiers of Brazil for their defense." Yet, as it was not "humanly possible" to provide the necessary people from Portugal itself or the adjacent islands (Azores and Madeira) without converting them "entirely into deserts," it was essential to abolish "all differences between Indians and Portuguese," to attract the Indians from the Uruguay missions, and encourage their marriage with Europeans.[7] He also secretly told Gomes Freire de Andrada to retain control of Côlonia until the missions were evacuated and in Portuguese possession.[8] Pombal's instructions to his brother, Mendonça Furtado, reflected similar objectives. He recommended that the Indians be freed from religious tutelage, miscegenation between the Portuguese and Indians be encouraged to insure continued population growth in the area, married couples be introduced from the Azores, and the importation of African slaves stimulated.

In practice, Pombal's instructions meant the suppression of the Jesuits' religious hold on the frontier. The interests of the state so defined collided with the most basic philosophical tenet of the Jesuits' protectionist Indian policy which had been devised precisely to isolate the Indians from exploitation by the settlers and integration with the Portuguese. The Jesuits believed, and with good historical precedent, that the removal of their protection would have disastrous consequences for the indigenous population

---

[5] For an excellent background on the Jesuits' missions, see Alden, *Royal Government*, pp. 63–66.

[6] Ibid., *Royal Government*, p. 86.

[7] "Carta secretíssima de [Pombal] para Gomes Freire de Andrada . . ." Lisbon, September 21, 1751, in Carneiro de Mendonça, *Pombal e o Brasil*, p. 188.

[8] See Alden, *Royal Government*, p. 90.

by opening the Indians to ruthless manipulation and decimation.[9] Pombal's imperial objectives, nevertheless, received warm commendation from Vienna. Duke Silva-Tarouca wrote enthusiastically to Pombal in 1752, "the Kings of Portugal could come to have an Empire like China in Brazil." Above all, an increase in population should be encouraged. "Moor, white, negro, mulatto, or mestizo, all will serve, all are men, and are good if they are well-governed." The vast Amazon basin should be secured. "Population is everything, many thousands of leagues of deserts serve for nothing."[10]

With the new delineation of the frontiers and the growing awareness in both Madrid and Lisbon of the strategic value of control over the interior and its river systems, it was perhaps inevitable that the great complex of Spanish and Portuguese Jesuit missions, which stretched from the mouth of the Amazon to the Rio de la Plata, should begin to appear as a threat to the interests of both the dominant European powers in South America. Pombal was acting, in effect, to secure the future of Portuguese America by encouraging an increase in the population. But since he did not believe that this objective could be realized in Brazil by massive European emigration, he aimed at removing the Indian population from religious protection so as to encourage their Europeanization through miscegenation.

The Indians of the Seven Jesuit Missions, moreover, had no desire to submit to Portuguese authority, which they perceived, again with ample historical precedent, to be their enemy. They considered themselves loyal vassals of the king of Spain, a fact repeatedly stressed by their *caciques* in letters to the Spanish authorities. Since the mid seventeenth century, moreover, the mission villages had been capable of defending themselves, and ready to do so, especially against the marauders from São Paulo. Pombal's policy of divesting the Jesuits of their spiritual authority within the communities was also doomed to failure since the Jesuit role as spiritual overlords was so intimately interwoven into the very fabric of community life that it was inseparable from their secular authority.[11] Under the terms of the treaty, the 30,000 Indians in the mission communities were expected to migrate with all their moveable goods from what is now part of Brazil's state of Rio Grande do Sul into lands now occupied by Argentina and Paraguay. But, rather than leave lands they had inhabited and tended for three generations, the Indians chose to resist.

The initial Spanish and Portuguese attempt to pacify the Guaraní resistance by force was a failure (1754), and the withdrawal of the European forces encouraged the spread of the revolt. The response from both European powers to this defiance was rapid and decisive. In January 1756, an allied Portuguese and Spanish military force of 3,700 men and nineteen pieces of artillery invaded the territory of the Seven Missions to enforce

---

[9] See D. Alden, "Economic Aspects of the Expulsion of the Jesuits from Brazil: A Preliminary Report," in *Conflict and Continuity in Brazilian Society*, ed. Henry H. Keith and S. F. Edwards (Colombia, SC, 1969), pp. 38–39; and Aurélio Porto, *História das missões orientais do Uruguai* (Rio de Janeiro, 1943).

[10] [Silva-Tarouca] to [Pombal] Vienna, August 12, 1752, *AAP*, pp. 323–329.

[11] See excellent discussion by John Hemming in *Amazon Frontier: The Defeat of the Brazilian Indians* (Cambridge, MA, 1987), pp. 1–80; and *Red Gold: The Conquest of the Brazilian Indians, 1500–1760* (Cambridge, MA, 1978), pp. 444–461.

the treaty stipulations, crushing the christianized Amerindian combatants, who never numbered more than 2,000. The Spanish and Portuguese victory was total. The mission forces had been used to oppose freelance raiders, not the organized forces of a European army.[12]

Tragically, neither of the new governments in Lisbon or Madrid had been happy with the 1750 agreement negotiated by their predecessors and which had proved disastrous for the Guaraní. The death of Carvajal, Queen Maria Bárbara, and eventually Ferdinand VI in Spain removed from the scene the Treaty of Madrid's major supporters, and Charles III reviewed the whole agreement. In September 1760 the Spanish ambassador told the Portuguese government that Lisbon's failure to give up Colônia obliged Charles III to rescind the treaty. Lisbon did not object. In February 1761 at Pardo, the Treaty of Madrid was abrogated, allowing the Seven Missions to continue under the jurisdiction of the Spanish Jesuit province of Paraguay. But, by then the damage had been done. The failure to resolve the boundary question peacefully led to a protracted period of undeclared warfare over the disputed southern frontier. And the image of militarized Indians under Jesuit control, unilaterally opposing the mandates of the Iberian monarchs had a significant impact on European minds. In *Candide*, Voltaire portrays a sword-wielding Jesuit riding on horseback.[13] The events surrounding the attempted implementation of the Treaty of Madrid, moreover, provided much grist to Pombal's propaganda mill and served to fortify his conviction that the presence of the Jesuits in Portuguese lands was an impediment to the realization of wider imperial designs.

As these events were unfolding Pombal was moving aggressively to reform Portugal's mercantile and imperial policy. In order to implement his ambitious agenda to protect the national interest Pombal threw his support behind the established Portuguese merchants in the metropolis against the interlopers and contrabandists who had disrupted regular commerce and credit. He hoped that by making imperial consolidation a profitable operation, he could link the interests of Portuguese entrepreneurs more closely to the interests of the empire.

In December 1750 the Crown, resolving a long dispute about the best method to raise taxes on Brazil's gold production (see fig. 24), accepted the proposition made by the inhabitants of Minas Gerais in 1734, which had offered to the Crown a basic minimum contribution of 100 *arrobas* (1465.6 kilograms) of gold per annum. This annual contribution was to be guaranteed by the municipal councils of the captaincy,

---

[12] See discussions by Magnus Mörner, *Region and State in Latin America* (Baltimore, 1993), pp. 29–32. The Jesuit Guaraní missions reached a demographic peak in 1732 with 141,182 Indians. By 1740 the number had fallen to 73,910 due to famine and epidemics and mobilizations required to suppress a revolt in Paraguay. The population had risen again to 88,828 by 1758 but by 1783 was 56,092 and by 1797, 45,700. The ending of the segregation policy of the Jesuits thus, in the long term, mainly postponed the problem of integration of the Indian population with other rural inhabitants. For a discussion of this see Magnus Mörner, *Region and State*, pp. 29–32.

[13] Voltaire, *Candide*, translated and edited by Robert M. Adams (New York and London, 1966), pp. 30–31.

whose task it was to levy a poll tax (*derrama*) to make up the difference should the quota not be filled. The new legislation also established foundry houses (*casas de fundição*) in the principal towns of the administrative districts (*comarcas*) where all gold had to be smelted. The administration of these foundry houses was to be placed in the hands of the most substantial local property owners nominated by a plurality of votes in the municipal councils and approved by the superior crown magistrate (*ouvidor*) of the district not, as had been normal practice, the crown magistrates. These foundry house officials were charged to work closely with the administrators of the *entradas*, the tax on goods entering the Minas Gerais region. These taxes were farmed out to the same merchants the government wished to involve in the administration of the gold smelting operation. The royal decree setting up the new system introduced vigorous measures to control contraband and provided incentives for those who cooperated with the authorities. Goldsmiths were expelled from the captaincy of Minas Gerais in 1751 in order to make fraud more difficult.[14]

The Portuguese state also intervened to protect and regulate the traditional staples of the Luso-Brazilian commercial system – sugar and tobacco. Inspection houses were established in the principal Brazilian ports with the objective of regulating supply and sustaining the prices of these colonial staples. Brazilian merchants and agricultural producers were encouraged to participate in all these new government organs.

As with the new institutions intended to improve the fiscalization of gold production in Minas Gerais, the Portuguese government encouraged local participation in the management of the staple trades. The inspectors were to include representatives of the Brazilian merchant community and of the sugar and tobacco producers, selected through their respective municipal councils by a plurality of votes. Protection was also afforded to the debtors of the hinterland.[15]

The government's aggressive new policies did not go unchallenged. The gold quota and *derrama* provoked a bitter controversy in the overseas council. The Brazilian-born Alexandre de Gusmão, a key negotiator for the Treaty of Madrid, felt the scheme had been "fabricated with more zeal than experience of the mines" and would fail, as all other methods had, to prevent contraband and fraud. He believed the tribute would in effect fall only on the miners, virtually exempting ecclesiastics, men of government, local magnates and merchants, who he said took most of the miners' gold in return for merchandise and foodstuffs. He saw grave danger in the process of *derrama*, the poll tax to make up the quota, which again he believed would fall heavily on the miners.[16] It

---

[14] "Alvará . . . para a cobrança do direito senhorial dos quintos . . ." December 3, 1750, BNLCP, codex 453, fos. 47–50v; "Bando publicado . . . para . . . sahirem . . . os Ourives," Vila Rica, July 31, 1751, IHGB, file 8, doc. 26; "Coleção da casa dos Contos de Ouro Prêto, documentos avulsos," ANRJ, files 99/3, 86/3, 94/2; AHU, codex 311/15; "Regimento das Intendencias e casas de fundição," in José Roberto Monteiro de Campos Coelho e Sousa, ed., *Sistema, ou colecção dos regimentos reaes, contem os regimentos pertencentes a fazenda real, justiças, e militares . . .* , 7 vols. (Lisbon, 1783) IV, pp. 503–516. Also A. J. R. Russell-Wood in *CHLA* II, pp. 547–600

[15] "Regimento . . . casas de inspeção . . ." April 1, 1751, IHGB, file 71, doc. 17.

[16] "Reparos sobre a dispozição da ley de 3 de dizembro de 1750," Lisbon, December 18, 1750, IHGB/AUC, 1-2-39, fos. 65, 80–87.

24 Gold mining in Brazil

was also unclear whether regulation and price control of sugar and tobacco alone would provide a real challenge to the stranglehold of foreign credit on the Luso-Brazilian system. The inspection houses were, in the broader Atlantic context, to some degree palliatives. They did not tackle the root causes of the difficulties facing the established agricultural and merchant groups in the colony, which, as Pombal had discerned while in London, lay in the dominance of the foreign merchants in the metropolis and the power of these merchants to extend long-term credit.

On the far-off, vast, and ill-comprehended frontiers of the Amazon, moreover, the sanguine hopes that the Indians, and most especially those of the Jesuit missions, would be peacefully assimilated and Europeanized was proving to be disastrously misplaced. In his instructions of 1751 Mendonça Furtado had been required to investigate "with great caution, circumspection, and prudence" the reputed wealth and capital of the Jesuits.[17] After his arrival in America, relations between Pombal's brother and the black robes steadily deteriorated. The colonists of the far north who had long felt themselves shut off from the benefits of Amazon trade did everything they could to

[17] "Instruçoes regias . . . para [Mendonça Furtado]," in *Correspondência inédita* I, pp. 26–31.

encourage the split between Mendonça Furtado and the Jesuits. In this they were aided in Lisbon by Paulo da Silva Nunes, who for fifteen years had represented the interests of the colonists of Maranhão in Lisbon with constant propaganda against the Jesuits.[18] Nunes claimed that the religious orders' protection of the Indians had deprived the colonists of workers and complained that because the price of imported African slaves was exorbitant they were unable to obtain substitute labor from this source.

While the Jesuits' enemies exaggerated their wealth, it was not inconsiderable. The Jesuits, by virtue of the number and value of their properties, the temporal government over numerous mission villages (*aldeias*), and the labor use of many other Indian settlements, possessed a capital and power long coveted by the Portuguese settlers of Grão Pará and Maranhão.[19] On the island of Marajó alone the Jesuits managed ranches containing over 100,000 head of cattle, and rural estates producing sugar. They also commercialized the fruits of Indian expeditions into the Amazon forests for native drugs, cloves, cacao, and cinnamon which were conveyed by fleets of canoes to the Atlantic seaboard where they were collected in the warehouse of the Jesuit *colégio*. Here they were exempt from taxation and customs dues and were marketed by means of a fair maintained while the Portuguese fleet was in port. At Belém the products were sold to ships' captains and commissaries from Portugal, and a smaller portion consigned to the metropolis in the name of the Society of Jesus and under its stamp. Like their colleagues elsewhere in Brazil, the Jesuits managed, in addition to their religious activities, a mercantile operation of considerable sophistication resulting from years of capital accumulation, reinvestment, and careful husbandry.

During 1754 Mendonça Furtado, in a series of letters to his brother, took up the pleas of the colonists that a commercial company be formed to facilitate the supply of African labor to the Amazon region. He believed African slave imports would relieve the pressure on the colonists to enslave and mistreat the native Indian population. He also wanted to see more investment in the Amazonian economy in order to develop its export potential, which he believed a monopoly company would provide. Mendonça Furtado, therefore, recommended the foundation of a privileged trading

---

[18] J. Lúcio d'Azevedo, *Os Jesuítas no Grão Pará, suas missões e a colonização* (Lisbon, 1901), pp. 196, 200, 248–249; "Cálculo das excessivas negociações que os Reverendos Missionarios, os seus Prelados e Comunidades fazem com o serviço dos Indios e Indias nas lavradoras e fábricas que tem 57 aldeos de S. Magistrada chamados as missões do Maranhão e Grão Pará junto a elles nos certões . . . ", n.d. [1755] IHGB/AUC, 1-1-8, fos. 290–309; Manuel Nunes Dias, "Fomento ultramarino e mercantilismo" II, *RHSP* 67 (July–September 1966), p. 96; Roberto C. Simonsen, *História económica do Brasil 1500–1820*, 5th edition (São Paulo, 1967), pp. 324–326, 329; Arthur Cezar Ferreira Reis, *A Amazônia que os Portuguêses revelaram* (Rio de Janeiro, 1956), p. 50. For further details of Jesuit activities in Amazonia and throughout Brazil, see the monumental study by Serafim Leite, *História da companhia de Jesus no Brasil*, 10 vols. (Lisbon and Rio de Janeiro, 1938–1950). For a judicious treatment of the expulsion of the Jesuits from Latin America as a whole, see Magnus Mörner's introduction to his collected readings in the Borzoi series, *The Expulsion of the Jesuits from Latin America* (New York, 1965), pp. 3–30.

[19] [Mendonça Furtado] to [Carvalho e Melo], January 24, 1754, *Correspondência inédita* II, pp. 460–464; Alden, "Economic Aspects of the Expulsion of the Jesuits from Brazil," pp. 25–65. Also "Rendimento dos bens sequestrados aos jesuitas do estado do Grão Pará e Maranhão," in Manuel Nunes Dias, *A Companhia Geral do Grão Pará e Maranhão (1755–1778)*, 2 vols. (Pará, 1970) I, pp. 179–191.

company for the region. To establish prosperity fully in Amazonia, however, he also believed it was essential to dislodge the Jesuits from the "absolute power" which he claimed their control of Indian labor and the strategic position of their settlements gave them over commerce and contraband. To assert secular authority, encourage commerce, as well as to furnish African labor on easier terms than those offered by private traders, Pombal's brother argued that the foundation of a company with "solid funds" appeared a logical solution. An abundant supply of Africans would obviate the need for Indian slavery and hence circumvent Jesuit influence, as well as provide crucial labor to work the land and augment commerce. This, in turn, would increase royal revenue and help finance the new defensive system to secure the frontiers of Portuguese America.[20]

Mendonça Furtado's proposition had met with a sympathetic reception in Lisbon. Already Pombal had experimented with the idea of a monopolistic company for Asian trade on the British model, but the idea from Pará provided a practical way of realizing an important part of his long-term intentions. Pombal acted quickly in 1755: the Company of Grão Pará and Maranhão was established and simultaneous legislation, on June 6 and 7, 1755, decreed the complete liberty and integration of the indigenous population, removing the religious and secular tutelage of the missionaries granted under the missionary regulation of 1680.

Even at the time, Mendonça Furtado was aware that so complete a break with tradition would not work. He advised Lisbon that

as one who had dealt with them [the indigenous population] on a day to day basis and who has lived in their settlements for two years, [that] the most pious intentions of his majesty will be frustrated if these miserable and rustic ignorants are totally placed in control of their own affairs . . . and since it is not possible to pass from one extreme to the other without seeking some means by which it is possible to obtain the objective [of the legislation] I see no more appropriate measure than to place in each settlement a man with the title of director.[21]

In fact, the Jesuits were quickly replaced by a system of state-appointed functionaries who were intended to provide a bridge between religious isolationism and secular integration. The directory system was infused with the high expectations of an enlightened government. In reality, it provided a means to subject the unfortunate indigenous population to the most extreme forms of exploitation and misuse.

The Company of Grão Pará and Maranhão was given the exclusive right to all commerce and navigation of the captaincies for a period of twenty years. Pombal also decreed the expulsion from the whole of Brazil of the *comissários volantes* at this time. The establishment of the monopoly company and the banishing of the small itinerant traders were key components of an overall policy with objectives well beyond

---

[20] [Mendonça Furtado] to [Diogo de Mendonça Corte Real], January 18, 1754, *Correspondência inédita* II, pp. 456–459; [Mendonça Furtado] to [Pombal], January 26, 1754, ibid., II, pp. 465–470.
[21] [Oficio do governador] May 21, 1757; J. Lúcio d'Azevedo, *Os Jesuítas no Grão Pará*, p. 286. For complete text of "Directório que se deve observar nos povoações dos indios . . . " Belém, August 17, 1758, see *Aula do Comércio*, ed. Marcos Carneiro de Mendonça (Rio de Janeiro, 1982), pp. 139–181.

the confines of Amazonia. Pombal hoped that by granting special privileges and protection to Portuguese entrepreneurs via such a mechanism as a monopoly company, he could help national merchant houses accumulate sufficient capital to compete more effectively with British merchants in the colonial trade as a whole and, by extension, in Portugal proper. By simultaneously striking at the itinerant traders he sought to remove one key linkage between the foreign merchants in Portugal and the Brazilian producers. The hidden objective of the Brazilian monopoly company was thus much broader than its regional focus might at first indicate. "One of the great public utilities that the commercial company will bring," Pombal wrote to his brother during August,

is the regulation of the quantities of merchandise in proportion to consumption . . . because lack of this just proportion resulted necessarily in the ruin of the commerce of the national merchants in benefit of foreign merchants and nations. For private nationals buying from the foreigners without rule or measure as much as the foreigners wished to credit them, introduced in one year goods requiring three years to consume and the national merchants were ruined because they could not sell with profit.[22]

Pombal, writing privately to Duke Silva-Tarouca, told him that his aim in establishing the Company of Grão Pará and Maranhão was "to restore to the market places of Portugal and Brazil the commissions of which they were deprived, and which are the principal substance of commerce, and the means by which there could be established the great merchant houses which had been lacking in Portugal."[23]

The establishment of the Grão Pará and Maranhão company and the abolition of the itinerant commissaries formed a two-handled lever to pry open the contraband–foreign merchant nexus. The establishment of the monopolistic company and the economic legislation of 1755 was a deliberate action by the state to rationalize the entrepreneurial structure in favor of the large established national merchants. The Company of Grão Pará and Maranhão, Pombal told Mendonça Furtado, "was the only way to revindicate the commerce of all Portuguese America from the hands of foreigners."[24] The objective of granting Portuguese merchants monopoly privileges was to help them accumulate sufficient capital to compete more effectively with foreign credit in every area of Luso-Brazilian commerce.

Pombal's monopoly company thus met objectives on several levels – not all of them made explicit. The fundamental objective in the colonial trade was to try to diminish the influence of the British, but the methods employed to achieve this aim were subtle, pragmatic, and enveloped in subterfuge. The unavoidable problem

---

[22] [Pombal] to [Mendonça Furtado] August 4, 1755, BNLCP, codex 262, fo. 107. Also for legislation on Indian emancipation see the important letter not published by Carneiro de Mendonça; discussed by Padre Helio Abranches Viotti, S.J. in "O pombalino império na Amazônia na regência de Francisco Xavier de Mendonça Furtado," *RHSP* 100 (1974), p. 322.

[23] Also [Pombal] to [Silva-Tarouca] November 3, 1755, and [Pombal] to [Silva-Tarouca], *AAP*, pp. 419–420.

[24] [Pombal] to [Mendonça Furtado] August 4, 1755, BNLCP, codex 26, fo. 90.

with the British–Portuguese relationship was that it was circumscribed by treaties that, for political and security reasons, the Portuguese wanted to maintain. One way of taking action against British influence, however, while avoiding open confrontation over the terms of the treaties, was to use a variety of techniques in Portugal and within the colonial setting to shift concessionary economic advantages away from foreigners to Portuguese merchant groups. In this respect the choice of the Amazon to begin the process was a very clever maneuver. The British did not perceive the threat to their interests until the end of the decade though in Vienna, Silva-Tarouca much appreciated the subtlety of Pombal's measures. These were precisely the type of great new dispositions of which he approved, and surrounded by the camouflage he recommended should always disguise innovations in government policy.

While these actions by the Portuguese government were seeking to contain and limit the role of foreign credit and participation in the Atlantic trade, the key components in the Anglo-Portuguese reciprocal commercial relationship were also subjected to increased state intervention. Pombal was giving close attention to the Port wine sector, which by 1755 had been facing four years of unsteady markets after three decades of unbroken prosperity. Between 1750 and 1755 the price of wine had fallen 8.61 percent annually, which produced recriminations between Portuguese producers and British shippers as well as between large and small producers, the former blaming the latter for saturating the market.[25]

In the upper Douro valley, the traditional source of the wine exported from Oporto, the major producers were large landowners – some secular, some religious orders. Substantial capital was needed to engage in wine production. It was necessary for the landowners to build and own lodges, presses, casks and vessels for transportation down the Douro river to Oporto. The more substantial of the aristocratic producers tended to live part of the year on their *quintas* upriver, and part of the year in Oporto, where they were influential in local government, regional affairs, and in the prestigious local sodalities. The president of the *misericórdia* in the 1760s, Dom António de Lencastre, for instance, came from an old noble family which owned large vineyards in the upper Douro. Other important families engaged in wine production included the Leite Pereiras, Pacheco Pereiras, Belleza Andrades, and the Sousas of Mateus.[26]

By the early 1750s, however, the traditional producers were facing a severe economic and entrepreneurial challenge from small producers who were selling from two to eight times more wine to the British merchants than were the big vineyard owners. Vine cultivation, moreover, had spread into many other regions of Portugal, and even Douro producers bought wine outside the traditional region and passed it off as Port. In 1755, the principal vineyard owners petitioned the government in Lisbon for relief and assistance. Again Pombal responded with speed, establishing

---

[25] See Borges de Macedo, *A situação económica*, pp. 48–49.
[26] Schneider, *Pombal e o vinho do Porto*, pp. 40–44, 55–84.

the General Company for the Agriculture of the Vineyards of the Upper Douro (Companhia Geral da Agricultura das Vinhas do Alto Douro) in 1756.[27]

The company statutes were largely based on a plan put forward by the large noble vineyard owners of the Douro, led by Luís Belleza de Andrade, who owned vineyards in Valdigem, Gouvães, and Ventezelo. Belleza had been active in promoting Port wine exports, and with other vineyard owners had sent a representative to Russia in 1755, in the hope of opening up a Baltic trade. In late 1755, Frei João de Mansilla, a Dominican theologian of Oporto, whose family owned vineyards in the Douro valley, suggested to Belleza and his colleagues that they establish an officially designated zone for Port wine production, and that any wine produced outside this demarcated area would be prohibited from the export trade. This idea became the basic component of the Douro company's monopoly and Mansilla, one of Pombal's most active collaborators and official representative of the company in Lisbon.

The Douro producers reacted enthusiastically when Pombal announced his planned company in 1756. A mix of investment in the company's first capital fund was solicited from both producers and Oporto businessmen. Luís Belleza de Andrade became the first president. To protect the larger estates, Pombal abolished all entailment yielding less than 100 *milréis* per annum in the north of Portugal, and 200 *milréis* in the south. He also issued legislation instituting strict primogeniture for entailed estates, prohibiting daughters from inheriting more than 4,000 *cruzados* unless there were no male heirs.[28]

The objective of the Upper Douro Company was essentially to protect the upper Douro vineyard owners from the vast expansion of vine cultivation by smaller producers which had occurred over the previous decades. The title of the company is almost invariably mistranslated (indeed it is very often mistranscribed even in Portuguese), transforming *vinhas* (vineyards) into *vinho* (wine), thus misrepresenting entirely the major objective of the company. The company established a restricted production zone and exclusive name (*nom d'appellation*) almost a century before the French. The demarcation of the upper Douro was the most important measure resulting from the company's establishment. At its widest, the demarcation was 16 miles, at its narrowest, less than a mile. This restricted area for export wine produced about 25,000 pipes in 1758, and the wines could be sold for between 25 and 36 *milréis* a pipe. Pombal and Mansilla established the first demarcation guidelines.

---

[27] The excellent study by Susan Schneider is based in large part on her careful use of the company's business records now held by the private company (the Companhia Velha) that succeeded the monopoly company established by Pombal. Included among these documents is the fundamental correspondence between Frei Mansilla in Lisbon and the administrators of the company in Oporto. Documentation from Pombal's personal archive containing complaints from the British factory, the statutes of the company, etc. are in BNLCP. Also, for an overview see António Barreto, *Um retrato do Douro* (Vista Alegre, 1984). A list of shareholders of the Douro company is printed by Borges de Macedo in *A situação económica*, pp. 135–139.

[28] *Alvará* of August 3, 1770, September 3, 1767, and August 17, 1761.

Thereafter three government commissions (1757, 1758, 1761) drew the final boundaries.[29]

Pombal's intervention in the northern wine-producing region was not unlike his intervention in the colonial entrepreneurial nexus, using state intervention, in effect, to protect the large export producers. All opposition was ruthlessly repressed on a day-to-day basis by the stringent enforcement of the Douro company's monopoly rights, and more generally by the vigorous exercise of military and judicial authority.[30] This policy, as with the protection afforded the producers of cash crops in Brazil, aimed at stabilizing prices and market conditions. But as John Croft, a British wine merchant, observed in 1788, the exclusive zone in the Douro included "the vineyards only of the principal Gentry and Religious Houses, excluding those of the menial Vintagers and Farmers."[31] And the demarcated zone included one very remarkable exception, the wine produced on Pombal's own estate at Oeiras, an estate bordering not the Douro river, but the Tagus some hundred miles to the south of the Port wine area. It was a lucrative arrangement for Pombal's property and added greatly to the wealth of his family.

The purpose of the company of the vineyards of the upper Douro was not to seize the Port wine trade from the British Port wine exporters. The privileged position Port wine enjoyed in British markets was, after all, a result of British tariff manipulation (in favor of Portuguese wine), and was exactly the sort of reciprocal and mutually beneficial trading of which Pombal approved. This access to the British markets he had no intention of disrupting. The state was intervening to protect agricultural producers by seeking to control production and thereby assure stable markets and prices. Father Mansilla put the policy with respect to the British succinctly: "The objective," he wrote to Pombal, "was to hurt them in such a way they cannot scream."[32] On the surface therefore, neither the Company of Grão Pará and Maranhão nor the Douro monopoly company posed any overt threat to British economic power in Portugal, and neither violated the treaties which circumscribed economic relations between Britain and Portugal. For a time, Pombal was able to disguise the full intent of these measures from the British. In this subterfuge he was assisted by a serious conflict within the British community in Portugal.

The great profitability of Luso-Brazilian commerce and contraband had produced a serious contradiction of function among the British merchants in Portugal and it was by the careful exploitation of this conflict that Pombal succeeded for a time in camouflaging the real intention of his measures. In Lisbon, the new "universal" traders had sought to capture control of the factory and to circumvent the control of the

---

[29] Alvaro Moreira da Fonseca, "As demarcações pombalinos no Douro vinhateiro," in *Anais do Instituto do Vinho do Porto*, 3 vols. (Oporto, 1949–1951).

[30] *Devassa a que mandou proceder sua Majestade no território do Alto Douro pelo desembargador António de Mesquita e Moura (1771–1775)*, organized by António Brás de Oliveira and Maria José Marinho, introduction by António Barreto (Lisbon, 1983).

[31] John Croft, *A Treatise on the Wines of Portugal* (Oporto, 1940) (facsimile of 1788 edition).

[32] Cited in Schneider, *Pombal e o vinho do Porto*, p. 169.

consul, an appointee of the British Crown. By doing so they hoped to neutralize the most powerful obstacle to the transformation of the factory from its original function as an organization of British factors engaged only in the British trade into a privileged and autonomous merchant corporation involved in the whole range of commercial speculation. Lord Tyrawly noted with disdain in 1752 the rise of a custom since he was "first at Lisbon . . . which is that upon all matters that arise they call a meeting of the factory . . . where any low fellow . . . has as much right to talk as much nonsense as if he was the head of the best house in Lisbon." William Mawman, a Lisbon merchant, in private correspondence with Lord Tyrawly described the attempt of the "Grumbletonians" party during a riotous general meeting in 1752 to intimidate the new consul, George Crowle, into confirming the powers they had wrung from his senile predecessor on his deathbed. The new powers were so extensive as to place effective control in the hands "of twelve men whose turbulent spirits, especially of some of them ye Lordship is fully appraised of." Crowle succeeded in thwarting the scheme but Mawman was not optimistic, reporting that "after much squabbling ye power of ye new committee were reduced. Bristow and I are of ye number of ye new members but whilst ye Sherleys, Burrells, King and Hake are of ye number I expect no good."[33]

One of the "turbulent spirits" Mawman mentioned is of particular interest – William Shirley. In 1753 Pombal, fearful that excessive demand for grain in Spain caused by crop failure would cause a dearth of grain in Portugal, forbade the re-export of wheat arriving in the Tagus.[34] Crowle supported the Portuguese government's measure. A violent dispute was provoked in the factory, with William Shirley leading the opposition. Crowle, acting with the Portuguese Judge Conservator, asked Pombal to banish Shirley from Portugal which Pombal was only too pleased to do. The Sicilian corn trade had been one of the "universal trading" enterprises condemned by Tyrawly, and the very collusion of British representative and Portuguese government was probably exactly what the universal traders feared after the visit of Lord Tyrawly, and one of the compulsions behind their attempt to take control of the factory. Influential pressure in London was to bring a reversal of the banishment order but the display of open faction within the British community in Portugal, involving the British Crown's own representative, only served to weaken the factory's case, to divert attention from the deeper intentions of Pombal's measures, and to confirm the aspersions concerning the role of the "universal traders" by the Portuguese government and Lord Tyrawly.

On one issue, however, the British authorities remained sensitive and vigilant. The Portuguese government, in its efforts to crack down on contraband, had confiscated the gold in the possession of one Humphrey Bunster and about to be remitted to Britain. The Humphrey Bunster affair opened a long and complicated test case since it established a precedent which could not fail to concern the British merchant

---

[33] Tyrawly papers, in Walford, *British Factory*, pp. 54–56.
[34] See Earl J. Hamilton, *War and Prices in Spain, 1651–1800* (Cambridge, MA, 1947), pp. 174, 198.

community in Portugal, challenging, as it did, a basic objective of mercantilist policy, the import of bullion into Britain from Portugal.

After the great earthquake of November 1, 1755, Pombal levied an extra 4 percent import tax across the board as a contribution to rebuilding the city. The British merchants strenuously objected to paying this levy. The members of the factory immediately saw the new tax as a breach of the Cromwellian treaty's secret article, and as a means of raising their complaints against Pombal before the London government. They were, they told London, "sensible that a breach of treaty was the only solid foundation upon which a national complaint can be granted."[35] A powerful memorandum was forwarded by the factory to Secretary of State Fox who immediately contacted the old Portugal hand, Lord Tyrawly, to advise him on the question. The report for Secretary Fox prepared by the former ambassador turned out to be distinctly unfavorable to the pretensions of the British merchants. Lord Tyrawly noted the dichotomy which had developed within the factory between the merchant's role as "universal trader" and as "British factor" and came down solidly on the side of the factors. Anglo-Portuguese trade returned to its more traditional patterns, Lord Tyrawly believed, so that the activities of the factory would be restricted to a "wholly British trade." Tyrawly reacted against the use certain British merchants were making of the factory, in fact, in much the way Pombal reacted against the use Portuguese speculators were making of the Brazil fleets, though his reasoning was decidedly more traditional than was that of Pombal, who understood the role of credit and invisible earnings. Tyrawly, in his report to London, even revealed a willingness to act in concert with Pombal and hinted that "new regulations" had been contemplated by them in 1752.[36]

Clearly, in the changed political environment of the 1750s the "universal traders" found themselves in a vulnerable position before the new activism of the Pombaline regime. The old-established British factors in Portugal might at times have been tempted to trade in non-British merchandise, and certainly entered into arrangements with *comissários volantes*, but they also had a regular and legal access to fleet traffic backed by treaty and tradition, as well as a strong interest in the smooth functioning of the fleet system itself. Thus, while it was far from true that only the universal traders had been linked to *comissários volantes*, it was a convenient fiction, and one that could be used to political advantage by the Portuguese government.

The Company of Grão Pará and Maranhão thus caused no head-on collision between the British and Portuguese governments because there was nothing in the company's statutes that directly attacked vital British interests. Although the directors of the company had to be Portuguese subjects or naturalized citizens, investment was open to all. Foreign investment was specifically welcomed and guaranteed protection against confiscation and reprisal in case of war between Portugal and the nation of the

---

[35] "Memórias do consul e factória britânica," BNLCP, codex 94, fos. 11, 37.

[36] "Considerations on the Affairs of Lisbon," Tyrawly papers in Walford, *British Factory*, pp. 54–70.

investor concerned.[37] As compulsory agents of exchange for the Brazilian far north, the company was peripheral to the main channels of trade, and in no way upset the equilibrium of Anglo-Portuguese commerce. The founding of the monopoly company served indirectly to undermine the interests of British merchants' houses in Portugal, but it avoided providing an excuse for the British government to intervene on behalf of its nationals and while the British certainly had lucrative indirect relations with the Jesuits, in both the north and south of Brazil, the British government could hardly be the Jesuits' protector since the Jesuits of all Catholic orders held highest place in the demonology of British Protestantism. Indeed, Pombal was well aware of this fact from his time in London and in his battle with the Society of Jesus had the Portuguese envoy in London collect information on the Jesuits' role in plots against the British Crown, including the infamous Guy Fawkes and his plot against Parliament. The company and the abolition of the *comissários volantes* was on the surface in no way detrimental to those British houses engaged in supplying British goods for regular fleet traffic, and only an attack on their interests would justify action from London.

From the Portuguese point of view, Pombal's policy was a practical and logical one within the terms of the Anglo-Portuguese economic relationship. The balance of trade might always have been unfavorable to Portugal but it was at base an exchange of manufactured goods for Portuguese raw materials and wine and, as such, though one-sided, mutually beneficial. The aim of a Portuguese economic nationalist would always be to achieve reciprocity in Anglo-Portuguese exchange, not its elimination. "It was not the treaty [of Methuen] that was the cause of such pernicious effects but the infractions and abuses," Pombal had written in his famous account of the grievances of Portuguese subjects in Britain.[38] He stressed to the British that all his measures had been taken with the treaties in view. His rules and economic laws, he claimed, were intended to facilitate their object, which was "reciprocal advantages by legal means." Any honorable businessman could see the benefits of the provisions he had made. The opposition, he said, came from those elements among the foreign merchants in Lisbon who were linked by interest to the contrabandists, and who were misusing their privileges as British citizens. They were not worthy of the protection of Great Britain. After all, he pointed out, Britain's own special envoy, Lord Tyrawly, had found they did not deserve such special consideration.[39]

Pombal's measures, in fact, were based on a careful assessment of the economic and diplomatic factors involved in the situation. For a small power like Portugal, he recognized that statesmanship lies as much in assessing the power and limitations of friends as in assessing that of enemies. Within the relationship with Great Britain there lay large room for maneuver, and Pombal realized that he could safely make major policy changes and take fundamental decisions on vital national interests without

[37] See discussion by Borges de Macedo, *A situação económica*, pp. 117–118.
[38] Cited by d'Azevedo, *Marquês de Pombal*, p. 211.
[39] "Cartas de Londres," BNLCP, codex 611, fos. 10–17.

calling the framework of the alliance itself into question. He had no intention of altering or dispensing with the ancient connection between Lisbon and London. If he could maintain the distinction between "measures rather to the disadvantage of the factory than to Great Britain," as the traveler William Dalrymple wrote, he knew that he ran no risk of a major clash with the British government.[40]

Pombal took much from classic mercantilist theory and practice in his policy-making, both from its British and its French or Colbertian origins, but the use of the term "mercantilism" to describe Pombal's policy is not entirely appropriate. Mercantilism, when defined narrowly, however, describes a policy whereby trade is regulated, taxed, and subsidized by the state to promote an influx of gold and silver — the objective of such state intervention being aimed more broadly at achieving a favorable balance of trade. Pombal's policy was more focused than this. Its objective was to use mercantilist techniques — monopoly companies, regulation, taxation, and subsidies — to facilitate capital accumulation by individual Portuguese merchants. This aid to individual Portuguese capitalists had wider objectives and consequences because it was part and parcel of a scheme to fortify the nation's bargaining power within the Atlantic commercial system.

The problem for an enlightened Iberian economic nationalist, which is perhaps a more accurate way to describe Pombal, was not so much to encourage the influx of precious metals; this was rarely a problem for Iberian economic policymakers given the fact that Spain and Portugal and their empires were the principal source of the world's bullion supply in this period. The dilemma was precisely the opposite, that is, policymakers needed to devise measures to retain capital within their own economic system and at the same time to multiply the positive and diminish the negative economic impact of being producers of precious metals. The theory and practice of mercantilism was, after all, the creation of bullion-poor northwestern Europe. The application of the theory and practice of mercantilism in the bullion-rich Iberian peninsula was bound to be partial because the end of the policy was fundamentally different from that sought by mercantilism's progenitors. The Iberians aimed to retain bullion, the northwest Europeans aimed to attract it.

Pombal's methods reflected, in fact, the peculiarities of Portugal's position within the Luso-Atlantic system, and the particular impact on Portuguese entrepreneurship of the Brazilian gold boom of 1700–1760. Essentially, the all-powerful minister, Pombal, placed the power of the state decisively on one side of the conflict that had developed between Portuguese entrepreneurs as a consequence of the gold boom. He chose the large, established Portuguese and Brazilian merchants over their smaller competitors because he saw the small merchants as mere creatures or commission agents of the foreigners. With support from the state he hoped the large Portuguese merchants would in time be able to challenge the foreigners at their own game.

His economic policy was a logical one in view of Portugal's position within the eighteenth-century international trading system. It protected mutually beneficial trade

[40] Major William Dalrymple, *Travelling Through Spain and Portugal in 1774* (London, 1777), p. 125.

(such as the Portuguese wine trade), but it also sought to develop a powerful national class of businessmen with the capital resources and the business skills to compete in the international and Portuguese domestic markets with their foreign, especially British, competitors. It was not an easy policy to pursue, at least overtly, because it was essential to achieve this outcome without bringing into question the political and military support that the treaties with Britain guaranteed and which was essential if Spanish ambitions were to be kept at bay. Duke Silva-Tarouca wrote to Pombal approvingly in November 1755, praising his "excellent measures." Pombal had become the Portuguese Colbert, the duke concluded.[41]

41 [Silva-Tarouca] to [Pombal], November 3, 1755, *AAP.*

4

Collaborators and conspirators

To end the rule of King Sebastião it is necessary to end that of King José.

(1758)[1]

Pombal's intervention in the Portuguese economy did not go unopposed. His creation of a designated zone in the upper Douro and the enforced rationalization of the entrepreneurial structure of the Luso-Brazilian merchant community by means of monopoly commercial joint stock companies and prohibitions on private trading provoked repercussions throughout Portuguese society. In effect, the Portuguese state had chosen to favor particular elements within patterns of conflicting interests. The result was to force those groups not favored into opposition and, at times, into collusion and conspiracy. The lament of the Brazil merchant to Alonso in an anonymous chronicle published in London in 1755 well represents the complaints of those who suffered from Pombal's economic policy during the 1750s.

The establishment of companies with such exclusive privileges has proved not only ruinous, by annihilating that spirit of enterprise and industry which results from the prospect of gain and is the support of thousands, but confines the wealth acquired by the trade of that part of the world to a few, which before was generally diffused throughout the Kingdom.[2]

Confining wealth to the few, however, was precisely what Dom Luís da Cunha had recommended in his *Political Testament*, and was at the heart of Pombal's scheme to develop a competitive Portuguese merchant class.

Pombal's measures, however, hurt many vested interests and the reaction was swift and angry. The promulgation of the Company of Grão Pará and Maranhão's monopoly privileges, the prohibition of the *comissários volantes*, and removal of Jesuit tutelage over the Indians provoked an immediate response from the dispossessed traders and Jesuits. Both found an organ for agitation in the Lisbon *mesa do bem comum*, a rudimentary commercial association. The *mesa*, established in the late 1720s, comprised a board of deputies representing the fraternity of Espírito Santo de

---

[1] Cited by Lúcio d'Azevedo, *O marquês de Pombal*, p. 171.
[2] *Adventures of Alonso: containing some striking anecdotes of the Present Prime Minister of Portugal* (London, 1755).

Pedreira.[3] Padre Bento da Fonseca, who represented the Maranhão missions in Lisbon, helped João Tomás Negreiros prepare a written protest against the company's privileges.[4] In the name of the *mesa do bem comum*, its lawyer, Nogueira Braga, sought an audience with the king and presented the Negreiros–Fonseca memorandum against the monopoly company. The seven of the *mesa*'s twelve deputies who took part in the audience with the king "indulged in the most virulent abuse of, and applied the most violent language to the Company of Grão Pará and Maranhão, predicting the most fatal consequences to the country," according to a contemporary.[5] Meanwhile, from the pulpit of the Basilica of Santa Maria Maior in Lisbon, the Jesuit Manoel Ballester, delivered a vehement attack on the monopoly, proclaiming that "he who entered it would not be of the company of Christ our Lord."[6]

Pombal acted swiftly in the face of these provocations. He immediately dissolved the fraternity of Espírito Santo as "prejudicial to the royal service, common interest, and commerce" and the deputies who had protested to the king were condemned to penal banishment. Among the confiscated papers of the *mesa* were documents that revealed the extent of Jesuit involvement. Pombal interpreted and dealt with the protest as if it were a conspiratorial uprising against royal power.[7] The *mesa do bem comum* was abolished in September 1755 and, in its place, Pombal established a *junta do comércio* or board of trade.[8] The new *junta* was charged with the regulation of "all affairs connected with commerce."[9] Headed by a *provedor* (superintendent), it was to consist of a secretary, advocate, and six deputies (four from Lisbon and two from Oporto). These officials had to be Portuguese born or naturalized subjects. The members of the *junta* were bound to strict secrecy in their deliberations.

Meanwhile, a serious popular reaction to the Douro company was developing in the north of Portugal, especially in the city of Oporto. Anger at the company was concentrated within several occupational groups adversely affected by the establishment of the upper Douro monopoly. The coopers, for example, whose guild had exclusive rights to cask production, feared the company's power to requisition their services. The company had been granted a monopoly of supply to the taverns and employed inspectors to control the quality of the wine sold at retail (and to verify that the wine sold was indeed company wine). The city tavern keepers were also adamantly opposed to the company's charter which reduced their number to 95, from an estimated 1,000 taverns in 1755. So intense was working people's hostility to the

[3] d'Azevedo, *Estudos*, pp. 54–56; also his *Marquês de Pombal*, pp. 138–140.
[4] d'Azevedo, *Os Jesuítas*, pp. 248–249. Padre Bento da Fonseca had long experience in Brazil and was author of a proposal in 1746 for the governance of the Indian communities. See "Parecer do Jesuíta Bento da Fonseca," *RIHGB* 68, 1, pp. 407–431. For the *regimento das missões* of 1680 see S. Leite, *História da companhia de Jesus no Brasil*, 10 vols. (Lisbon/Rio de Janeiro, 1938–1950) IV, pp. 369–375.
[5] António Carreira, *As companhias pombalinas* (Lisbon, 1983), pp. 35–38, 303–329.
[6] d'Azevedo, *Estudos*, p. 60.
[7] Pombal called the protest a *sublevação* in a private letter to his brother on August 5, 1755. See *Correspondência inédita* II, pp. 784–789.
[8] Originally the *mesa* was substituted by a *junta* of businessmen, Junta de Homens de Negócio, in September 1755. The statutes of the *junta* were promulgated in December 1756.
[9] *Estatutos da junta do comércio*, Sept. 30, 1755; and *Alvará porque . . . he por bem confirmar os estatutos da junta do comércio*, December 16, 1756, BNLCP, codex 453, fos. 128–147.

company that Belleza de Andrade advised Pombal in October 1756 that "only fear prevented them from revolting."[10]

Four months later Belleza's fears proved justified. On February 23, 1757, according to the account of the municipal government, some 5,000 rioters besieged the house of Bernardo Duarte de Figueiredo, Judge Conservator of the Douro company. They forced him to concede the freedom to buy and sell wine as had been the case before the company's establishment. The mob next stormed Belleza's mansion and ransacked the company's archives along with the mansion.[11] Pombal reacted to the uprising, which dissipated as quickly as it had arisen, with ferocity – treating the event as an act of *lèse-majesté* and giving full power to João Pacheco Pereira de Vasconcellos to head an official investigation. Pacheco Pereira was a director of the Douro company, judge of Oporto customs house and a rich landowner of the Douro valley.

The tribunal sat from April to October 1757 and tried 478 people; only 36 were absolved. The court condemned 375 men, 50 women and young boys: a total of 442 people. Some escaped and were hanged in effigy, but on October 14, 1757, thirteen men and one woman were hanged, their quartered limbs placed on spikes for fifteen days. Ten women and 49 men were exiled to Africa and Portuguese India and the remaining prisoners were flogged, sent to the galleys or imprisoned. Most lost all their goods through confiscation. Oporto (see fig. 25) was placed under a state of siege; people could not hold meetings after dark, wear capes, carry arms, or loiter. To enforce these restrictions 2,000 troops were billeted in Oporto, adding to the already existing 2,400 troops in the city.[12] These forces were commanded by João de Almada e Melo, Pombal's cousin, who became in effect *de facto* ruler of the north, surviving even Pombal's own fall from power in 1777.

The creation of the monopoly companies also provoked some unintended consequences. With the new definition of frontiers mandated by the Treaty of Madrid and the growing awareness of the strategic value of the interior, it was perhaps inevitable that the great complex of Spanish and Portuguese Jesuit missions should have begun to appear as a threat to the interests of both the dominant powers in South America. The Society of Jesus was one of the more visible casualties of the events that were set in motion by the imperial pretensions of Pombal's administration, the frontier demarcations, and by the attempts to nationalize sectors of the Luso-Brazilian commercial system. Given Pombal's desire to populate and exploit so great a tropical and subtropical region, to encourage European–Indian marriages, and to consolidate national territories, the clash with the Jesuits must appear an almost inevitable by-product. The Jesuits straddled the frontiers at the two most vital and sensitive points in Pombal's imperial system in the Amazon and in Paraguay and Uruguay. Pombal urged his brother in 1755 to use "every possible pretext to separate the Jesuits

[10] Cited in Schneider, *Pombal e o vinho do Porto*, pp. 97–129.
[11] Fernando de Oliveira, *O motim popular de 1757: uma página na história da época pombalina* (Oporto, 1930).
[12] "Sentença de Alçada que o Rei Nosso Senhor mandou conhecer da rebelhão sucçedada na cidade de Porto em 1757" (Lisbon, 1758), BNLCP, codex 456. See also Flavio Gonçalves, "A arte no Porto na época do marquês de Pombal," in *Pombal revisitado* I, pp. 103–130.

from the frontier and to break all communication between them and the Jesuits of the Spanish dominions."[13] The Jesuits' Indian policy, moreover, stood in the way of the desire to populate and Europeanize the interior by assimilation, and the Indian, both Mendonça Furtado and Pombal believed, must be made to constitute the "principal force and principal riches for the defense of the frontiers."[14]

The missions' exemption from contribution to the state in the far north also provoked acute tension between them and a colonial administration. The fiscal exemptions enjoyed by the Jesuits were especially irksome to Pombal's brother because one of his major objectives was to construct and finance an extensive network of fortifications and to do so out of the meager resources of the local treasury. The Jesuits' real and supposed wealth and exemptions left them very vulnerable since their activity was by no means confined to the missions but included vast holdings in urban and rural property. These included some of the greatest landed estates in all the Americas, the Fazenda of Santa Cruz in the captaincy of Rio de Janeiro, for example, extending over 100 square leagues and worked by a thousand slaves.[15]

The Jesuits' principal constituencies in Brazil were either the Amerindians or the sons of the colonial elite who relied for their children's education on the Jesuits' network of colleges. The philosophical debate over education had also left the Society of Jesus vulnerable to charges of obfuscation in the age of Enlightenment, despite the Jesuits' long tradition of scholarship and educational excellence. And intrachurch rivalries and jealousies enabled action against them to be dissociated from any feeling that the church itself was under attack. Indeed, some of the Jesuits' most outspoken enemies came from within the ecclesiastical establishment. Comparatively few in numbers in 1750, there were 474 Jesuits in the province of Brazil and 155 in the province of Maranhão. The colonists were, of course, not averse to the idea of obtaining choice properties at giveaway prices once the Jesuits had been expropriated, and had long complained of the irritating obstacle the Jesuits represented by standing between them and cheap Indian labor.

It was the Jesuit reaction to the Madrid agreements, however, that made the chances for a peaceful solution to the tension between the Society and the Pombaline state problematical. In opposition to the secular rulers of South America the Guaraní missions took up arms. Such treacherous activity in Pombal's eyes was compounded by signs of Jesuit collusion with the British who, according to the French minister in Lisbon, complained about the persecution of the Jesuits with whom they had "great and profitable commercial business."[16] *The Annual Register* in London noted in 1758 that the Jesuit settlements of Paraguay were reputed to have an area of "beneficial

---

[13] [Pombal] to [Mendonça Furtado], March 17, 1755, *Correspondência inédita* II pp. 668–673.

[14] Ibid.

[15] On the Fazenda of Santa Cruz, see Richard Graham, "Slave Families on a Rural Estate in Colonial Brazil," *JSH* 9, 3 (Spring 1976), pp. 382–402.

[16] *Quadro elementar das relações políticas e diplomáticas de Portugal . . .*, ed. Visconte de Santarém and L. A. Rebello da Silva (Lisbon and Paris, 1842–60) XVIII, p. 369.

25 Oporto: a scene near the riverfront, late nineteenth century (Arquivo Nacional de Fotografia)

commerce" for British traders.[17] And even from Vienna, Duke Silva-Tarouca pointed out to Pombal in February 1758 that "it was not evangelical spirit that armed with muskets eighty or a hundred thousand Indians, and erected an intermediate power from the River Plate to the Amazon, which one day could be fatal to the interested and dominant powers of South America."[18] In the *mesa do bem comum* affair, Pombal was convinced that the Jesuit missions of Grão Pará and Maranhão had resorted to intrigue against a project he regarded as essential to the battle against foreign domination of the economy. As opposition grew, the minister moved to consolidate his own power. The Jesuits, who had long performed the key role of confessor to the royal family, had been expelled from their position in September 1757 and replaced by priests in Pombal's confidence.[19]

[17] "An Account of the Political Establishment of the Jesuits in Paraguay," *The Annual Register for 1758* (London), pp. 362–367.
[18] [Silva-Tarouca] to [Pombal], Vienna, February 18, 1758, *AAP*, pp. 386–387, 395.
[19] Montalvão Machado, *Quem livrou Pombal*, pp. 94–95.

The socio-economic situation in Portugal had strictly limited the group from which Pombal could choose his collaborators. Given the dominance of foreigners in commercial activity in Lisbon and Oporto, the Portuguese were limited almost exclusively to internal and colonial trade. Only a handful of Portuguese merchant houses in Lisbon had the experience of exchange business, modern double-entry bookkeeping methods, and general commercial expertise to engage in business with foreign markets. Among them the most notable were the Lisbon houses of Bandeira and Bacigalupo, Born and Ferreira, and Emeretz and Brito, and, even in these businesses, the Portuguese were in partnership with foreigners.

It was among these few Portuguese merchants, however, that Pombal found three of his most active collaborators. José Rodrigues Bandeira became the first *provedor* of the new *junta do comércio* and director of the Pernambuco Company. António Caetano Ferreira and Luís José de Brito were both to play significant roles in the formulation and execution of economic policy. A second potent group of entrepreneurs came from the Cruz family, brought into the minister's favor by the activity of the Oratorian, António José da Cruz. José Francisco da Cruz, a merchant with interests in Bahia and in the tobacco trade, was closely involved in the formulation of the statutes of the Company of Grão Pará and Maranhão and became *provedor* and deputy of the company, administrator of the customs house in Lisbon, and was a close adviser on financial matters to Pombal in many different capacities. His brother, Joaquim Ignácio, who had made a most profitable marriage to an immensely rich Brazilian heiress, succeeded him in all his posts. The fourth brother, Anselmo José, succeeded to the Cruz fortune and became contractor to the tobacco monopoly. His daughter married Geraldo Wenceslão Braamcamp, director of the Pernambuco Company and deputy to the *junta do comércio*, later to become Anselmo José da Cruz's heir.[20]

One of the most important instruments used by Pombal to assist capital formation among the Portuguese merchants was the careful farming of royal contracts. The tobacco monopoly was one of the major and most lucrative of the royal monopolies farmed out to private businessmen. João Gomes de Araujo and João Marques Bacalhau, both close associates of Pombal, were important functionaries of the tobacco *junta*, and the office of *provedor* of the *junta do comércio* remained in the hands of the tobacco interests throughout Pombal's rule. José Rodrigues Bandeira was one of the major tobacco exporters in Portugal.[21]

Pombal also used colonial contracts to advance his policies of concentrating wealth in the hands of a new Portuguese business class. Ignácio Pedro Quintela, a tobacco trader and a member of both Brazil companies, held the contract of *dizimos* in Bahia. The right of collection of *dizimos* in Brazil had been relinquished by the church in return for fixed salaries paid by the state. The tax collection was farmed out by the overseas council in Lisbon to private individuals, usually on a three-year basis. During

[20] Borges de Macedo, *A situação económica*, pp. 141–143, 293–294. Ribeiro Júnior, *Colonização e monopólio no nordeste Brasileiro*, pp. 92–96. Ratton, *Recordações*, pp. 190, 192, 257, 259, 261; d'Azevedo, *Estudos*, pp. 50–51.
[21] "Livros dos contratos," AHU, codex 298, fos. 23, 34, 93 and codex 299, fos. 16, 22, 52.

1754 and 1755 Quintela also held the rights to the collection of duties on all nonfleet shipping entering Rio de Janeiro. In a similar way, José Rodrigues Esteves, another director of the Pernambuco Company, held the right to the duty paid on slaves entering Bahia.

The establishment of the Brazil companies was closely linked to initiatives concerning manufacturing industries. In 1757 the *junta do comércio* took over the administration from the bankrupt silk factory in the Lisbon suburb of Rato. The factory had been founded during the 1730s by Cardinal da Mota and two French entrepreneurs, Roberto Godin and Sibert. Capital had been raised, a company formed, and a large building constructed. The early years were difficult and during the 1740s the company's deficits were considerable. The royal takeover placed the *junta do comércio* in control and determined that the directors of the factory should be chosen equally from among the deputies of the *junta* and from the directors of the Company of Grão Pará and Maranhão. The statutes were drawn up under the influence of José Rodrigues Bandeira and among the first directors were João Rodrigues Monteiro and José Moreira Leal representing the *junta*, and for the Company of Grão Pará and Maranhão, José Francisco da Cruz and Manoel Ferreira da Costa. The silk factory's products were granted exemption from duties at the customs house.

The type of manufacturing agglomeration envisioned for the factory was based partly on the industrial configuration of the period. Pombal also drew on his own assessment of the causes for the success of manufacturing enterprises in Britain. Instead of large capital expenditures on plant and equipment such as had been undertaken at the foundation of the silk factory at Rato, he had seen industrial concentrations in Britain grow from individual units where initially only a small outlay had been necessary and returns were immediate.[22] The concept of manufactory as a coordinating center resting firmly on the household producer was systematically applied to the Royal Silk Factory in 1766, and of the small units of production taken under its control, only part were involved in silk production *per se*. By 1776 the Rato factory consisted of the central building with manufacturing, accounting, and retailing functions, and an associated network of dependent individual workshops in other parts of the city. At the factory itself at least 91 looms were in operation and perhaps over 200 looms dispersed in a large number of small units of production. These independent producers were integrated with the factory for marketing and dependent on it for their supply of raw material. The Royal Silk Factory in 1776 encompassed not only silk manufactures, but sealing wax, lacquer, and stockings – in all some thirty units of production employing 3,500 workers.

It was the close connection between the factory and the monopolistic company which was of most significance. The presence of the same powerful directors at the head of both enterprises created a close and profitable relationship between them and allowed for a fluidity of funds and aid which was mutually beneficial. The Company

---

[22] "Estatutos da real fábrica das sedas, estabelecida no subúrbio do Rato," Lisbon, August 6, 1757, BNLCP, codex 453, fos. 152, 158–165. See also Borges de Macedo, *Problemas*, pp. 70–72, 96–98.

of Grão Pará and Maranhão paid no dividends until 1759, and it is probable that capital from this source was secretly used to encourage the manufacturing enterprise. The company's monopoly also provided an assured and protected market, particularly after the establishment of a second company in the important and populated market of Pernambuco and Paraíba during 1759.[23] As the British factory complained, the

companies have solely the permission and privilege to supply the Brazils [within their monopoly area] and some of the directors openly declared, that their views and design are to prefer the exportation of the commodities of their own country's produce, which consequently must find a sale, when no other goods are in competition with them either in quality or price.[24]

Both Brazilian companies favored Portuguese manufactured goods, and well they might for it was the same group of investors, directors and merchants who benefited at each stage of the process. The growth in the export of raw cotton stimulated by the companies in Brazil, and the flexible interpretation of the function of the silk factory, saw the creation of a lucrative triangle which brought profits at all points: as interest on the loans that stimulated the production of commodities that were then shipped to the metropolis in company ships where the raw materials were manufactured in company-supported workshops, and shipped back again on company ships to the colonial consumer, who bought them on company credit.[25] The lucrative triangle was not the only part of the system (raw cotton after the Peace of Paris provided a profitable re-export business) but it was a vital core. During the early years it gave a powerful boost to both commercial and manufacturing activities, not to mention to the capital accumulation of the new Pombaline merchant oligarchy.[26]

Pombal's attempt to introduce new business practices was very clearly demonstrated in his attitude toward the upper Douro landowners. He placed four noblemen on the company board of directors. The reason, as he explained it, was to encourage cohabitation. "Where the nobility serves with men of business promiscuously and indiscriminately," he wrote, "it destroys the irrational and very prejudicial preoccupation that commerce is mechanical." The election of aristocrats to the board was desirable, he continued, "so that every two years, four or five nobles will leave trained in this very important science through the practice gained in the job."[27] One of the

[23] Borges de Macedo, *Problemas*, p. 147. Also Ribeiro Júnior, *Colonização*, pp. 61–74.
[24] *Memórias do consul e factória britânica*, BNLCP, codex 94, fo. 25v.
[25] "Documentos referentes a indústria de extração da seda e seu privelegio na América Portuguêz," IHGB, file 107, doc. 4, 10; "Mapa de todas as fazendas que a Companhia Geral de Pernambuco e Paraíba tem extraido das fábricas do Reino e exportado para as conquistas desde o seu estabelecimiento até 31 de deziembro 1777," IHGB/AUC, 1-2-11, fo. 239.
[26] "Resumes do estado da companhia geral do Grão Pará e Maranhão no fim de 1770," AHU, codex 1187. For Ratton's calculations of profits gained by company stockholders see Ratton, *Recordações*, p. 180; also Manuel Nunes Dias, "A junta liquidatória dos fundos das companhias do Grão Pará e Maranhão, e Pernambuco e Paraíba, 1788–1837," *Revista Portuguêz de História* 10 (1963), pp. 153–201, and Ribeiro Júnior, *Colonização*, pp. 114–115, 164–169.
[27] These quotations are from Schneider, *Pombal e o vinho do Porto*, pp. 97–129, 169. For a list of the titles created during the Pombaline period, see Montalvão Machado, *Quem livrou Pombal*, p. 180.

26 Pombal, from a contemporary engraving

most significant initiatives of the *junta do comércio* was to establish a school of commerce (*aula do comércio*), the statutes of which were promulgated in April 1759. This school was to teach Italian double bookkeeping methods and was to give preference to sons of Portuguese businessmen in its three-year course of study.

Pombal also facilitated social mobility by granting noble rights to merchants and sought to raise taxes "without differences and without privileges whatsoever."[28] Like his mentor, Dom Luís da Cunha, Pombal believed the expulsion of the Jews and the discrimination against "New Christians" had stunted Portuguese enterprise. The statutes of all his commercial companies used the allure of ennoblement as an incentive to invest. The companies' statutes not only offered to non-noble investors certain exemptions and privileges which were the prerogative of the nobility and the magistracy, but also admitted them to membership of the military orders. As to the nobles who invested, the fact of involvement in commercial matters was held not to prejudice their status but actively to aid its advancement.[29] Magistrates were also permitted to become shareholders in the companies, making that involvement entirely compatible with the exercise of their administrative or legal functions.[30]

To the old aristocracy Pombal himself was an upstart. In the face of virulent opposition he had married into the Arcos family. His activity at the academy of history had been interpreted as an insidious attempt to gain intelligence on the ancient houses of Portugal.[31] Even the Austrian envoy complained that only one of Pombal's diplomatic representatives was "a person of distinction."[32] The opposition to Pombal's social engineering was strongest among the self-styled *puritanos* of the Portuguese nobility. "Puritanism" in Portugal referred to the old concept of "purity of blood," that is, the absence of Jewish or Moorish ancestry, a condition which since 1496 was required for office-holding and state honors.

Professor Oliveira Marques has pointed to the division of the Portuguese nobility into two groups in the eighteenth century. On one side stood a sector which was, in the view of its members, the defender of blood and lineage, the old methods of government, and was linked to landed property and agriculture. On the other side stood a more open-minded group who accepted the elevation of men of letters, even businessmen and bureaucrats, to noble status, who looked to trade and profit and saw England and Holland, not Spain and France as their models. Dom João V's reign had witnessed the beginning of a reassertion of state and hence bureaucratic power at the expense of the old nobility. This process of change in favor of the new nobility was greatly accelerated by Pombal and the renewal of the aristocracy during his period of preeminence very extensive. In the twenty-seven years of Pombal's rule, twenty-three new titles were granted, and twenty-three were extinguished – in this way, about one-third of the nobility was of new blood by 1777.[33]

---

28 Cited by d'Azevedo, *Marquês de Pombal*, pp. 125–126.
29 For a more detailed and documented discussion of this important aspect of Pombal's administrative and fiscal reforms, see Borges de Macedo, *A situação económica*, p. 50.
30 "Companhia Geral . . . do alto Douro, instituição," paragraph 39, BNLCP, codex 453, fos. 96–112; "Companhia Geral de Pernambuco, instituição," paragraph 33, BNLCP, codex 453, fos. 275–290.
31 For a comprehensive collection of documents relating to the *aula do comércio* see Marcos Carneiro de Mendonça, *Aula do comércio* (Rio de Janeiro, 1982).
32 See d'Azevedo, *Marquês de Pombal*, pp. 148–149.
33 Oliveira Marques, *History of Portugal* I, p. 398. Also Nuno Gonçalo Monteiro, "O poder senhorial, estatuto nobiliárquico e aristocracia," in José Mattoso, ed., *História* v, pp. 333–379.

I *Concordia Fratrum*:
Pombal with his two brothers, Paulo de Carvalho, cardinal Inquisitor General,
and Mendonça Furtado.
Ceiling painting in the Oeiras palace

II *Azulejo* panel from the Palácio Correio-Mor

III The Oeiras palace of the marquês de Pombal

IV Lisbon before the earthquake: the royal palace and square, 1693
(Jorge de Brito Collection, Cascais)

V Lisbon after the earthquake:
colored prints from "eye-witness" paintings by Jacques Philippe le Bas, 1757
(Museu da Cidade, Lisbon)

(a) the royal opera house

(b) the tower of São Roque

VI Lisbon before and during the earthquake.
Etching by Mateus Sautter, late eighteenth century (Museu da Cidade, Lisbon)

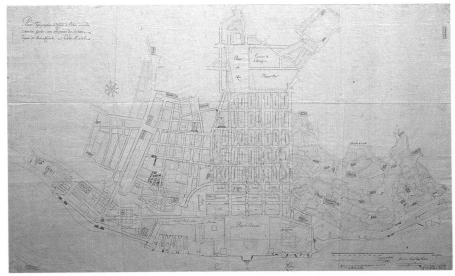

VII Plan of the city of Lisbon in accordance with the new alignment,
planned by the architects Eugenio dos Santos and Carlos Mardel
(Instituto Geográfico e Cadastral, Lisbon)

VIII The royal palace of Queluz, near Lisbon (garden façade, 1747–1752)

IX Jeweled miniature by A. Castriotto showing Dom João V
taking chocolate with the Infante Dom Miguel, 1720

X Allegory of the acclamation of Dom José I.
Painting attributed to Francisco Vieira Lusitano, *c.* 1750
(Ministry of Foreign Affairs, Lisbon)

XI Portrait of Pombal in later life,
attributed to Joana da Salitre, *c.* 1769 (Museu da Cidade, Lisbon)

The *mesa do bem comum* affair, the attack on contraband, and the regulation of colonial commerce had already brought an identity of interest between the dispossessed itinerant interlopers, their British creditors, and the Jesuits. The favors bestowed on Pombal's collaborators now also produced an identity of interest with the discontented nobles, for the group opposed by the interlopers and supported by Pombal also represented a potent challenge to aristocratic privilege. The reaction was not slow in developing.

The crisis came to a head with the attempted regicide in September 1758. King Dom José was returning to his palace after an evening visit to his mistress, who was the wife of Marquês Luís Bernardo of Távora, when his carriage was fired upon. The king was wounded sufficiently seriously for the queen to assume the regency during his recuperation. There was official silence on the incident until early December, when, in a large dragnet operation, a substantial number of people were arrested, including a group of leading aristocrats. The most prominent prisoners were members of the Távora family, the duke of Aveiro and the count of Atouguia. The residences of the Jesuits were simultaneously placed under guard.[34] The king appointed a commission of inquiry on December 9, 1758, granting the presiding judge wide authority to remove even the minimal protections afforded by the Portuguese legal code.[35] With such broad terms of reference, the tribunal acted with dispatch. The interrogations were carried out before the secretaries of state, including Pombal himself in his role as secretary of the kingdom (*Reino*).[36] On January 4 a supreme Junta da Inconfidência was nominated whose responsibility would be to pass judgment. Dominated again by Pombal, among the nine judges joining him on this *junta* was João Pacheco Pereira de Vasconcellos, who had presided over the trial of the Oporto rioters.[37]

On January 12 the prisoners were sentenced. The crimes of which they were convicted were defined as *lèse-majesté*, treason, and rebellion against the king and the state. The duke of Aveiro was to be broken alive, his limbs and arms crushed, exposed on a wheel for all to see, burnt alive, his ashes thrown into the sea. The marquês de Távora Velho was to suffer the same fate. The marquesa de Távora was to be beheaded. The limbs of the rest of the family were to be broken on the wheel, but they were to be strangled first, unlike the marquês and the duke, whose limbs were to be broken while they were still alive. The sentence was carried out the next day in Belém (figs. 27 and 28).

---

[34] "Alvará porque . . . he servido declarar que todos os ministros, e officiaes de justiça e fazenda ou guerra he permitido negociar por meyo da companhia geral do Grão Pará e Maranhão, e qualquer outros por V. M. confirmados . . . " January 5, 1757, BNLCP, codex 456, fo. 138.

[35] For a discussion of the Távora case, see *O processo dos Távoras*, ed. Pedro de Azevedo (Lisbon, 1921); sixteen of the thirty-five people called before the tribunal were subjected to torture.

[36] The interrogations comprise the bulk of *O processo dos Távoras*, pp. 11ff.

[37] The Junta da Inconfidência comprised Dr. João Pacheco Pereira de Vasconcellos, João Marques Bacalhau, Manuel Ferreira de Lima, Ignácio Ferreira Souto, João Ignácio Dantos Pereira, António Alvares da Cunha e Araíyo, José Costa Ribeiro, and José António de Oliveira Machado.

27 The execution of those convicted of the assassination attempt on Dom José I. Engraving
c. 1759 (Biblioteca Nacional, Lisbon)

The treatment of the conspirators was not out of keeping with eighteenth-century
European practice. In 1757, the unsuccessful assassin of Louis XV of France, Robert-
François Damiens, was subjected to every form of physical punishment then in use,
until the *coup de grâce* was finally administered hours later. What was unusual in the
case of the Távoras and the duke of Aveiro was the status of the victims. The duke of
Aveiro, Dom José Mascarenhas, was the most powerful noble in Portugal after the
royal family itself, and president of the supreme court. The marquês of Távora Velho
was a general, director general of the cavalry, and had served as viceroy of India. The
count of Atouguia was responsible for the palace guards of the king.

The Távora case provoked much interest and comment in the rest of Europe.
George II was especially "desirous of being informed of the particulars of the
conspiracy," Mr. Hay, the British envoy in Lisbon, responding to the king's inquiry,
wrote secretly to London on February 10, 1759.

(a)

(b)

(c)

(d)

28 The execution of the duke of Aveiro

(a) the execution of the duke

(b) the Jesuits accused of regicide in a contemporary broadsheet

(c) the statutes of the University of Coimbra (1772)

(d) the statutes of the College of Nobles (2nd edn 1771, first published March 7, 1761)

there is a circumstance that seems to have been industriously concealed, but is not therefore the less credited, and which is the only one that accounts for the treacherous behavior of the Tavora family . . . The king's intimacy with the young marquês's wife, which began during the time the general was viceroy of India . . . .

Mr. Hay added that "when the rest of the relations were confined, this lady was sent to a convent, not a very strict one, where it is said she lives very much at her ease."[38] The relationship was, in fact, even more complicated than Mr. Hay intimated, since the young marquês' wife was also his paternal aunt, an arrangement by no means uncommon among the Portuguese high nobility and the royal family itself. The king's daughter, Maria, was to be married a year later to his brother Pedro.

The day before the spectacular punishment of the aristocrats and others found guilty of attempted regicide, eight Jesuits were arrested for alleged complicity, among them Padre Gabriel Malagrida, a Jesuit missionary and mystic. Malagrida, who had been born in Italy, had gone to Brazil in 1721, working in Maranhão. After a brief sojourn in Lisbon between 1749 and 1751, he returned to Brazil where he ran afoul of Pombal's brother. Malagrida had also published a pamphlet on the Lisbon earthquake, *Juizo da verdadeira causa do terremoto* (The True Cause of the Earthquake), attributing the disaster to divine wrath. Pombal had gone to great lengths to explain the earthquake as a natural phenomenon. For the state to act against the Jesuits Pombal needed papal dispensation. But for the church to turn the Jesuits over to the secular authorities would have implicitly recognized their guilt and this the papacy was not prepared to do. Pombal turned instead to Dom João Cosme da Cunha, archbishop of Évora who issued a pastoral letter against the Jesuits, written by the Brazilian, Frei José de Santa Rita Durão, author of the famous poem *Caramurú*. Dom Cosme was a member of the Távora family, but he became one of Pombal's most sycophantic followers, receiving many important positions over the course of the next twenty years.[39] Pombal personally denounced Malagrida to the Inquisition, at the head of which he had installed his brother, Paulo de Carvalho.[40] A royal *alvará* on September 3, 1759 declared the Jesuits to be in rebellion against the Crown, reinforcing the royal decree of July 21 of the same year, which ordered the imprisonment and expulsion of the Jesuits in Brazil.[41] By March and April of the following year 119 Jesuits had been expelled from Rio de Janeiro, 117 from Bahia, and 119 from Recife. The order's

[38] See Guilherme G. de Oliveira Santos, *O caso dos Távoras*, p. 15: "Em processo simplesmente verbais, e summarissimos pelos quais consta de mero facto de verdade das culpas, observados somente os termos de Direito Natural, e Divino, sem alguma attenção as formalidades, ou nullidades provenientes das Dispoziscoens de Direito, commun e Patrio: Porque todos Hey por dispensadas neste cazo, para nelle se proceder tambem sem a limitação de tempo, e sem determinado numero de testemunhas que se achão estabelecidos sobre as Devassas ordinarias." Full text in *O processo dos Távoras*, p. 5.
[39] For good discussion of this episode see Tarcisio Beal, "Os Jesuítas," p. 45.
[40] Denunciation by Pombal in ANTT, in Inquisition papers, no. 18, proceeding no. 8064, fos. 1–6. Listed in *RHDI/M de P* I, pp. 370–376.
[41] See discussion by John Hemming *CHLA* II, pp. 542–545.

vast properties in Brazil, Portugal, and throughout the Portuguese empire were expropriated.[42]

The garroting and burning (judicial murder might be a more appropriate phrase) of Malagrida, the half-mad old Jesuit on September 20, 1761 in the Lisbon Rossio was the final straw to many Europeans, who saw only Portugal's backwardness and Pombal's tyranny. It was a curious historical irony, however, that the last individual burnt at the stake by the Portuguese authorities at the instigation of the Inquisition should have been a priest and a member of an order which had been at the very spearhead of the Counter-Reformation. As if to emphasize the point, the Cavaleiro de Oliveira, a Portuguese adventurer who had recommended that Dom José establish a Lusitanian church on the model of the Church of England, and who later became a Lutheran, was burned in effigy beside the Jesuit.[43] In fact, the two men were condemned for exactly the opposite reasons: the Cavaleiro de Oliveira for saying the earthquake was a punishment for Portugal following an erroneous religion and worshipping idols, and Padre Malagrida for saying the earthquake was divine punishment for Portugal's abandonment of the true religion.

Pombal used the assassination attempt on Dom José I as a means to crush both aristocratic opposition and the Jesuits in Portugal. He also used the occasion to strike at the small traders whom he accused of plotting with the Jesuits against his plans, abolishing their guilds, and hence their representation.[44] About the Malagrida case Voltaire wrote, "thus was the excess of the ridiculous and the absurd joined to the excess of horror [*Ainsi l'excès du ridicule et de l'absurdité fut joint à l'excès d'horreur*]," and the European reaction was sufficiently critical for Pombal to find it necessary to print the sentence against Malagrida in French with a justification for the sentence.[45]

Pombal's fears of conspiracy were not, of course, entirely unfounded, and on past experience the opposition of the nobility and the Jesuits was not something to be treated lightly. The news of the failure of the Távora–Aveiro assassination plot was greeted with undisguised dismay by those interests not favored by the Pombaline state. In Grão Pará the Jesuits were noticeably absent from the service of thanksgiving for the king's safety.[46] After the conspiracy trial a 72-page pamphlet appeared in London

---

[42] "Ley porque Vossa Maestade he servida exterminar, proscrever, e mandar expulsar dos seus Reinos e Dominios, os Religiosos de companhia denominada de JESU . . . " September 3, 1759, BNLCP, codex 453, fos. 291–294. Also discussion by Alden, *CHLA* II, pp. 612–619.

[43] Claude-Henri Frèches, *Voltaire, Malagrida et Pombal* (Paris, 1969).

[44] For a remarkably detailed Jesuit account of these proceedings, see José Caeiro, s. J., *Jesuítas do Brasil e da India, primeira publicação após 160 anos do manuscrito inédito* (Bahia, 1936); and *História da expulsão da Companhia de Jesus da província de Portugal* (Lisbon, 1991). For an equally detailed eyewitness account by a Jesuit expelled from the Amazon, see Anselmo Eckert, *Memórias de um Jesuíta, prisioneiro de Pombal* (Lisbon, 1987).

[45] "liste des personnes qui ont été condamnées à l'act public de Foi, célèbré dans le cloître du couvent de s Dominique de Lisbonne le 20 septembre 1761" (Lisbon, 1761).

[46] d'Azevedo, *Os Jesuítas*, pp. 306–307. J. R. do Amaral Lapa, *Livro da visitação . . . da inquisição do estado do Grão Pará* (Petropólis, 1978).

refuting the accusations in detail. The author was William Shirley, "late of Lisbon, Merchant."[47] The London *Annual Register*, to which Shirley contributed, believed the problems of Portugal could be resolved easily. It was to be accomplished by "reinstating matters on their natural basis."[48]

Pombal, moved rapidly, as always, to consolidate his position. During 1758 the temporal power of the Jesuits was suppressed throughout Brazil, and the directory system of Indian secular control designed by Mendonça Furtado for Grão Pará and Maranhão, made applicable in all Portuguese America.[49] On September 3, 1759 the Portuguese government decreed the proscription and expulsion of the Society of Jesus from the whole empire, prohibiting any communication, either verbal or in writing, between Jesuits and Portuguese subjects. In 1760 the Pará company's ship, *Nossa Senhora de Arrábida*, removed the last Jesuits of Maranhão into exile.[50] And from the dark waters of the Távora–Aveiro affair Pombal moved forward in a self-conscious attempt to remold the Portuguese nobility. The attack on noble tax privileges, the qualification of commercial men for public office, the corresponding permission for public men to involve themselves in commercial matters, and the use of ennoblement as an incentive to investment in the privileged companies, now became part of a wider policy. The College of Nobles chartered in 1761 and endowed in 1765 from, among other sources, the confiscated properties of the house of Aveiro and the Jesuits (fig. 29), was to purge the nobility of the "false persuasion" that they could live "independent of the virtues." Together with Pombal's second son, among the first pupils were the two children of the archetypal Pombal collaborator, José Francisco da Cruz, a self-made man, ennobled by investment in the Company of Grão Pará and Maranhão, the statutes of which he had helped Pombal formulate.[51]

Pombal's conflict with the Jesuits, like the Lisbon earthquake, brought Portuguese affairs to the center of European concerns. The Portuguese were the first to begin a movement which would bring about the expulsion of the Jesuits from all of Catholic Europe and led to the suppression of the order by the pope himself. The spark for these extraordinary repercussions had been set by a combination of factors, including Pombal's plan for economic regeneration through the rational exploitation of the colonies and the challenge to Britain's economic power. A geopolitical conflict over frontiers and the security of the empire, in which the Guaraní missions in particular opposed Portugal's decisions by force of arms, had aggravated the conflict. The

---

[47] *Observations on a pamphlet lately published, entitled the genuine and legal sentence pronounced by the high court of judicature of Portugal upon the conspirators against the life of his most faithful majesty . . .* by William Shirley late of Lisbon, merchant (London, 1759). Shirley's *Observations* had been published by *The Annual Register for 1759* (London), p. 222.

[48] *The Annual Register for 1770* (London), pp. 10–11.

[49] For the directorate see John Hemming, *Amazon Frontier*, pp. 40–61.

[50] Prado Junior, *A formação do Brasil contemporâneo* (São Paulo, 1963), p. 89.

[51] Rómulo de Carvalho, *História da fundação do Colégio Real dos Nobres de Lisboa 1761–1772* (Coimbra, 1959), pp. 119–121, 182; *História dos estabelecimentos científicos, literários, e artísticos de Portugal nos successivos Reinados da Monarchia* I (Lisbon, 1871); BNLCP, codex 455, fo. 69.

29 A pair of silver-gilt figurines by Ambroise Nicholas Cousinet, confiscated from the duke of Aveiro (Museu Nacional de Arte Antiga)

security of the regime itself was jeopardized by the attempted regicide. But it was the conflict with Pombal which began the process that led to the Jesuits' demise. They met their match in a powerful and ruthless minister who would not tolerate dissent, for whom *raison d'état* was supreme policy, and who did not hesitate to act when challenged. That a dispute in Portugal served as a catalyst for the expulsion of the Jesuits from Spain and later France owed much, of course, to the receptivity to Pombal's actions by European enlightened opinion, the intricacies of church politics, and the diplomatic acquiescence of the Catholic monarchs. But European opinion alone would not necessarily have been sufficient to destroy so powerful a religious order. The Catholic monarchs were quick to follow Portugal's example, to be sure, but it is not at all clear that any of them would have acted had Portugal not acted first. On June 6, 1759 the future marquês de Pombal was granted the title of count of Oeiras by the king for services rendered in the judgment of the would-be assassins.[52] Among the Portuguese aristocrats and their children imprisoned in the fortresses of the ports of Lisbon and Setúbal was Dom Manuel de Sousa, the cousin and brother-in-law of the Duke Silva-Tarouca (both had married princesses of Holstein). Pombal wrote privately to his old friend in May 1759 to tell him of the arrests. Dom Manuel de Sousa was to die in jail before he was formally charged with any crime: his two sons were released from the fortress at Setúbal into house arrest on the Portuguese rural estate of the Princess of Holstein, doubtless out of deference to Silva-Tarouca and the Empress Maria Theresa. But the old friendship was not renewed and two hundred years later, descendants of Silva-Tarouca, as do the descendants of many Portuguese aristocrats, remember Pombal with rancor.[53]

---

[52] *O processo dos Távoras*, index, p. 214.
[53] [Pombal] to [Silva-Tarouca], Ajuda, May 3, 1759, *AAP*, pp. 420–422.

5

Reform

[Pombal] . . . has become the most despotic minister there ever has been, not only in Portugal, but I shall say, in all of Europe.

Papal Nuncio in Lisbon to Vatican Secretary of State (1759)

Do not alter anything with force or violence . . . when reason allows and it is necessary to banish abuses and destroy pernicious customs . . . act with great prudence and moderation, a method which achieves more than power . . .

Pombal to Luís Pinto de Sousa Coutinho (1767)

The 1750s had seen important initiatives in several areas of state policy – some of which resulted from planning, others had been driven by unforeseen developments. In economic and social policy Pombal embarked on an ambitious plan to reestablish national control over the riches flowing into Lisbon from Portugal's overseas dominions. To do this he adapted many of the techniques he had seen elsewhere in Europe, especially in Britain and Austria, to the peculiarities of the Portuguese situation. Pombal had also been faced with implementing the Madrid Treaty which involved a major effort to delineate and survey the vast frontiers of Brazil. In both cases the Jesuits provided major obstacles to his plans. On the southern border of Brazil a military campaign had been needed to defeat the Jesuit missions. In the Amazon the missions ran into a headlong conflict with Pombal's brother, where their opposition to his broader imperial policy proved disastrous for the missionaries. In the midst of these struggles the Lisbon earthquake struck. Pombal's rapid response to the crisis served to propel him into virtual supreme power and gave him the authority to achieve a radical reconstruction of the city. The disenchantment of the *puritanos* among the Portuguese nobility, upset by their exclusion from office and by the favors bestowed on merchants and businessmen, the escalating dispute with the Jesuits, and the distress of small merchants and tavern keepers excluded by the new monopolies, combined to provoke a series of violent reactions, riots, and assassination attempts. Pombal reacted ferociously to these events, not only against the popular classes but also against the high nobility and the Jesuit order.

One immediate consequence of Pombal's drastic measures was to clear the way to government action on several fronts. The 1760s thus marked a period of consolidation and amplification of the reforms initiated during the previous decade. These included the erection of a new system of public education to replace that of the fallen Jesuits; the assertion of national authority in religious and church administration; the stimulation of manufacturing enterprise and entrepreneurial activity; and the strengthening of the state's taxing authority, military capabilities and security apparatus. In each case the legislation needed for these measures was encapsulated within a reformed, codified, and systematized set of public laws where the reasoning was clearly outlined, justified, and explained. Pombal also fortified his own position. The crime of *lèse-majesté* was expanded to include attacks against the king's ministers. And Pombal obtained for himself a personal corps of bodyguards, something unseen in Europe since the primacy of Richelieu in France. In 1760 Pombal had established the office of general intendant of police of the court and kingdom. These measures gave the state the organizational means to combat crime and banditry as well as provide surveillance over enemies of the government. The first intendant was Inácio Ferreira Souto, a personal friend of Pombal and a member of the tribunal which had condemned the duke of Aveiro and the Távoras.[1]

Colonial policy, however, continued to receive high priority. Pombal's brother, Mendonça Furtado, had returned from Pará in 1759. With his practical experience of Brazilian frontier conditions and intimate involvement in the affairs of the Company of Grão Pará and Maranhão, he joined Pombal's cabinet in Lisbon with direct responsibility for the overseas dominions.[2] Within a month, using the prototype of the first Brazil company, the statutes of a new commercial company were promulgated. Pombal now moved to extend his scheme to reestablish national control over the economy to cover one of the principal centers of Brazilian commerce and production – the sugar-exporting captaincies of Pernambuco and Paraíba. The objectives remained similar to those intended for Amazonia, yet Pernambuco and Paraíba were old established communities, long at the center of the Brazilian colonial economy and the location of the great struggle with the Dutch during the previous century.

In Pernambuco the company was allowed to sell only at wholesale while customs duties in the metropolis were manipulated to encourage a diversification of production in Brazil by developing the cultivation of colonial commodities other than sugar which could be profitably re-exported. The Pernambuco company, like its forerunner, was intended to encourage the importation of African labor. The company's directors asserted in the 1770s that, with the foundation of the company, the "fraudulent commerce many foreigners were making in other ports of Brazil had ceased in Pernambuco, and following the laws of solid commerce the forwarding of European goods had been regulated to the value of the products of the respective

[1] See José Subtil, "Os poderes do centro," in Mattoso, ed., *História* IV, pp. 174–176.
[2] *Alvará de nomeação . . . de* [Mendonça Furtado], July 19, 1759. *Correspondência inédita* III, p. 1228.

colonies."[3] Pombal also set up a company for the Trade of the Mujaos and the Macuas (Mozambique) and in 1773 a company for the Royal Fisheries in the kingdom of Algarve which controlled the tuna, corvine, and sardine fisheries of the south.[4]

The monopolistic companies of the far north and the northeast of Portuguese America did have a considerable impact on their regions. Those excluded by the monopolies were far from happy but were unable, while Pombal ruled, to give voice to their protests. In Pará and Maranhão capital mobilized by the Crown in association with private investors provided essential credit for the import of African slave labor and European goods. No less significant was the initiation of new export commodities. By 1760 the export of cotton had begun from São Luís, the capital of Maranhão, for example, and in 1767 the export of rice. Cotton production soon exceeded metropolitan demand and provided valuable re-exports to Rotterdam, Hamburg, Genoa, Rouen, Marseilles, and London.[5] Exports from Belém, especially cacao, also increased in volume and value.[6] Unusual for a mercantilist age, the Portuguese government encouraged processing and manufacturing to take place in the colony. In Maranhão, for example, rice processing mills were established and skilled technicians imported from Europe. In Pará the company went so far as to set up a cotton mill in order to produce cloth for the local military forces. The company, sensitive to the originality of its actions, defended this policy on the grounds that "the establishment of such workshops was always useful to the state for it impeded the flow of money to foreigners."[7] Within a decade a 43,400 ton merchant fleet of 124 craft had been built up and was carrying European goods, Amazon products, and African slaves along trade routes that embraced Bissau, Angola, Europe, the Brazilian littoral, and the Indian Ocean.[8] As Pombal had envisioned in a letter to his brother in 1755, the company was contributing "to consolidate the establishment of the empire that the King our Lord had determined to found in these captaincies."[9]

In Pernambuco the company used its capital and credit to assist the sugar mill owners of the region. Goods and slaves were advanced to farmers and sugar producers at a 3 percent interest rate.[10] Direct company investment rehabilitated many old sugar mills and established new ones. The company's administrative board estimated in 1780 that to the 207 mills in existence at the time of the company's

---

[3] "Demonstrações da junta [company of Pernambuco]," IHGB/AUC, 1-2-11.

[4] Oliveira Marques, *History of Portugal* 1, p. 388.

[5] Manuel Nunes Dias, "Fomento e mercantilismo: política económica portuguesa na baixada Maranhense, 1755–1778," V. Colóquio internacional de estudos Luso-Brasileiros, *Actas*, 3 vols. (Coimbra, 1965), II, pp. 17–99.

[6] Manuel Nunes Dias, "As frotas do cacao da amazônia 1756–1773: subsídios para o estudo do fomento ultramarino português no século XVIII," *RHSP* 50 (April/June 1962), pp. 363–377.

[7] "Apontamentos vários sobre a companhia do Grão-Pará e Maranhão," IHGB/AUC, 1-1-8 fo. 18.

[8] Manuel Nunes Dias, "A tonelagem da frota da Companhia Geral do Grão-Pará e Maranhão," *RHSP* 52 (January/March 1964), p. 131.

[9] [Pombal] to [Mendonça Furtado], August 4, 1755, *Correspondência inédita* II, p. 789.

[10] António Carreira, "A companhia de Pernambuco e Paraíba: alguns subsídios para o estudo da sua acção," *RHES* 11 (January–June, 1983), pp. 55–88.

establishment, including those ruined or out of action, it had added 123 mills, forming some 390 functioning and producing sugar for export. Tobacco cultivation was also reestablished by subsidies and guaranteed prices to farmers. To make Pernambucan hides competitive with those of the Spanish provinces, they were exempted from customs duties.[11]

The creation in Lisbon of a royal treasury (Erário Régio) in 1761, however, was the key element in Pombal's overall effort of rationalization and centralization.[12] Here all the Crown's income was to be concentrated and recorded. Pombal appointed himself inspector general of the treasury, a position which was designed to be closest to the monarch and by implication that of chief minister. The aim of the treasury was to centralize jurisdiction for all fiscal matters in the *exchequer* and make it solely responsible for the different sectors of fiscal administration from customs house revenues to the farming of royal monopolies. The creation of the royal treasury marked the culmination of Pombal's reform of the revenue and collection machinery of the state. With high salaries for officials, modern double-entry bookkeeping techniques, regular statements of balance, the royal treasury was, like the *junta do comércio*, bound to a strict secrecy in its dealings.[13] The new organization, which conducted its business with great efficiency, was controlled by Pombal's close collaborator, José Francisco da Cruz, the first treasurer general.[14]

Just as the Pombaline state engaged in propaganda to enhance its image and influence opinion elsewhere in Europe, so too did its legislation outline in sometimes tiresome detail for domestic audiences the objectives and antecedents of the policy changes, as well as the substance of the measure itself. In this respect the corpus of legislation establishing secular authority over the areas which had previously fallen under papal or ecclesiastical jurisdiction required special argumentation.[15] In no other European country had the Counter Reformation been so thoroughly embedded, or the order that so exemplified the ultramontane claims of papal supremacy – the Jesuits – been so warmly received, or the control of the Jesuits so strongly established over the education of the elite. The Portuguese quarrel with the Jesuits was, as a consequence, of more than local interest. The Vatican, for its part, was thoroughly horrified by developments in Portugal. Ambassador Almada told Pombal that Rome believed he intended to introduce the "Protestant religion" into Portugal.[16] The Papal

---

[11] "Demonstrações da junta [company of Pernambuco] 1780," IHGB/AUC, 1-2-11; Ratton, *Recordações*, p. 182. Carreira, *Companhias pombalinas*, pp. 217–251.

[12] Fernando Tomaz, "As finanças do estado pombalino, 1762–1776," in *Estudos e ensaios* (Lisbon, 1990), pp. 355–388. For projected building for Royal Treasury see Mattoso, *História* IV, pp. 235 and 237.

[13] See *Inventário do fundo geral do Erário Régio*, organized by Alzira Teixeira Leite Moreira (Lisbon, 1977).

[14] *Exposição histórica do ministério das finanças* (Lisbon, 1952), pp. 25–26; Smith, *Pombal* II, p. 60; Borges de Macedo, *A situação económica*, pp. 48–49; António Manuel Hespanha, "A Fazenda," in Mattoso, *História* IV, esp. pp. 235–239.

[15] For a detailed discussion of the important legal formulations of the Pombaline state, especially the law of August 18, 1769, see António Resende de Oliveira, "Poder e sociedade: a legislação pombalina e a antiga sociedade português," *RHDI/M de P*, pp. 117–142; quotation from p. 141.

[16] [Almada] to [Pombal], September 15, 1759. ANTT, Min Just, part 11.

Nuncio in Madrid, Lazzao Opizo Pallevicini, was instructed (1760) by cipher to warn the Spanish monarch, Charles III, that "in that Kingdom [Portugal] . . . occult Hebrews and obvious heretics . . . benefit in every way from the greatest favor of the minister [Pombal]."[17] The struggle with the papacy was an inevitable result of Pombal's expulsion of the Jesuits.

The occasion for the break with Rome, as so often in such cases of regalist and ultramontane conflict, was a dispute over a papal dispensation for the marriage of Dona Maria, princess of Brazil and the heir apparent, to her uncle, the king's brother, Dom Pedro. In the face of Roman foot-dragging and a perceived insult to the Portuguese monarch's dignity, the Papal Nuncio was expelled from Portugal on June 15, 1760. On July 2, the Portuguese envoy and all the Portuguese in Rome were expelled, including Pombal's eldest son, Henrique. The break between Lisbon and the Vatican lasted nine years, an important period during which Pombal moved to create a secular state fortified by a systematic rejection of papal claims to jurisdiction. Again Pombal turned to precedent. *Placet*, the right to exclude ecclesiastical documents; *exequatur*, the power to approve the delivery of papal documents to their Portuguese recipients; and the overall claim of *recursua ad principem*, the power of royal courts to hear appeals from ecclesiastical courts, had all been claimed by Portuguese monarchs since the thirteenth century, and provided the occasion for perennial disputes between Catholic monarchs and the papacy. Pombal used all these justifications to place the church firmly under state control.[18]

Equally important was Pombal's secularization of the Inquisition. From 1684 to 1747, 4,672 persons were sentenced by the Inquisition and 146 burned at the stake (see figs. 30 and 31). From 1750 to 1759, there had been 1,107 sentences and 18 burnings. The Inquisition's police powers had already been appropriated by a new intendant general of police in 1768. Pombal also abolished the distinction between "old" and "new" Christians and the book censorship role, previously the responsibility of the Inquisition, was given over also in 1768 to a newly created royal censorship board (*real mesa censória*). And, in 1769 Pombal moved against the Inquisition itself, destroying its power as an independent tribunal and making it dependent on the government and ordering that all property confiscated by the Inquisition was henceforth to accrue to the national treasury.[19] He appointed his brother, Paulo de Carvalho, to be Inquisitor General. Public *autos da fé* ceased, along with the death penalty. Malagrida, the last victim, was burned in 1761.[20]

There are interesting parallels between the Austrian reforms and Pombal's measures. In Vienna, the principal mechanism of educational reform had been the creation of

---

[17] Cited by Miller, *Portugal and Rome*, p. 109.

[18] See Cândido dos Santos, "António Pereira de Figueiredo, Pombal e a *Aufklärung*, ensaio sobre o regalismo e o jansenismo em Portugal na segunda metade do século XVIII," *RHDI/M de P* 4, 1 (1982), pp. 167–203; also, Zílie Osório de Castro, "O regalismo em Portugal: Antonio Pereira de Figueiredo," *Cultura* 8 (1987), pp. 357–411.

[19] See discussion by Montalvão Machado, *Quem livrou Pombal*, p. 118.

[20] Oliveira Marques, *History of Portugal* 1, p. 402.

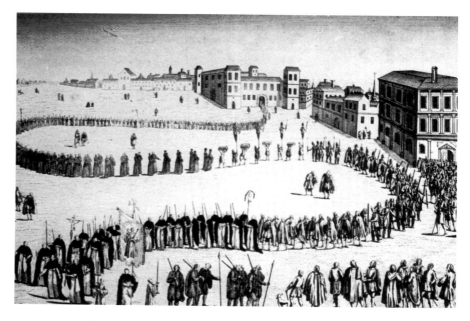

30 Procession of the Inquisition through the Rossio, Lisbon

the book censorship commission (Bucherzensurcommission), in 1759/1760 under
Pombal's old friend and doctor from his Vienna days, Gerhard van Swieten. These
reforms had been aimed principally at the Jesuit monopoly and based on much the
same philosophical ground as the reforms in Portugal, especially the writing of
Muratori.[21] In Portugal the *real mesa censória* (the royal censorship board) established
eight years later, was intended to provide a mechanism to secularize the long-
standing religious control and prohibitions which had governed the introduction of new
ideas into the country. Thus the *real mesa censória* superseded the Inquisition and
became the judge of what was deemed acceptable for the Portuguese reading public.

The censorship of the state in this instance was paradoxically intended to provide a
means of stimulating enlightenment. The *mesa* often released books to their owners or
booksellers which had been banned previously by the Inquisition – among them
Voltaire's *Œuvres* (theater), Richardson's *Pamela*, Montesquieu's *Esprit des lois*, and
Locke's *Essays on Human Understanding*. But the limitations placed on readership are
also illuminating. Works which were deemed harmful to religion remained excluded;
and in 1769 the royal censorship board requested catalogues of "all the book shops,
printing houses, publishers, and libraries containing all the books printed or in
manuscript that they possessed." Works considered to contain "irreligion and the
false philosophy of the books of the so-called 'philosophes' whose atheism and

---

[21] Beales, *Joseph II* I, pp. 441–443; also G. Klingenstein, *Staatsverwaltung und kirchliche Autoritat im 18
Jahrhundert* (Vienna, 1970).

 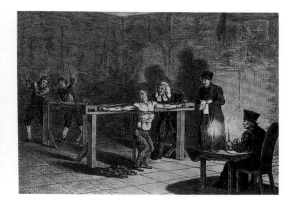

31 The Inquisition in action: four engravings from George Landemann's *Historical, Military and Pitoresque Observation on Portugal* (1821)

materialism" remained formally condemned.[22] But the principal censors were drawn from the reforming wing of the church – including the erudite Frei Manuel do Cenáculo Vilas Boas (1724–1814), the confessor of Prince Dom José; Padre Inácio de São Caetano, confessor to the Princess Maria and the royal princesses; Padre António Pereira de Figueiredo, the Oratorian; and the Brazilian-born Dr. Francisco de Lemos and his brother the jurist João Pereira Ramos de Azevedo Coutinho.

António Nunes Ribeiro Sanches (1699–1783), in his *Cartas sobre a educação da mocidade* (1760), proposed the total separation of church and state.[23] The writings of António Pereira de Figueiredo and João Pereira Ramos de Azevedo Coutinho provided the justification for secular claims over church matters and the seizure by the state of jurisdiction previously considered to be within the spiritual arena. Azevedo Coutinho's task was to justify the installation of bishops without recourse to Rome.

[22] For relevant archival sources see Calazans Falcon, *A época pombalina*, p. 444.
[23] See António Nunes Ribeiro Sanches, *Cartas sobre a educação da mocidade*, in *Obras* (Coimbra, 1959), first edition 1760. Also discussion by António Novoa, *Le Temps des professeurs*, pp. 132–134.

The French experience proved especially attractive to the Portuguese ecclesiastical reformers. There was, in fact, some substance to the fears that the Portuguese had become Jansenists or Gallicans, as Rome darkly hinted. Pombal was kept closely informed of the activities of the schismatic church of Utrecht by means of correspondence with the Jansenist, Gabriel Duparc de Bellegarde, via Figueiredo and Cenáculo, a correspondence facilitated by the Van Zeller family which had originated in the Low Countries. As Pereira wrote to Cenáculo on February 14, 1776, "Yesterday I received a letter and package of important papers from my friend Bellegarde of Utrecht. And today I went to the Marquês (de Pombal) and gave him the same letter to read in which he is spoken of with such appreciation ."[24] Pombal and his ecclesiastical collaborators, in fact, took and adapted from others what suited their purposes which were, in essence, regalist and Catholic. That is, they accepted the supremacy of the state, but did not wish to see Catholicism overthrown. They wanted papal authority circumscribed and a greater autonomy for national churches, the fraternal orders and regular clergy purified and their numbers limited, and they wished to achieve this by expanding the power of the bishops. In Germany the ideas contained in *De status ecclesiae et legitima potestate Romani pontificis liber singularis* by Nicolaus von Hontheim (1701–1770), published in 1763 under the pseudonym of Justinus Febronius, opposed the monarchical concept of the papacy. It was a book Pombal ordered translated and published in Portuguese as *Do estado da igreja e poder legítimo do pontífice Romano*, 2 volumes (Lisbon, 1770). The policy here reflected a common interest among the eighteenth-century Catholic rulers: known as Gallicanism in France, Febronism in Germany, Josefism in Austria, and Regalism in the Iberian peninsula. In all cases the policy involved the affirmation of the rights of the state over those of the church.[25] A series of books and letters by the Oratorian António Pereira de Figueiredo was especially influential in Portugal. The first two editions of his *Tentativa teológica* (Lisbon, 1766) were rapidly sold out, 1,600 copies in all; António Ribeiro dos Santos' *De sacerdotio et imperio* (Lisbon, 1770) also met with considerable commercial success in the market-place.[26] This book was dedicated to Joaquim Inácio da Cruz, Ribeiro dos Santos' protector and Pombal's close collaborator, and Ribeiro dos Santos' book was intended as a key document for the reform of the teaching of common law at Coimbra, laying out the jurisdictional limitations of state and ecclesiastical power. In his theory he drew extensively on the work of the Italian reformer, António Genovesi (1712–1798), who believed the church should be autonomous and separated from the state, with its concerns limited to doctrine and the

[24] See *RHDI/M de P* I, pp. 194–195.
[25] António Pereira de Figueiredo's *De suprema regum* (1765) also had a large impact outside Portugal, with editions in Latin and French, where it was praised in the semi-clandestine organ of the French Jansenists, as well as an edition in Italy and Leipzig. Cândido dos Santos, "António Pereira de Figueiredo, Pombal e a *Aufklärung*: ensaio sobre o regalismo e o jansenismo em Portugal na segunda metade do século XVIII," in *RHDI/M de P* I, pp. 167–203. Also see *RHDI/M de P* I, pp. 174–175, 185.
[26] José Estêves Pereira, *O pensamento político em Portugal no século XVIII, António Ribeiro dos Santos* (Lisbon, 1983), p. 87.

sacraments, even religious education he believed should be the responsibility of the state. Genovesi saw Britain as a model in terms of economic development and wished to see its techniques adapted to Neapolitan conditions.[27]

As in other areas of Pombal's activities, these moves did not go unopposed. The bishop of Coimbra, D. Miguel da Anunciação, who was a member of the Távora family, took a lead in condemning the regalist writings the new royal censorship board had specifically approved. On his own initiative, and in a clear challenge to the new censorship board's area of competence, he issued a pastoral letter linking the works of Febronius to the *Encyclopédie* and other works of the Enlightenment.[28] The censorship board reacted with fury. Their ruling took the bishop of Coimbra to task precisely for making this linkage: "A scandalous mixture of the materialist and libertine writer with the wise and Catholic Du Pin and Febronio . . . in order to cause injury to those who adopt their sane and important doctrines." Louis Elies DuPin (1657–1719), a French theologian and historian, had been a fervent advocate of Gallicanism, opposed the primacy of the pope, and was a champion of ecumenical unions between the Catholic, Anglican, and Orthodox churches. His works had long been on the index of published works. The censorship board ordered that the bishop's pastoral letter be torn up and burnt in the Praça do Comércio, which was done on Saturday, December 27, in the presence of the criminal magistrate, Pina Manique.[29]

Like so many of Pombal's opponents, the offending bishop was swept into jail for his temerity. Pombal dispatched eighty cavalry soldiers and a judge, surrounded the bishop's palace and took him into custody. The offending ecclesiastic was conducted under military escort to Lisbon, where he was imprisoned in the fort of Pedrouças. Pombal told the chapter of the cathedral of Coimbra that the bishop was dismissed by the civil authorities and that the bishopric of Coimbra was vacant. He then proceeded to install Francisco de Lemos (1732–1814), one of his closest advisers and apologists to the "vacant" position. The pope, however, did not approve this nomination even though Dom Francisco de Lemos began to serve as bishop of Coimbra immediately and in this role he acted as the reforming rector of the university.[30] Pombal, who found his regalism challenged by leading members of the Oratorian community, reacted against his old friends with no less ferocity than he did against his old enemies. He demanded that "so venomous and poisonous a plant be torn up from its roots."[31]

Educational reform, in fact, became a high priority in the 1760s.[32] The expulsion of

---

[27] Banha de Andrade, *Vernei*, pp. 299–300.

[28] Montalvão Machado, *Quem livrou Pombal*, pp. 130–131. Also *Colecção dos negócios de Roma*, part 3, pp. 299–314.

[29] For a full text of the opinion of the *real mesa censória* (the examiners were Desembargador João Pereira Ramos, Frei Manoel do Cenáculo, Frei Inácio de S. Caetano) in *RHDI/M de P* I, pp. 288–298. For a very comprehensive discussion of this episode see Manuel Augusto Rodrigues, "Pombal e D. Miguel da Anunciação, Bispo de Coimbra," in *RHDI/M de P* I, pp. 207–298.

[30] See documents and discussion in Montalvão Machado, *Quem livrou Pombal*, pp. 130–136.

[31] See Pombal quotation in Banha de Andrade, *Contributos*, p. 426.

[32] José Ferreira Carrato, "The Enlightenment in Portugal and the Educational Reforms of the Marquis of Pombal," in *Studies on Voltaire and the Eighteenth Century*, ed. Theodore Beterman (Oxford: The Voltaire Foundation, 1977), vol. 167.

the Jesuits had left Portugal bereft of teachers at both the secondary and university levels. The Jesuits had run 34 colleges in Portugal and 17 residences. In Brazil they possessed 25 residences, 36 missions, and 17 colleges and seminaries.[33] Pombal's educational reforms aimed for three principal objectives: to bring education under the control of the state, to secularize instruction, and to standardize the curriculum.[34] As with so many of Pombal's measures, the initial experiments had occurred in Brazil. In 1758, Pombal's brother introduced the directory system to substitute secular administrators for the Jesuits where Jesuit control over the Indian villages had been abolished in the royal decrees of June 7, 1755. The directors were intended to occupy the missionaries' places and two public schools were to be established in each Indian village, one for boys, the other for girls, where the boys would be taught reading, writing, and counting, as well as Christian doctrine, while the girls would have counting substituted by cleaning, sewing, and other tasks "suitable for that sex." The directors, unlike the missionaries, were to impose on the Indian children the use of Portuguese, and prohibit the use of their own language.[35]

Not surprisingly, in his educational reforms, Pombal drew directly on the recommendation of the Jesuits' old enemies, especially on Luís António Vernei, by now a paid consultant to the Portuguese government. Vernei was persistent to a point of irritation (especially to Ambassador Almada) in his pressure of honoraria and emoluments. By the 1770s Vernei was receiving stipends from his membership in the Order of Christ, his absentee archdeaconship of Évora, from the Church of Santa Maria of Beja, and as an honorary deputy of the treasury of the ecclesiastical court of Consciência e Ordens, as well as from the sale of his book in Lisbon which from January 1764 to August 1773 brought him 1,378,510 *réis*.[36] The subtitle of Vernei's famous work, the *Verdadeiro método de estudar*, in fact, summed up the radicalism as well as the limitations of Pombal's pragmatic educational philosophy. It was a method "intended to be useful to the Republic, and the Church, commensurate to the style, and necessity of Portugal."[37]

To implement the educational reform, Pombal had first established a position of director of studies (July 6, 1759) to oversee the establishment of a national system of secondary education. To the post he appointed Dom Tomás de Almeida, a principal of the Patriarchal church and nephew of the first patriarch of Lisbon. (A "principal" of the Lisbon Patriarchy was a position intended to duplicate the role of the Roman Curia in a Portuguese setting.)[38] Later a *junta* for the provision of

---

[33] Beal, "Os Jesuítas," p 80.

[34] See the comprehensive discussion of the reform program in the excellent book by António Novoa, *Le Temps des professeurs*, 2 vols. (Lisbon, 1987) I, pp. 95–315.

[35] Banha de Andrade, *Contributos*, pp. 596–597.   [36] Banha de Andrade, *Vernei*, pp. 231–2.

[37] "para ser útil a Republica, e a Igreja, proporcionado estilo, e necessidade de Portugal," frontispiece in Vernei, *Verdadeiro método*.

[38] See Banha de Andrade, *Contributos*, pp. 591–594. Complete text of directory law in Carneiro de Mendonça, *Aula do comercio*, pp. 141–178, 179–181.

learning (*junta da providência literária*) was formed to prepare for the reform of higher education.

As director of studies, Dom Tomás de Almeida oversaw the establishment of the new state system of secondary education. His tasks involved coordination, preparing annual reports, inspection, and the administration of the system. The new professors were to be paid by the state, teachers were to pass a public examination in order to obtain their positions, and the professors were to enjoy "privileges accorded to nobles in common law."[39] The royal decree nominating Dom Tomás de Almeida had specifically cited the "critical logic of Vernei and Genovezi," and the director of studies was given the exclusive right to print books. The new regius professors in Coimbra and Évora were to be granted use of the houses of the expelled Jesuits.[40] After the reform of the secondary school system, António Pereira de Figueiredo's books on grammar and composition were required in all state schools in Portugal and Brazil.[41]

In 1771 the director of studies was replaced by a Royal Censorship Board and the state system was expanded to incorporate schools of reading, writing, and calculating, and to increase the number of classes of Latin, Greek, rhetoric and philosophy. The system was also extended to the overseas territories.[42] The legislation of 1772 included a national plan relating the schools and professors to the socio-economic situation of the regions and establishing a financial base for the system through the introduction of a new tax or literary subsidy to pay for it.[43]

The royal decree creating the state-run system envisioned 526 positions of instructor and 358 professors (236 of Latin, 38 of Greek, 49 of rhetoric, 35 of philosophy). The instructors were to receive stipends of 40–60,000 *réis* depending on location. A professor of Latin in a town, for example, was to earn 100,000 *réis*. These were not generous sums. The minimum needed to sustain a peasant's family in the Alentejo was 25 thousand *réis*. In some places, however, the new state schools were successful. In Beja, between 1774 and 1776, the royal college enrolled 220 students whose average age was between 8 and 12 years. The whole system was to be financed by a new tax, a literary subsidy (*subsídio literário*) based on wine and *eau de vie* in Portugal and the Atlantic islands. In Asia and Brazil the tax rested on meat and *eau de vie*. (Pablo de Olavide in Seville raised a similar tax to finance his new university.)

A leading figure in these educational innovations was Frei Manuel de Cenáculo Vilas Boas (1724–1814) (fig. 32). The son of a candlemaker, Cenáculo was educated by Oratorians in Lisbon where he studied with Father João Baptista. He had joined the third order of St. Francis in 1739. From 1740 he was a resident in Coimbra, where

---

[39] See António Novoa, *Le Temps des professeurs*, pp. 142–149, where he analyzes the annual reports prepared by Dom Tomás de Almeida.

[40] Calazans Falcon, *A época pombalina*, pp. 432–433.

[41] *Exercicios da lingua Latina e Portuguesa*, 2nd edition (1765) and *Novo método da gramática latina* (Lisbon, 1752); see Banha de Andrade, *Vernei*, pp. 186, 262.

[42] António Novoa, *Le Temps des professeurs*, p. 168.

[43] Ibid., pp. 172–173.

he eventually became a tutor of theology in 1749. He became part of the reaction against scholasticism, embracing the ideas of Descartes and Newton. In 1750 he visited Rome and in 1755 moved to Lisbon.[44] Cenáculo was a brilliant scholar and was an expert in Greek, Syriac, and Arabic. In the area of educational reform, he was one of Pombal's closest collaborators. Cenáculo became the reforming provincial of the third order of St. Francis, president of the Royal Censorship Board, confessor and preceptor to the Prince Dom José, the king's grandson, and first bishop of Beja. He was also a major influence in the reform of the University of Coimbra.

Cenáculo also became president of the *junta do subsídio literário* in November 1772. The income from the literary tax was considerable, with annual revenues averaging 92,3030$191 *réis* between 1774 and 1793 and expenses 88,520$294 *réis* in the same period. Of the revenue, 83 percent came from Portugal proper and 1.6 percent from the overseas territories, which was four times what they received in return in expenditures. Since the tax fell on wine and *eau de vie* the contribution of the northern provinces of Portugal and the rural areas was disproportionately high, whereas the expenditures were heavily concentrated in the urban areas and the south. Lisbon, for example, which contributed 0.19 percent to the receipts, received 15.12 percent of the expenditures.[45]

In his role of president of the royal censorship board, Cenáculo took on the functions of what Professor J. Marcadé defines as "if not a ministry then certainly a veritable commission of national education."[46] In 1771 the censorship board's attributes were enlarged to encompass the oversight of the College of Nobles, all primary and secondary schools and the University of Coimbra.[47] The *real mesa* applied previous censorship for all books printed in Portugal, and *a posteriori* censorship on all foreign works. The books accumulated as a result of these activities, together with the library of the Oratorians and the libraries of the Jesuit colleges suppressed in 1759, were later to form the basis of the first public national library in Portugal, as Cenáculo had envisioned.[48] Cenáculo also organized the libraries of the Convento de Jesus of Lisbon, which later became the library of the Academy of Sciences, the library in Beja, and another in Évora.[49]

As in other areas Pombal took from the example of others what suited him.[50] Despite claims and fears in Rome and more traditionalist circles, the activities of the Royal Censorship Board were exemplary in this respect. Dominated by reform-minded

---

[44] Marcadé, *Cenáculo*, pp. 5–16.

[45] For a very detailed discussion of salaries and comparisons with other occupations see Novoa, *Le Temps des professeurs*, pp. 236–252. Also António Alberto Banha de Andrade, *A reforma pombalina dos estudos secundários (1769–1771)*, 2 vols. (Coimbra, 1981, 1984). For an analysis of budgets, see António Novoa, pp. 208–209.

[46] Marcadé, *Cenáculo*, p. 67.

[47] This role probably explains his correspondence with the count of Campomanes (1723–1806) who was developing similar projects in Spain.

[48] Marcadé, *Cenáculo*, p. 70.

[49] Montalvão Machado, *Quem livrou Pombal*, p. 150.

[50] For a discussion of Pombal's eclecticism, see Calazans Falcon, *A época pombalina*, pp. 430–431.

RETR: DO EXC:
E R:S: D.F: M: DO CE:
NACULO BISPO DE BEJA,
CONF: E M. DO SER: S: D.JO:
ZE. PRINCEPE DA BEIRA,
PREZ. DA REAL MEZA CEN:
SORIA CAPELLAO MOR DAS
ARMADAS REAES, CONS: DO S
OFFICIO, E DA CRUZ. EZAMIN:
SYNODAL DO PATRIAR. E DAS
ORDENS MIL: M.JUB: E D CO.
NIMBRICENSE, DEF: G: DE TODA
A ORDEM DE S.FRAN: PROC: E
CHRONISTA DA ORDEM DA PENIT

32 Frei Manuel do Cenáculo Vilas Boas (1724–1814). Painting by António Joaquim Padrão (Museu Rainha D. Leonor, Beja)

ecclesiastics, its members carefully analyzed the literary production of the high Enlightenment (and some works of a less elevated nature) and equally carefully removed from the Portuguese editions whatever they deemed detrimental to Catholic dogma or, as was sometimes the case, they restricted circulation to those who they believed should be aware of the offending works in order to be better able to refute their message. If measures of Pombaline organs such as the censorship board seem cautious and contradictory to Enlightenment purists, they seemed eminently dangerous, even sacrilegious, to traditionalists. Vernei, for example, was viciously attacked by the Jesuits and their apologists, both when his book was published and no less once his recommendations were promulgated into law. The Portuguese reformers were not freethinkers to be sure – they were seeking to promote what they believed would be useful to the state. In the context of northwestern Europe this cautious approach appeared self-defeating, but in the context of eighteenth-century Portugal it was a major innovation.

In 1768 Cenáculo was chosen as confessor to Dom José I's grandson, Prince José (who became the heir apparent after the succession of his mother to the throne in 1777) (fig. 33), and in 1770 the prince's preceptor, a position he held for seven years. The curriculum he supervised included geometry, geography, and law at the king's request, and the king laid out detailed instructions for his grandson's education.[51] The 9-year-old prince rose at eight o'clock in the morning, went to mass at nine and had two sessions of lessons each day in the morning from ten o'clock to a quarter past twelve and during the afternoon from three to four o'clock. Cenáculo personally taught geometry and the history of Portugal. In the prince's library Cenáculo placed *Les Aventures de Télémaque* of Fénelon, *De copia verborum* of Erasmus, *L'Histoire universelle* of Bossuet, and *Histoire ecclésiastique* of the abbé Racine.[52] Prince José always retained a high regard for his tutor. Frei Manuel do Cenáculo outlined in some detail in his private diary in 1772 how he organized the prince's instruction in order to prepare him for rulership. He regarded the examination of the preambles to the laws promulgated by Dom José I as a starting point because they outlined the "causes which had reduced the Portuguese monarchy to such decadence and the dispositions contained in them revealed the remedies by which such inveterate and deplorable ills could be cured." He divided these laws into several categories with specific examples in each general category. First in order of priority he placed the laws and procedures concerning respect for civil authority, public security and criminal justice, and his example was the law of July 28, 1751 which established the state's power to hold prisoners without interference from any other authority. Second he placed the question of the administration of state finances, and used as example the law of

[51] The instruction for the education of his grandson, December 7, 1768 in IHGB, file 61, doc. 4. Discussed by Maria Beatriz Nizza da Silva, "A educação de um príncipe no período pombalino," in *RHDI/M de P* I, pp. 377–383.
[52] See "Livros que tenho dado en sua alteza para a sua instrução e curiosidade," in "Excertos do 'diário' de Dom Frei Manuel do Cenáculo," notes of João Palma-Ferreira, in *Revista da biblioteca nacional* 2, 1 (1982), pp. 17–35, especially p. 21; also Marcadé, *Cenáculo*, pp. 60–65.

33 (a) Prince Dom José, grandson of King José I and heir apparent to Dona Maria I

(b) Infanta Dona Maria Benedita, aunt and wife of Prince Dom José

December 1, 1750 concerning the collection of the royal fifth on gold production. Third he discussed the laws concerning education, using as examples the laws of 1759 and 1760 concerning public education.

His fourth category concerned the military and his fifth, commerce and navigation. The sixth division concerned agriculture, the seventh the rebuilding of Lisbon and the eighth division looked at ecclesiastical affairs. In this final category he used as examples the laws of September 3, 1759 concerning the expulsion of the Jesuits and the conservation of the papers relating to this expulsion, the law of June 14, 1760 expelling the Papal Nuncio, and other dispositions taken against papal powers.[53] After Cenáculo's semi-disgrace following Pombal's downfall, Prince José made a point of commenting in public that, "other than being born a prince, everything else that made me respectable in the eyes of the world I owe to that great man."[54]

At base, the Pombaline educational reform had a highly utilitarian purpose – to produce a new corps of enlightened officials to staff the reformed state bureaucracy and church hierarchy. It was to be here, from among these freshly minted bureacrats

[53] "Excertos do 'diário' de Dom Frei Manuel do Cenáculo," pp. 22–23.
[54] Marcadé, *Cenáculo*, p. 66.

and clerics, that the Pombaline reforms would find their perpetuators and defenders. The center of the reform process, however, was the thorough revamping of the University of Coimbra in 1772. After the death of Clement XIII, Francisco de Lemos was confirmed as bishop of Coimbra by his successor, Clement XIV, who was anxious to reestablish the broken relationship with Portugal. In order to prepare the new statutes of the university, a *junta da providência literária* was created in December 1770. The ubiquitous and pliant Dom João Cosme da Cunha was the president of the *junta* and Francisco de Lemos became the reform rector. Francisco de Lemos, together with his brother, composed the new statutes of the university, João Pereira Ramos, coordinating the juridical part in close collaboration with the marquês de Pombal and Francisco de Lemos concentrating on the new statutes relating to the natural sciences and mathematics.[55] Frei Cenáculo was also a member of the *junta da providência literária*.[56] Pombal's personal intervention had placed Cenáculo on this commission, where Pombal took an active part in discussions, presiding over some sessions of the *junta* himself.[57] The university was closed down during the final stages of the reform and Pombal personally supervised the inauguration of the reformed institution during a 32-day stay in Coimbra from September to October, 1772. The key individuals who assisted him were José Seabra da Silva, his coauthor of the *Dedução cronológica*, Frei Manuel do Cenáculo, João Pereira Ramos, D. Francisco de Lemos, Pascoal José de Melo Freire, António Nunes Sanches, Jacobo Castro Sarmento and, of course, Vernei.

The reform aimed to keep but modernize the faculties of theology and canon law, to incorporate the study of Portuguese sources in the faculty of law curriculum, to update thoroughly the faculty of medicine by the return of the study of anatomy through the dissection of corpses (previously prohibited in Portugal for religious reasons), the study of hygiene "because it is easier to conserve health than to recuperate it once lost," to adopt Harvey's discoveries concerning the circulation of blood, Albinus' theories in anatomy, Boerhaave's in pathology, and van Swieten's in pharmacology.

In addition, two new faculties were created, those of mathematics and philosophy. Philosophy was to incorporate not only the traditional subjects of metaphysics and logic and ethics but also the new natural sciences, which used observation and experiment. The elaborate plans for the university included a series of new and impressive buildings designed in a neoclassical style by the English military architect Colonel William Elsden, who had accompanied Count Lippe to Portugal, where he

---

[55] Montalvão Machado, *Quem livrou Pombal*, p. 151. For comments in Cenáculo's diary concerning the meetings of the *junta* in the house of Pombal and other locations to discuss the reform see "Excertos do 'diário' de Dom Frei Manuel do Cenáculo," pp. 23–35. These remarkable diary entries give an intimate inside view of the discussions in the *junta da providência literária* as well as other conversations with Pombal and observations by Cenáculo on the various individuals concerned with the reform program, their internal jealousies and rivalries, and the direct participation of Pombal in many of these decisions over curricula, and the source of advice and books used.

[56] Marcadé, *Cenáculo*, pp. 73–77.

[57] Ibid., pp. 83–84; also Dom Francisco de Lemos, "A reforma da universidade de Coimbra," *Memórias da Academia Real das Ciências*, series 7 (1895).

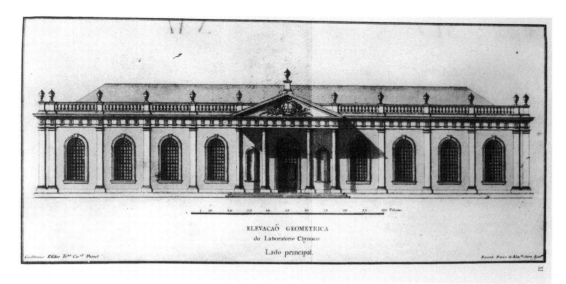

ELEVAÇAÕ GEOMETRICA
do Laboratorio Chymico.
Lado principal.

34 William Elsden's façade for the chemistry laboratory, Coimbra

remained, becoming Quartermaster General of the Portugese army in 1771. These plans encompassed a series of laboratories (figs. 34–36), an observatory, a university press, and a botanical garden.[58] The physics laboratory was fitted with the most recent equipment. The new curriculum and the provision of the laboratories was exceptionally advanced for the epoch.[59] Pombal, as with the plans for the reconstruction of Lisbon, took a direct personal interest in all stages of this planning. In October 1773, for example, he criticized the first plans for the botanical garden, which he considered too ostentatious. He wanted a garden for the "instruction of boys, not for the ostentation of princes or individuals."[60] As with Lisbon, the new construction at Coimbra was linked to the promotion of industrial development. The ceramic tiles and *azulejos* produced for the new building included a series of representations of the buildings themselves (fig. 35b).[61]

The first work printed by the *junta da providência literária* was a comprehensive justification for the reform placing the blame for the universities' decadence on the Jesuits, and maintaining a clear regalist position with respect to Rome. The papacy, however, was in no mood to quarrel again with Pombal and the process was now well under way whereby the pope himself would soon acquiesce in the suppression of the Jesuit order. The three published volumes of the university's new statutes were

---

[58] See *Riscos das obras da universidade de Coimbra* (Coimbra, 1983).
[59] Rómulo de Carvalho, *História do gabinete de física da universidade de Coimbra* (Coimbra, 1978).
[60] M. Lopes d'Almeida, *Documentos da reforma pombalina*, 2 vols. (Coimbra, 1937–1979) I, pp. 22–23.
[61] Matilde de Figueiredo, *Da cerâmica Coimbrã: uns notáveis azulejos do Museu Nacional Machado de Castro* (Coimbra, 1982).

35 The chemistry laboratory of the University of Coimbra, designed by William Elsden
(a)   view of the façade
(b)   panel of *azulejos* representing the façade (Museu Nacional Machado de Castro, Coimbra)

36 Façade of the chapter house at Coimbra by Elsden

received in Rome without censure.[62] The classic statement of purpose for the university reform process, however, came from the pen of Francisco de Lemos himself:

One should not look on the university as an isolated body, concerned only with its own affairs, as is ordinarily the case, but as a body at the heart of the state, which through its scholars creates and diffuses the enlightenment of wisdom to all parts of the monarchy, to animate, and revitalize all branches of the public administration, and to promote the happiness of man. The more one analyzes this idea, the more relationships one discovers between the university and the state: the more one sees the mutual dependency of these two bodies one on the other, and that science cannot flourish in the university without at the same time the state flourishing, improving and perfecting itself. This understanding arrived very late in Portugal, but at last it has arrived, and we have established without doubt the most perfect and complete example in Europe today.[63]

[62] *Compêndio histórico do estado da universidade de Coimbra, no tempo da invasão dos denominados Jesuítas, e dos estragos feitos nas ciências e nos professores e directores que a regiam, pelas maquinações e publicações dos novos estatutos por elles fabricados* (Lisbon, 1771). For discussion of Rome's reaction to the *compêndio* and the statutes see Beal, "Os Jesuítas," pp. 97–101.

[63] *Relação geral do estado da universidade, 1777* (Coimbra: facsimile reproduction, 1983), p. 232.

In his economic reforms Pombal always faced the problem of Portugal's limited entrepreneurial capacity. No less critical were the problems of finding suitably qualified individuals to carry forward the transformation of the educational and administrative structures of the country. The creation of human capital was, in fact, a slower process than the accumulation of wealth via the manipulation of tariffs, or the concession of lucrative monopolies. In the area of educational reform he tried to make use of foreigners, especially Italians, and to rotate from institution to institution the few modern-minded individuals he had at his disposal. The first state school within which experimental physics was introduced, for example, was the College of Nobles of Lisbon, and the fate of scientific education at the college is exemplary of the mixed impact of many of Pombal's endeavors. The idea was to provide the children of the nobility with professional skills needed in government or in military service. António Nunes Ribeiro Sanches in his *Cartas sobre a educação da mocidade* (Paris, 1759) had recommended the value of physics in the educational curriculum as well as the use of scientific apparatus with which the teachers could demonstrate the

properties of the elements, optics, mechanics and statics . . . so as to see by means of the use of these instruments that results were caused not by miracles but through the effects of nature . . . [and] . . . the pupils would see the proofs of what they were taught.

But the College of Nobles, the statutes of which were promulgated in 1761, only opened its doors in 1766, and the classes in experimental physics only lasted between 1768 and 1772, when all scientific education was dropped and the instruments in the laboratory were moved to Coimbra. The Italian professor of experimental physics, Giovanni Antonio dalla Bella, who had arrived in 1766, was responsible for the purchase of instruments, in part from England and in part by commissioning instruments constructed in Portugal. The collection which went later to Coimbra is reputed to be one of the most complete of its type in Europe of the period.[64] The young prince Dom José had his own physics laboratory at the Royal Palace of Ajuda in Lisbon. William Beckford, who met the prince a year before he succumbed to smallpox, observed that the very first thing the prince had spoken of was his physics laboratory.[65]

The effort made by Pombal to create an enlightened generation of bureaucrats and officials was to benefit his successors, but in his own administration he relied on a very small group of collaborators. These included members of his family and relatives, a handful of enlightened gentry and aristocrats such as the morgado de Mateus and the marquês de Lavradio, reform-minded clergy of modest origins or colonial back-grounds such as Cenáculo and Francisco de Lemos, and foreign experts such as Vandelli and Stephens. Many of these men accumulated several positions just

---

[64] Pombal had sought his professors for the college in Italy via Abbé Jacopo Facciolali at Pádua, see Rómulo de Carvalho, *História da fundação do Colégio Real das Nobres de Lisboa*, pp. 49–69.

[65] *A corte da rainha D. Maria I: correspondência de W. Beckford* (Lisbon, 1981); also Rómulo de Carvalho, *A física experimental em Portugal no século XVIII* (Lisbon, 1982), pp. 80–84.

37 The University of Coimbra (photograph by Jean Dieuzaide)

as Pombal's business associates accumulated positions in the management of fiscal and commercial affairs. After December 1770 Cenáculo, for example, served as principal consultant to the *junta da providência literária*, the commission responsible for the reform of higher education, in addition to all his other appointments. Cenáculo's multiple jobs, of course, meant that supervision of some of his responsibilities proved to be impossible. His secretary, Alexandre Ferreira da Faria Manuel, was accused of selling off books deposited with the royal censorship, including "six *Belisaires* by Masmontée, six *Lettres persanes*, five *Histoire des Indes de l'abbé Raynal*" for a total of 103,000 *réis*. The latter, curiously, was a book prohibited in Portugal.[66]

With his powerful will and ruthlessness, Pombal was able to mobilize these scarce human resources and succeed in putting into practice a series of extraordinary measures. But his reduced base of operations in terms of personnel was always a fundamental threat to the long-term success of his reforms.

There were also limits to what could be accomplished by legislation. António Ribeiro Sanches, reviewing a copy of the law prohibiting discrimination against those of Jewish origin like himself, wrote in his diary, "but can this law extinguish from the minds of a people, ideas and thoughts they have acquired from their earliest years?"[67] Sanches, of course, hit on the key point of weakness of enlightened social engineering. The legal formulations of the Pombaline state were justified as an application of natural law, a secularized system which was a logical construct where reason rather than faith or custom defined justice or injustice.[68] To provide justification for these new criteria for legal interpretation, Pombal enacted in 1769 a "Law of the Good Reason" (Lei de Boa Razão) instructing that henceforward all law was to be construed on "good reason," without which it would not be valid.[69] The radical renovation of judicial training after 1772 at Coimbra was the complement to this enactment.[70] Yet, in practice the explicit constructs of the state were underpinned by the unstated networks of personal relationships, clientelism, and self-interest. Such self-interest was clearly seen by Pombal as a means to fortify the objectives of the state in economic policy, as well as in administration. Yet, to work, this required a vision that set the national interest above private interests. While Pombal ruled, this overall objective prevailed. But it did so at the cost of continuous personal intervention and much repression. And as Pombal grew older, and as his brothers died, he became more and more repressive, suspicious of even his closest collaborators should they show too much independence or oppose his desires.[71] Pombal's own view of his historical role was also by no means neglected by his friends. In 1770 the great painting of Pombal by the fashionable artist, Van Loo (1707–1771), was commissioned and paid for by the two holders of the monopoly of the brazilwood trade, Gerard de Vismes (1713–1795), a merchant of Huguenot origins, who owned an estate at Benfica, and David Purry, a wealthy Swiss businessman born in Neuchâtel, and who had arrived in Lisbon after

[66] Marcadé, *Cenáculo*, p. 78.

[67] Cited by António José Saraiva, *Inquisição e Cristãos-Novos*, 4th edition (Oporto, 1969), p. 317.

[68] For an excellent discussion of Ribeiro Sanches' reaction to Pombaline legislation concerning the new Christians based on the comments and analysis contained in his private diary in the collections of the Bibliothèque de la faculté de médecine, Paris, MS 2015, see Maria Helena Carvalho dos Santos, "Ribeiro Sanches e a questão dos judeus," in *RHDI/M de P* 1, pp. 117–142; quotation from p. 141.

[69] Oliveira Marques, *History of Portugal* 1, p. 407.

[70] See Guilherme Braga da Cruz, *O direito subsidiário na história do direito português* (Coimbra, 1975).

[71] For attack on Oratorians, see "Processo pombalino contra os Oratorianos," in Banha de Andrade, *Contributos*, pp. 675–687.

the earthquake.[72] Van Loo never, in fact, came to Portugal, but his great painting, entitled *The Marquis of Pombal Expelling the Jesuits*, of Pombal with the Tagus behind him, the plans for the new Praça do Comércio in his hand and the plans for the façades for the new College of Nobles and the Board of Trade at his feet, set the image of Pombal which remains most prominently in the public mind to this day (see frontispiece).[73]

[72] See *Marquês de Bombelles: journal d'un ambassadeur de France au Portugal*.

[73] The title is, in fact, anachronistic since Sebastião José de Carvalho e Melo did not become marquês de Pombal until three years after the portrait was executed.

6

War and empire

Portugal must be regarded as an English colony.

Duc de Choiseul (1762)

If the commerce of Britain fails by encouraging that of France and Spain, adieu to the liberty of your country.

Mr. Punch to the King of Portugal (1762)

In 1762 outside events intervened to complicate and transform Pombal's intentions. The diplomatic revolution in the European alliances of the mid-1750s and the subsequent Seven Years War at first did not involve Portugal directly. Pombal believed, in fact, that he could avoid participation in this broader European and colonial embroglio and sustain the traditional policy of Portuguese neutrality. Pombal's brother, Mendonça Furtado, had written that Portugal should not object to the French and British "breaking one another's heads" as long as Portugal was not drawn into their conflicts.[1] But it was not to be. Both Pombal and his brother, and even Duke Silva-Tarouca, miscalculated the chances of Portuguese involvement in the Seven Years War.[2] Portugal's relations with Austria were obviously adversely affected by the changed European situation, and with the accession of the Bourbon Charles III in Spain in 1759, Portugal's position became precarious as the conditions were created for the Third Family Pact between France and Spain (August 1761). French objectives, which now extended to the Iberian peninsula, involved shutting British commerce out of the Continent, including closing British access to the Atlantic ports of Portugal, thereby forcing Portugal from its neutrality into the broader struggle. With French encouragement and to enforce these demands, in 1762 Spanish forces entered Portugal on two fronts.[3]

---

[1] [Mendonça Furtado] to [Pombal], November 22, 1755, *Correspondência inédita* III, p. 876.

[2] For example, [Silva-Tarouca] to [Pombal], Vienna, April 1, 1758, *AAP*, p. 397.

[3] There is a good account of the war as it affected Portugal in D. Francis, *Portugal, 1715–1808*. Also A. Christelow, "French Interest in the Spanish Empire During the Ministry of the Duc de Choiseul (1758–1771)," *HAHR* 21, 4 (1941), pp. 515–537.

The Spanish invasion of 1762 brought a shattering challenge to the basic assumptions on which for a decade the Portuguese government had based its policies. Above all, it once again reminded all of the military and political dependency of Portugal on Britain, something Pombal had tried repeatedly to reduce. What was worse, in the face of the total inadequacy of Portugal's military preparedness, British assistance was required to repel the invasion. British aid did not come without vocal protest in the House of Commons.[4] In case the lesson of events should be lost on the government in Lisbon, they were summarized in an anonymous open letter to the Portuguese king entitled *Punch's Politiks* published in London in 1762. In the pamphlet Punch warned that, should Spain and France gain control of Lisbon, the British might be content to claim direct access to Brazil with the Portuguese monarch safely conveyed across the Atlantic out of harm's way. Thus the "previous steps taken by his Portuguese Majesty" would be "an immediate withdrawing on board the British fleet, with his treasures, and all that of his family and faithful subjects . . . to the Brazils." The conquerors would be left with "the shell to subsist on when the kernel is taken away." Punch's "fairy dream," for such it was described, was intended to convey a warning to Pombal. "If the commerce of Britain fails by encouraging that of France and Spain," Punch told the king of Portugal, "adieu to the liberty of your country."[5] The British minister in Lisbon, Mr. Hay, reported tersely to London during October 1765, "[Pombal] seems to lay it down for a maxim, that it is the undoubted interest of Great Britain to assist Portugal upon every emergency, at the same time that almost every innovation in the commerce for these past ten years tends evidently to the lessening of that interest."[6]

By the early 1760s, in fact, British official and merchant circles had realized at last the true objectives of Pombal's commercial companies and economic legislation. During 1763 Mr. Hay placed before the government in London a detailed synopsis of the Pombaline system as he saw it. Pombal "looks upon the Portuguese here as no more than shopkeepers, and the Brazil merchants no more than commissaries or factors to the foreigners," he pointed out. "This put this minister upon a scheme to put the trade into the hands of the natives, and to make them the importers and wholesale traders in foreign goods . . . [T]he design is to establish an active trade among the subjects of Portugal, and to make foreign factors useless."[7] The merchants of the British factory in Lisbon, shaken out of their complacency, petitioned the government in London and underlined the long-term potentialities of Pombal's measures, particularly if

---

[4] The king's message recommending support for Portugal was presented to the House of Commons on May 11, 1762 and opposed by Mr. Clover, spokesman of the London merchants (T. C. Hansard, *The Parliamentary History of England from the Earliest Period to the Year 1803* xv [London, 1818], pp. 1221, 1222, 1224).

[5] *Punch's Politiks* (London, 1762), introduction and pp. 40–45.

[6] Quoted by Allan Christelow, "Great Britain and the Trades from Cadiz and Lisbon to Spanish America and Brazil, 1759–1782," *HAHR* 27 (February 1947), p. 12.

[7] Quoted by Smith, *Pombal* ii, p. 46.

monopoly companies were established in Bahia and Rio de Janeiro. These "intended companies," the merchants reported,

> . . . if effected will change the circulation and channel of trade from the hands of British subjects to Portuguese, and consequently we shall be deprived of the great advantage of our commission business and other profits that arise from the sale and purchase of our commodities . . . It will force the major part of the British merchants and factors now residing in Portugal to leave the country.

To emphasize its disquiet the factory went so far as to publish their petition in London, along with confidential memoranda of the past several years, doubtless in order to bring pressure to bear on the British government and Parliament.[8]

Pombal, when requesting British military assistance in 1762, was careful not to invoke the Anglo-Portuguese treaties, a fact the British minister in Lisbon noted with unease. Mr. Hay recognized that this deprived the Spanish and French of the argument they had used to justify their invasion of Portugal, which was that the Anglo-Portuguese treaties were offensive and not defensive in nature. But Pombal's request on the basis of "the common cause" had the further effect of depriving the British of the opportunity to hold Portugal to closer observance of what the British regarded as obligations in the commercial sphere, where they now recognized Pombal was intent on challenging their dominant position. The wider British conflict with France and Spain, however, required that Portuguese requests be attended to as Pombal had surmised, since the British had no desire to see Lisbon's port in enemy hands. Pombal requested the British appoint Lord Tyrawly, who had proved so sympathetic to his policy in 1752, to be commander of the expeditionary forces sent by London to Portugal's assistance.[9] Tyrawly was dispatched as requested but he was, by now, a quarrelsome old man, too sick even to mount a horse, and soon requested to be released from the responsibility, though one of his numerous Portuguese-born illegitimate children, Colonel John O'Hara, was to distinguish himself in the campaign. The British government sent to replace Tyrawly an officer of considerable reputation, Wilhelm Graf von Schaumburg-Lippe, who arrived in Portugal in late July. Graf Lippe was a grandson of George I through an illegitimate line, and he was accompanied to Portugal by the king's brother-in-law, Prince Charles of Mecklenberg.[10]

The war itself was a dilatory affair with each side's weaknesses proving more significant in engagements than their respective strengths. Both sides relied extensively on foreign troops and officers, though Portuguese popular opposition to the Spaniards proved decisive in places, especially in the north. Peace in the wider conflict, in any case, came in November before the end of the year, and the peninsular campaign of

---

[8] "Memórias do consul e factória britânica," BNLCP, codex 94, fos. 24, 24v, 25v. *Occasional Thoughts on the Portuguese Trade and the Inexpediency of Supporting the House of Braganza on the Throne of Portugal* (London, 1767) recommended the sacrifice of Portugal in the interest of an alliance with Spain.

[9] See discussion by David Francis, *Portugal: 1715–1808*, pp. 146–147.

[10] Christa Banaschik, *Wilhelm Graf von Schaumburg-Lippe in Portugal, 1761–1777* (Osnabrück, 1974).

1762 remained very much a sideshow at the tail end of the Seven Years War. The recourse to British assistance, however, had considerable significance for Portugal, since it forced Pombal to much greater discrimination and caution in his dealings with Britain, as well as revealing the deplorable conditions of Portugal's defenses. At Pombal's request Graf Lippe remained a year after the peace and set about a thorough reform of the Portuguese military establishment.

British recognition of the possible impact of the Portuguese government's economic measures, together with the clear demonstration of the dependence of Portugal on Britain, however, served to rekindle with a new virulence those fears which twenty years before first led Pombal to make his detailed and comprehensive investigation of the causes of Britain's commercial superiority. The consequences of the Seven Years War, therefore, were paradoxical. Portugal had been defended, but British intentions were more distrusted than ever before. The demands of war on the treasury, moreover, had compelled Pombal to institute a comprehensive tax on all income and production by reviving the *decima*, an emergency tax granted in the mid-seventeenth century to the Portuguese monarch by the Cortes following the restoration of Portuguese independence. And, shocked by British military successes overseas, especially in the Caribbean and Canada, Pombal urgently extended to Brazil many of the administrative, fiscal, and military reform measures being implemented in Portugal itself.

Britain's striking preponderance in world affairs at the end of the Seven Years War, in fact, turned Pombal's recurrent concern with British expansionist intentions into a near obsession about the vulnerability of Portuguese America. Pombal viewed the British victories against Spain's empire as a potential threat to Portuguese America as well. The world-wide dimension of British planning and capabilities had been startlingly revealed during the Seven Years War by Lord Albemarle's capture of Havana in 1762 and the capture of Manila by Admiral Cornish and General Draper using forces of the British East India Company. The vulnerability of the west and east coasts of the Americas to a strategy conceived in world terms by a European power which was also fast becoming an Indian-based Asiatic power was clearly demonstrated. Thus, when in 1763 the British began the systematic exploration of the Pacific, it was not only the Spaniards whose fears seemed realized.[11] The *rapprochement* between Madrid and Lisbon was aided by Pombal's sympathetic reaction to the Madrid uprising of 1766 which had shaken Charles III's regime; the so-called Squillace revolts against the king's Italian ministers. Pombal had seen a striking resemblance to the plots against his own reform programs. He closed the borders and offered Portuguese troops to Charles III to quell the disturbances. The subsequent expulsion of the Jesuits from Spain on the pretext that they were responsible for the uprisings also brought Pombal into a *de facto* anti-Jesuit alliance among the European Catholic monarchs. Pombal was not, however, averse to profiting from Spain's difficulties and he advised the viceroy

---

[11] For an excellent discussion of legacies of the Seven Years War, especially for British and French policy, see H. M. Scott, *British Foreign Policy*, pp. 29–52.

of Brazil, the count of Cunha, to take every possible advantage of the situation.[12] Meanwhile, in London the Prince of Masserano, the Spanish ambassador, was busy bribing clerks at the British Admiralty. Madrid, anxious to attract Portugal into an anti-British coalition, forwarded these purloined documents to Pombal. Pombal wasted no time in sending them on to the count of Cunha in 1767.[13] The British, "their natural arrogance" heightened by successes during the Seven Years War, would use "any occasion or pretext to conquer the overseas dominions of all the other European powers," Pombal told the viceroy in his covering letter. "Two most powerful monarchies had been laid low, and Havana, always reputed to be impregnable, taken." There was a clear pattern in all this to Pombal. First the British had attacked Cartagena in 1741, then Havana in 1762; how long before Rio de Janeiro followed, he asked. "If the British establish themselves in the Rio de la Plata they would make themselves masters of all Paraguay and Tucuman, of all Chile and Peru, in a word of all Spanish America, and as a necessary consequence of all the state of Brazil," he concluded. "We must defend ourselves," Pombal wrote, "first with policy, until where it will extend no further, and after, as a last resort, with force."[14] His fears in the 1760s, especially over British ambitions in the river Plate region, very much revived the concerns he had expressed to Lisbon during the 1740s when he was Portuguese envoy to the Court of St. James.

The years immediately following the Seven Years War, in fact, saw Pombal involved in a complex multi-layered game of eighteenth-century diplomacy, all sides pursuing policies on several fronts at the same time and often with the same partners. The hope on the Spanish and French side was to move Portugal away from its alliance with Britain; and on Pombal's side it was aimed at getting the British to support his ambitions in South America – especially, in defense of the Portuguese claim to the "natural" frontier of the La Plata. Choiseul, who was Louis XV's leading minister from 1758 until the end of 1770, well aware that "[Pombal] loses his head whenever there is talk of Jesuits," was willing to explore the possibilities of taking some advantage from this fact. After the humiliations of the Seven Years War, when France had seen her position in India virtually destroyed, Canada lost together with part of Louisiana, France's Continental interests were subordinated to the struggle with Britain overseas.

[12] See D. Alden, *Royal Government*, p. 107.

[13] Harlow, *Second British Empire* I, pp. 49, 220, II, pp. 252–255, 281, 300, 632–633; R. L. Schuyler, *The Fall of the Old Colonial System* (New York, 1945), pp. 80–82. Pombal and the king had both expressed their wish to see the two peninsular powers make common cause in the Old World and the New against the "common enemy," the British, during conversations with the Spanish ambassador in Lisbon, the marqués de Almodóvar. [Marqués de Almodóvar] to [marqués de Grimaldi], Lisbon, May 8, 1767, AHN, state file 4536 (2). Shortly thereafter, Grimaldi forwarded copies of the Prince of Masserano's gleanings in London to Lisbon for Pombal's attention. [Grimaldi] to [Almodóvar], San Ildefonso, August 6, 1767, AHN state file 4536 (2), and [Grimaldi] to [Almodóvar], San Lorenzo, November 13, 1767, AHN, state file 4536 (2).

[14] "Instruções officiaes," April 14, 1769, Marcos Carneiro de Mendonça, *O marquês de Pombal e o Brasil* (São Paulo, 1960), pp. 31–44; "Relação das instruções de ordens que expediram ao conde da Cunha," June 14, 1767, *RIHGB* 35, pt I (1872), pp. 227–326.

The British were meanwhile instructing their representatives secretly in Lisbon and Madrid to obtain the best information they could on the strengths and weaknesses of Spanish and Portuguese territories in the New World and the "strength and amount of discontent which are supposed to prevail there."[15]

In fact, Pombal's concerns about British intentions were largely misplaced and the careful assessment of the Anglo-Portuguese alliance which underlay Pombal's economic policies during the 1750s was more soundly rooted in reality than was his post-war obsession with British objectives and their supposed collaboration with the Jesuits in South America. In the pamphlet, *Punch's Politiks*, the British position was more accurately summarized: Punch had argued that Britain "knows her own interest too well" to search for a universal empire; "commerce is her support and extent of territory, her trade neglected, must be her downfall."[16]

A great deal of subterfuge had always characterized Pombal's relations with the British, but his imputation of equal dissimulation to them in their dealings with Portugal over Brazil overestimated the British government's subtlety. The "most declared unity" he perceived between the British and the Jesuits, as well as the supposed designs of Britain on the Portuguese empire in America, had little substance. The voyages of Captains Byron and Cook which so concerned him were motivated by science as much as by imperial expansionism, and had as their motivation a desire to explore the Pacific and seek out the great southern continent that many believed at the time existed beyond the southern sea. So esoteric an objective for so avaricious a power only provoked contemptuous disbelief in the suspicious mind of the Portuguese minister. The South Sea objective he held was an "appearance" only, for the expeditions were intended against Brazil and the Spanish dominions in that part of the world.[17]

British ambitions to break into the Pacific did provoke an acute conflict with Spain over the Falklands. Captain Byron, in 1765, had explored the islands and declared them to be British territory.[18] The British relationship with Portugal and hence with Brazil was governed, however, by quite different criteria from those governing the relationship with Spain and Spanish America. The acute dependency of Portugal on Great Britain meant that while all factors in the situation remained stable, it was essentially true, as Punch had told Dom José I in 1762, that Portugal "can never have reasons to fear encroachment from her."[19] Martinho de Melo e Castro, the Portuguese envoy in London, insisted that Pombal's obsession with British intentions was misplaced. The French and Spanish were Portugal's principal enemies, he insisted.[20] Portugal had no more "ready or solid resources than her own forces," Melo e Castro pointed out. As far as Britain was concerned, it would be only "when she saw

---

[15] Alden, *Royal Government*, p. 111, n. 123.
[16] *Punch's Politiks*, p. 54.
[17] Carneiro de Mendonça, *Pombal e o Brasil*, pp. 33, 36–37.
[18] See R. E. Gallagher, ed., *Byron's Journal of his Circumnavigation, 1764–1766* (Cambridge, 1964).
[19] *Punch's Politiks*, p. 54.
[20] [Martinho de Melo e Castro] to [Pombal], September 26, 1764, BNLCP, codex 611, fos. 262–266.

Portugal powerful and resolute that she would treat her as an ally, and not as a dependant."[21] The British themselves, to add insult to injury, drew Pombal's attention to the weakness of Brazilian defenses by forwarding a confidential British intelligence report to Pombal on the "deplorable condition" of Brazil's coastal fortifications. The author claimed that he would consider himself "deserving of everlasting infamy if I do not with one Battalion of infantry make myself master of Rio de Janeiro in 24 hours." He recommended that the "reformation already begun there [in Portugal] be extended to the coast of Brazil," in order to prevent "these valuable possessions from falling into the hands of the French and Spaniards."[22]

The ambiguities of Pombal's attitude toward his powerful maritime ally was ironically most acute in the region where he most feared its presence. The Spanish threat on the southern frontier of Brazil, in fact, made the retention of British goodwill by Portugal essential. But Pombal's economic policies and the changed diplomatic situation that followed the Peace of Paris found the British very unwilling to involve themselves in a quarrel with Spain for the sake of securing Portugal in possession of her colonies. Pombal's requests that Britain require Spain to uphold the stipulations of the Peace of Paris in South America were answered with a superb irony which could hardly have been lost on the all-powerful minister in Lisbon. "The court of Portugal would not wish British troops to be sent to defend the mines and govern the ports and coast of Brazil," the British government observed sardonically, "the deplorable situation of Brazil could do nothing but incite her enemies to conquer her."[23] In response, Pombal told the British minister in Lisbon that "England and Portugal were like man and wife, who might have little domestic disputes among themselves, but if anybody else came to disturb the peace of the family they would join to defend it."[24] He was mistaken. To many in Britain, Portugal, if anything, was the member of a harem. There always existed the possibility for the introduction of new and more voluptuous companions. Even Spain herself might be one of them.

The changed international situation following the Peace of Paris in 1763, however, had clearly limited Pombal's room for maneuver. British power had been formidably demonstrated, both in the Americas and in Portugal. British unhappiness with Pombal's economic policies had been made more than clear in London, and greater circumspection was clearly required in dealing with London. It is not clear, in fact, if Pombal ever contemplated extensions of the monopolistic company scheme to Bahia and Rio de Janeiro. The British merchants had complained, nevertheless, that, if created, the companies would completely exclude British trade from Brazil. In the 1700s numerous British pamphlets attacked Portugal's new economic policies. One of these, *Occasional Thoughts on the Portuguese Trade* (1767) anticipated Adam Smith in

---

[21] [Melo e Castro] to [Pombal], April 7, 1766, BNLCP, codex 611, fo. 383.

[22] Extract of a letter to Mr. Greenville, dated Rio de Janeiro, October 14, 1764, BNLCP, codex 612, fo. 61.

[23] [Pombal] to [Conde da Cunha], November 18, 1765, IHGB, file 11, doc. 12; [Melo e Castro] to [Pombal], March 20, 1765, BNLCP, codex 612, fos. 62–64.

[24] Quoted by Smith, *Pombal* II, pp. 51–52.

questioning the real value to Britain of the Portuguese connection and urged a renunciation of Britain's old ally in favor of an alliance with Spain.[25]

Pombal, however, moved aggressively to improve Brazil's defenses. His immediate postwar action in 1763 was to move the capital of Brazil south to Rio de Janeiro from the city of Salvador da Bahia. Rio de Janeiro provided a better center if the southern frontier was to be secured. Taking the advice of London seriously, he informed the new viceroy that "Eight unarmed British men-of-war would be sufficient to conquer Rio de Janeiro." On the defense of that magnificent harbor and city, he added, "depended the security of this precious continent."[26] To spearhead the military reorganization, he sent to Brazil several of the officers who had come to Portugal to participate in the military campaign led by Graf Lippe, including an Austrian-born general, Johann Heinrich Böhm, and Jacques Funck, a Swedish fortification expert who had been Graf Lippe's adjutant general. These reform-minded military specialists became chief of staff and chief of engineering and artillery, respectively. The colonial garrison was later reinforced by three of the best Portuguese regiments (Maura, Bragança, and Estremoz). Pombal also sent to Brazil two of the more effective Portuguese aristocrats who had worked with Graf Lippe, Dom Luís António de Sousa, morgado de Mateus, who was appointed governor of the reestablished captaincy of São Paulo in 1765, and the marquês de Lavradio, who became governor of Bahia in 1768 and later viceroy of Brazil in Rio de Janeiro in 1769.[27]

Lavradio's appointment embodied some of the ambiguities of Pombal's relationship with the Portuguese aristocracy and their relationship with him. Lavradio's mother was sister to the late duke of Aveiro and his grandfather had been the first patriarch of Lisbon; Pombal's first director of studies in his educational reform, Dom Tomás de Almeida, was Lavradio's brother. The morgado de Mateus summarized the instructions Pombal had given him as follows: "The spirit . . . may be reduced to three principal points," he noted, "the first, to secure the frontier, the second, to people it in order that it may defend itself, and third, to make profitable use of the mines and utilities which might be discovered in this vast continent."[28] Pombal also made use in Brazil of the first students to graduate from the College of Nobles. Dom Luís Pinto de Sousa Coutinho (who graduated in 1767) was appointed governor and captain general of the Mato Grosso. "Do not alter anything with force or violence," he told the young aristocrat as he embarked for the far interior of Brazil. "When reason allows and it is necessary to banish abuses and destroy pernicious customs to the benefit of King, Justice and the common Good, act with great prudence and moderation, a method which achieves more than power . . . In whatever resolution your excellency intends observe these three things: Prudence in deliberation, dexterity in preparation,

---

[25] Alden, *Royal Government*, p. 110.

[26] Instruções, June 20, 1767, in Carneiro de Mendonça, *Pombal e o Brasil*, p. 64.

[27] For a comprehensive account of the viceroyalty of Lavradio see Alden, *Royal Government*.

[28] Antunes de Moura, *Morgado de Mateus*, p. 89. For a comprehensive account of the government of the morgado de Mateus see Heloísa Liberalli Bellotto, *Autoridade e conflito no Brasil colonial: o governo do morgado de Mateus em São Paulo* (São Paulo, 1979).

38 (a) the Bahia regiment of black soldiers   (b) Bahia regimental uniforms

perseverance to complete."[29] This was ironic advice from a minister who was known throughout Europe for his harsh destruction of the aristocratic plotters against the king, and the expulsion of the Jesuits, but it encapsulated the caution Pombal always displayed in his dealings with colonial interests.

As in Portugal proper, in Portuguese America the military and fiscal reforms were intimately linked. Pombal sought to standardize military procedures on both sides of the Atlantic. The troops of Portugal and Brazil henceforth, he instructed the governors of the Brazilian captaincies, were to "constitute one . . . army under the same rules, with identical discipline, and without any differences whatever."[30] The new military structure envisioned cooperation between the various administrative divisions of Brazil. "Rio de Janeiro has a pressing obligation to aid all the other captaincies of Brazil," Pombal told the governor of São Paulo in 1775, "as each of them to aid mutually one another and the said Rio de Janeiro . . . In this reciprocal

[29] [Pombal] to [Luís Pinto de Sousa Coutinho], 1767. Carneiro de Mendonça "O pensamento da metrópole em relação ao Brasil," *RIHGB* 27 (1962), pp. 56–61.
[30] "Relação das instruções," *RIHGB* 35, pt 1 (1872), pp. 227–326.

union of power consists essentially the greatest force of a state and in lack of it all weakness."[31] The need for cooperation in military affairs was repeated time and again to all the governors in Portuguese America, for in its realization lay "one of the most important dispositions . . . for the defense, preservation, and security of all and each of them."[32] "The instructions of the Marquis of Pombal" were intended, the governor of Goiás was informed in 1771, "to establish for the government of all Portuguese America, a political, civil, and military system, applicable to all of the captaincies of that continent according to the situation and circumstances of each of them."[33] The governor of Mato Grosso was told in the same year that Pombal's measures were intended "to establish the *sistema fundamental* which today forms the government of Portuguese America."[34]

Like many of Pombal's measures, the directives from Lisbon were overambitious and they were imperfectly implemented, but important changes were achieved. At the captaincy level auxiliary cavalry and infantry regiments were raised throughout Brazil. In Minas Gerais, for example, thirteen regiments of auxiliary cavalry were organized, their colonels chosen from among the "principal men of greatest credit and fidelity in the captaincy." The Minas Dragoons, the captaincy's paid regular force, was reorganized into eight companies and salaries standardized.[35] In addition, companies of irregular foot troops were established to mobilize black and mulatto populations of the urban and rural population in a manner pioneered by the French and British with their American Indian auxiliaries (fig. 38).[36]

Simultaneously, the overseeing powers and new bookkeeping methods of the royal treasury were imposed throughout the colony. Exchequer boards (*juntas da fazenda*) were established in each Brazilian captaincy. Each *junta* was responsible for providing to the royal treasury in Lisbon standardized statements of receipts and expenditures on a regular timetable. As had happened in Lisbon, the colonial *juntas da fazenda* were encouraged to appoint officers from among the local "prudent and wealthy men" of the region, in particular, the most opulent of the local merchants.[37] The provision of suitably attractive salaries was intended to allow such men to bring their commercial expertise to the exercise of public affairs much in the manner that the Cruzes and Bandeiras had brought theirs to fiscal and economic policy making in Lisbon.[38] In the

---

[31] "Instrução militar para uso do governador . . . de São Paulo," June 24, 1775. Marcos Carneiro de Mendonça "O pensamento da metrópole em relação ao Brasil," *RIHGB* 227 (Oct.–Dec. 1962), p. 54.

[32] "Instruções para o governador . . . Minas Gerais," 1775, ibid., pp. 54–55.

[33] "Instruções para o governador . . . Gerais," 1771, ibid., p. 53.

[34] "Instruções para o governador . . . Mato Grosso," 1771, ibid., p. 52.

[35] "Instruções para D. António de Noronha, governador e capitão general da capitania de Minas Gerais," Jan. 24, 1775, *Anuário do museu da inconfidência* II (Ouro Prêto, 1953), pp. 177–182.

[36] "Quadros das forças de mar e terra existentes nas capitanias de Rio de Janeiro, Sta. Catarina, Rio Grande, Minas Gerais, e na Praça da Colonia disponiveis para a defesa da fronteira do sul," 1776, IHGB, file 44, doc. 8.

[37] [Pombal] to [marquês de Lavradio], March 31, 1769, BNLCP, codex 458, fos. 147–148.

[38] "Apontamentos vários sobre a Companhia do Grão-Pará e Maranhão," IHGB/AUC, 1-1-8, fo. 46; "Memórias do Consul e factória britânica," BNLCP, codex 94, fo. 24v. 31; codex 453, fos. 328–333.

face of massive fraud and considerable scandals which had rocked the old system of administration Pombal had dispatched accountants from Lisbon to Bahia to work with Lavradio who, as governor general of Bahia, was in charge of setting up the new fiscal system.[39]

In the principal Brazilian gold production region, Minas Gerais, a *junta da fazenda* was established in 1765, received detailed instructions on procedure during 1769, and took its final administrative form in 1771. Here, as elsewhere, expenditures were to be divided into four categories: military, ecclesiastical, civil, and extraordinary expenditures. The Minas *junta* was to be made responsible for the disposal of the captaincy contracts which, in the case of Minas Gerais, involved the important *entradas* taxes on goods crossing the captaincy's border and the local *dizimos* or tithes, as well as lesser passage tariffs. Because of the economic importance of Minas Gerais, these involved considerable revenues, and such important taxing powers had previously been retained within the competence of the overseas council in Lisbon. Pombal was here delegating for the first time to a constituted body, which welcomed local participation, responsibility for the regional *exchequer* and for all expenditure and revenue collection, excepting only that of the royal fifth. The collection of the fifth remained under the control of the foundry houses and was a royal revenue which could not be touched by the local *junta* and was remitted in its entirety to Lisbon. The intendant of the foundry house, however, was *ex officio* a member of the *junta*.[40]

In 1771 Pombal also abolished the contract system under which the specially demarcated diamond district of the Serro do Frio had been administered since 1740 (fig. 39). The diamond administration was now placed under the direct control of the royal treasury in Lisbon. A restrictive set of regulations was promulgated for the management of the diamond district and the mining and disposal of the diamonds. These measures were aimed at regulating production in keeping with the demands of the European market. In the Serro do Frio the district was placed under the administration of an intendant and fiscal (revenue inspector) together with three treasurers (*caixas*). These *caixas* were to be wealthy local residents nominated by the Lisbon directors and were to enjoy the same status and respect as directors of the Brazil companies.[41]

The involvement of colonial bigwigs in the administrative and fiscal organs of local government was characteristic of Pombal's reforms in Brazil. Local magnates had likewise been encouraged into posts of leadership in the colonial military establishment. Even within the magistracy men were appointed to powerful judicial positions within regions where they also retained widespread financial interests. Ignácio José da Alvarenga Peixoto, a Brazilian graduate of the University of Coimbra who had

---

[39] See Alden, *Royal Government*, p. 25.

[40] [Pombal] to *junta da fazenda*, Minas Gerais, Lisbon August 22, 1775, CCBNRJ, 1-9-23; also carta regia, March 6, 1765, CCBNRJ, 1-1-14 and 1-10-3.

[41] Joaquim Felicio dos Santos, *Memórias do distrito diamantino da comarca do Serro Frio*, 3rd edition (Rio de Janeiro, 1956), pp. 172–177; "Regimento para os administradores do contrato dos diamantes," Lisbon 1771, BNLCP, codex 691, fo. 2.

39 Diamond works in Brazil

(a)   general mining works

(c)   tobacco merchants and Rio de Janeiro slave porters

(b) searching for diamonds by hand

(d) the public punishment of slaves in Rio de Janeiro

composed fulsome poems in honor of Pombal and his family, was appointed *ouvidor* (superior crown magistrate) of the *comarca* of Rio das Mortes in the south of the captaincy of Minas Gerais. He chose this position specifically because of his vast landed and mining interests there.[42]

Protecting and stimulating the economic potential of Brazil and continuing its commercial benefits to national merchants remained a high priority. After the Peace of Paris, Pombal sought to achieve these objectives by reinforcing the traditional exclusion of foreigners, by major changes in the maritime connections, and by the stimulation of new primary exports. The ports of Brazil, long a favored stopping point for European shipping bound for Asia, would be closed to foreign vessels except for the most urgent humanitarian reasons. "All the world knows that the overseas colonies are founded as a precious object of utility of the metropolis . . . from which essential certainty result infallible maxims universally observed in the practice of all nations," Mendonça Furtado commented when the British complained of restrictions placed against East India vessels watering in Brazilian ports.[43] To stimulate Portuguese shipping, Pombal abolished the fleet system to Rio and Bahia in 1765 and permitted ships to sail at their own convenience. In 1766 when freight charges were regulated and lowered and the freedom of intercoastal shipping decreed,[44] the British envoy in Lisbon, Mr. Hay, at once congratulated Pombal: "I could not help telling him that freedom was the soul of commerce, and therefore, every liberty which could be allowed must be beneficial to the trade and credit of the nation."[45] There was more to the deed, however, than Mr. Hay noticed in his enthusiasm for the freedom of trade. Abolition of the fleets served to facilitate the access of Brazilian products to European markets and augment their competitiveness by avoiding the long delays of the old system. Brazilian producers saw quicker returns on their investment and a consequent alleviation of their debt position.

After 1763 the local administration in southern Brazil also began to assume some of the economic functions that the Brazil companies were performing in Amazonia and Pernambuco. The new viceroy, the marquês de Lavradio, was relentless in his encouragement of new commodities and more efficient methods both in Bahia and in Rio de Janeiro. He appointed João Hopman, a Dutch entrepreneur of thirty years' residence in Brazil, as "inspector of new plantations and farms." He ordered coffee plants and distributed them, to Hopman, among others. He sought out information in Santa Catarina on cheese and butter production. He insisted that wheat be planted in proportion to cultivated land and had mulberry trees introduced. Viceroy Lavradio also developed a system of subsidy to farmers who experimented with new primary products through a system of guaranteed prices, having come to the conclusion that

---

[42] M. Rodrigues Lapa, *Vida e obra de Alvarenga Peixoto* (Rio de Janeiro, 1960), pp. x, xxvii.

[43] "Note and counternote," Melo e Castro to British envoy in Lisbon, March 20, 1772 and May 11, 1772, BNLCP, codex 638, fo. 210.

[44] *Alvará* September 27, 1765 and decree June 2, 1766, private collection Brazil.

[45] Quoted by Christelow, "Great Britain and the Trades from Cadiz and Lisbon,", p. 15.

the rigidity of the colonial entrepreneurial framework discouraged Brazilian merchants from risking the export of new products to Europe which had not been ordered in advance by their correspondents in Lisbon and Oporto.[46] In this manner he was able to develop indigo and cochineal production with some success; indigo to such an extent that by 1779 it formed in value 16.8 percent of the total export from Rio de Janeiro to Lisbon, and 20.6 percent of Rio's exports to Oporto.[47]

While in Bahia, Viceroy Lavradio had formed a company to establish a canvas factory.[48] Once in Rio, he encouraged the entrepreneur Manuel Luís Vieira to set up a rice-processing plant.[49] By 1774 the viceroy was able to send to Lisbon a portion of silk made from the fiber of a new species of silkworm. With Hopman, Lavradio discovered the plant *quaxima* from which a good flax for cord and canvas could be extracted, and in 1778 Lavradio forwarded to Lisbon four *arrobas* of the improved plant and three pieces of linen prepared by Hopman.[50] In the captaincy of São Paulo the governor, the morgado de Mateus, opened up the iron mines at Sorocaba and by 1765 he was able to send Pombal a sample of the first iron forged by Domingos Ferreira Pereira. Eleven years later Ferreira Pereira obtained permission to establish a foundry with exclusive privileges to mining and smelting in the captaincy.[51] The new manufactories in America were aided directly by the Lisbon *junta do comércio*. Manuel Luís Vieira and his partner Domingos L. Loureiro, for example, received exclusive privileges from the *junta* for ten years of rice production in 1776. In Bahia José Ferreira Leal received in 1767 support for the manufacture of rigging. The *junta do comércio* also aided in the establishment of the leather factory of Feliciano Gomes Neves in Rio de Janeiro during 1760 and of Costa Moreira and Company in Pernambuco in 1772.[52] All of these developments in manufacturing and processing activities contradicted classical mercantilist practices and marked a major innovation in Portuguese colonial policy.

It was the continuing undeclared war in the south, however, which was to have the most immediate impact on the reform policies of Pombal in Brazil. The breakdown of the Madrid agreements in 1761 had provoked a major Spanish offensive to expel the Portuguese from Colônia and the lands they had settled to the south of the island of Santa Catarina during the 1750s. Santa Catarina itself had been the objective of a major official colonization scheme by the Portuguese during these years which had

[46] Dauril Alden, *Royal Government*, especially pp. 353–87.

[47] Calculated on the basis of tables in "Memórias políticas e económicas . . . para uso do vice-rei, Luís de Vasconcellos, 1770–89," *RIHGB* pt 1 (1884), pp. 25–52.

[48] D. José d'Almeida, *Vice-reinado de D. Luís d'Almeida Portugal, marquês de Lavradio* (São Paulo, 1941), p. 15. Also Alden in *CHLA* II, pp. 601–660.

[49] Dauril Alden, "Manuel Luís Vieira: An Entrepreneur in Rio de Janeiro during Brazil's Agricultural Renaissance," *HAHR* 39 (November 1959), p. 521.

[50] d'Almeida, *Vice-reinado de D. Luís d'Almeida Portugal*, p. 42.

[51] Américo Brasiliense Antunes de Moura, *Governo do morgado de Mateus no vice-reinado do conde da Cunha: São Paulo restaurado* (São Paulo, 1938), pp. 130–131.

[52] "Lista das fábricas instaladas com participação da junta do comércio," doc. 7, in Borges de Macedo, *A situação económica*; also see BNLCP, codex 456, fos. 183–4.

seen the importation of 4,000 married couples from the Azores. But the main frontier of settlement had been the region of Rio Grande with its vast hinterland of pastures and prairie, an area abounding in cattle and a source of hides and cereals exported to Rio, to the north of Brazil, and inland to São Paulo and the Minas Gerais. The Rio Grande area and Santa Catarina were placed under the authority of Rio de Janeiro. Colônia fell to the Spaniards in 1763 and when a naval relief force of British and Portuguese ships failed to retake it, the Spanish moved north up the Atlantic coast and succeeded in conquering much of Rio Grande just as peace was about to be made in Europe. The Peace of Paris technically was intended to reestablish the status quo ante, but left room for both Spain and Portugal to interpret its stipulations with respect to South America in their own interests. Spain did return Colônia though they established a blockade which made life very difficult for the inhabitants. Madrid held on to Spanish gains in Rio Grande, however, claiming that the Treaty of Paris did not apply to Rio Grande since this area had not been subject to any existing treaty conditions according to Madrid's interpretation. As a result for a decade the Portuguese and Spaniards confronted each other on either side of the narrow channel leading to Lago de Patos.[53]

The broader European objectives of Portuguese policy restrained any immediate Portuguese counteroffensive in the south. The anti-Jesuit struggle and the common desire of Portugal, Spain, and France to pressure the papacy over the Jesuit question meant that Pombal sought to avoid provoking the Spanish in the disputed southern borderlands in South America. Spain was itself anxious to preserve the uneasy peace with Portugal because of the coincident dispute with Britain over the Falkland Islands. On the ground in Brazil, however, Pombal encouraged surreptitious preparations, since he believed conflict could recur and regarded the retaking and securing of Rio Grande as essential to protecting São Paulo and Minas Gerais from Spanish ambitions. The governor of São Paulo was, in fact, aggressively expanding the area of Portuguese control toward Paraguay.[54]

In 1773, however, the Jesuit question was resolved when the Society of Jesus was suppressed by the pope. In the same year, the British warned Pombal that the Madrid government was concentrating forces in the north of Spain for potential deployment to South America. Pombal ordered the three Portuguese regiments in Rio to be sent south to Rio Grande where they were to be placed under the command of General Böhm. He also ordered the strengthening of the defense of Santa Catarina and dispatched under various subterfuges a naval squadron to Brazil, where it was to be commanded by a foreign naval officer, Robert MacDouall. Reinforcements were also sent from the Azores to Rio and troops deployed from Bahia to replace the European regiments now under Böhm's command in Rio Grande.

---

[53] For an excellent description of these events see Alden, *Royal Government*, esp. pp. 100–101.
[54] For a discussion of the Falklands see Scott, *British Foreign Policy*, pp. 144–154; also see detailed discussion of the activities of D. Luís de Souza Botelho Maurão, morgado de Mateus as governor of São Paulo by Heloísa Liberalli Bellotto, *Autoridade e conflito no Brasil colonial*.

The worry in Lisbon over Spanish intentions was further aggravated when news reached Lisbon of a huge Spanish troop and ship build-up in Cadiz – destined, as it turned out, to meet with disaster in an assault on Algiers, but which Pombal assumed was a cover for an expedition to South America and the Rio de la Plata. More mobilizations were demanded in Brazil, especially in Minas Gerais and São Paulo, both of which were ordered to provide troops for the Rio Grande and Rio de Janeiro. Governor Roche of Colônia was meanwhile secretly instructed to evacuate the outpost. Its defense was "chimerical and impossible," Pombal had concluded; but this decision was to be hidden from the Spaniards as well as Colônia's inhabitants: the objective was to entice the Spanish into an attack which could then be used to solicit British assistance.

The Spanish disaster in Algiers, however, once again shifted the balance in Europe. Now Madrid sought a negotiated settlement, rather than a military solution; and Pombal, sensing their weakness, countermanded his order: the bewildered garrison troops evacuated from Colônia had just disembarked in Rio when they were ordered back aboard their troopships for the return to Colônia. General Böhm, meanwhile, having eventually mustered his forces, struck a decisive blow against Spanish positions in the Lago dos Patos, reestablishing Portuguese control. This setback was too much for Madrid.

The early 1770s had seen a gradual improvement in relations between Britain and Spain. King George III had gone so far as to tell the Prince of Masserano in 1771 that the crisis over the Falkland Islands had been "like a lovers' quarrel; the lovers quarrel so that they will have the pleasure of making up and reaffirming their love."[55] After 1775, moreover, British foreign policy was subordinated to the exigencies of the war in the thirteen colonies, which required that Britain seek to avoid the intervention of the Bourbon powers, France and Spain, on the side of the colonists and to prevent them from seeking to take advantage of British preoccupation with the American rebels to avenge their losses during the Seven Years War. The danger of the escalation of the dispute in South America was thus a major concern to London, and the British were determined not to allow Pombal to provoke the Spaniards into an attack which would have provided an excuse for Pombal to evoke the defensive alliance between the two countries. London was aware, however, that an attack by Spain on Portugal in Europe would be more difficult to ignore. Thus, they encouraged France to restrain Spain while they tried to encourage Pombal to take a more moderate position. Pombal was equally anxious for British support and Portugal was the first to respond to British requests that the European ports be closed to the North Americans: in July 1776 Portugal closed her ports to American shipping.[56]

London was preoccupied with the colonial upheaval in British North America and seeking Spanish neutrality in this conflict made it clear to Madrid that it would not involve itself in supporting the Portuguese position in South America. Charles III and

[55] Cited by H. M. Scott, *British Foreign Policy*, p. 168
[56] See ibid., p. 222.

his new colonial minister, the activist José de Galvez, consequently, seeing a chance to restore the balance in the border dispute, ordered a huge Spanish expeditionary force to set sail to seize southern Brazil – the island of Santa Catarina in particular – and resolve the old territorial dispute by force of arms. The Spanish armada consisted of 116 ships, including 20 warships, 10,000 troops, 8,500 sailors and six months' supplies. It was the largest force Spain had ever sent across the Atlantic. By way of comparison, Portugal's navy in this period numbered 15–17 capital ships. ("Capital ships" in contemporary calculations, referred to ships mounting 50 guns or more and which were able to fight in the eighteenth-century "line ahead" formation.) The British navy through the 1760s and 1770s maintained a "two power standard"; that is, the size of the British fleet should be equal to the combined strength of the French and Spanish fleets, numbered in excess of 120 ships of the line. The Spanish commander was Don Pedro de Cevallos, who was also secretly nominated first viceroy of the new viceroyalty of the Rio de la Plata. He took Santa Catarina after perfunctory opposition by the Portuguese and the flight of MacDouall's small squadron before the huge Spanish fleet. Yet Cevallos failed to retake Rio Grande after a violent storm dispersed his ships.[57] Colônia was taken and its defenses destroyed. The Spanish failure to secure Rio Grande, however, redeemed Portugal's honor from an otherwise gloomy series of setbacks and defeats.

Although Brazil was, by the Pombaline period, the most important of Portugal's overseas dominions, the Asian and African territories had not ceased to be objects of imperial concern to the government in Lisbon. Portugal retained the fortified city of Mazargon on the Moroccan coast and its defense was an expensive drain on the royal treasury until Pombal ordered the complete withdrawal of the garrison and Portuguese population in 1769. The Portuguese possessions in the east still extended from east Africa to southeast Asia to China. The population of Macao numbered some 12,000 in the second half of the eighteenth century and the three small Goan cities each contained 10,000 inhabitants, though the largest city in Portuguese Asia was Daman with between 20,000 and 30,000 inhabitants (fig. 40).[58] Mozambique island had a population of around 10,000.

The struggle with the Spaniards over the disputed southern borderlands of the La Plata region between 1763 and 1777 had inhibited Pombal's reform program in Brazil, and his ambitious projects for Asia were no less affected by the war around the frontiers of Goa with the Marathas which, after 1756, consumed resources and energy Pombal had hoped to devote elsewhere.[59]

The defense of Goa was largely financed by the Saraswat Brahmin Hindus who had long comprised the commercial elite of Goa. The Portuguese succeeded in defending

[57] For an outstanding description of these events, see Alden, *Royal Government*, pp. 224–246.
[58] Unpublished paper by Rudy Bauss, cited in full in fn. 60.
[59] Rudy Bauss has drawn attention to a major study by Mira Pinto Mascarenhas, "The Pombaline Era in Goa, 1750–1777" (unpublished M.A. in history, University of Bombay, 1977) which regrettably I have not yet been able to read.

40 Goa, from a painting of the late eighteenth century (artist unknown)

Goa and even incorporated some additional territory (the so-called new conquests) as a protective buffer against the Marathas, though they were no doubt indirectly assisted in this by the defeats the Marathas were suffering in this period at the hands of the British, who by the end of the Seven Years War had established themselves as a formidable power in India.

The commerce of the Portuguese territories in Asia and east Africa was completely dominated by Asian merchants, and the Chinese likewise dominated the trade of Macao. Pombal's attempt to establish a commercial company of Asia in 1753 had failed and with the retention of the heavily taxed annual ship duty from Goa to Lisbon (paying 30 percent export and import duties as opposed to 5 percent duties charged in French, British, and Muslim ports in Asia) trade was brought virtually to a standstill in the 1770s. The Pombal regime took drastic steps, nevertheless, to reform the Portuguese administration in their India enclaves. The suppression of the Inquisition and the expulsion of the Jesuits both had a major impact in Goa. Between 1600 and 1773, of the over 4,000 cases examined by the Inquisition in Goa, 121 individuals had been burnt. Since both Inquisition and Jesuits had been the most relentless enemies of Hinduism in the Portuguese territories, their elimination brought a marked degree of religious toleration to the Portuguese territories in Asia, or at least brought a major shift in official attitudes. As in Portugal, changing actual behavior proved more difficult. The expulsion of the Jesuits, as in Portugal, however, also created a crisis for the educational system. The elimination of one of the largest religious landowners in the interior territories, as it did in Brazil and Portugal, opened lucrative opportunities for the commercial elite, the Saraswat Brahmins in particular in the case of Goa.

To fill the educational vacuum, classes in navigation were established in 1759 and institutionalized in 1774 with courses in arithmetic, geometry, and algebra among other topics. In 1773 a school of regimental artillery was established. Pombal also decreed that classes in medicine and surgery be taught. Drawing on the example of the College of Nobles in Lisbon, a college for Indian boys and clergy was established in Goa. As in Portugal, secular education in Goa was subsidized by a literary subsidy.

Among the more remarkable of Pombal's measures was a frontal attack on the racial prejudices of the Goa clergy. Race relations were codified in a decree of April 2, 1761 and an instruction in 1774. These reforms were aimed at Catholics not Hindus, yet within the Catholic community they foresaw radical changes.

All my subjects born in Portuguese India and my other dominions in Asia, being baptized Christians . . . enjoy the same honors, dignities, prerogatives and privileges as those enjoyed by the natives of this kingdom [Portugal] without the slightest difference. Not only are they already qualified for all these honors, dignities, enterprises, posts, callings and jurisdictions, but I do seriously recommend to the viceroys of that state [India] its ministers and officials, that . . . preference be given to the natives of the respective territories, so long as they are qualified for them . . .

Pombal was even more explicit in his instructions to the governor José Pedro da Câmara in 1774.

His majesty regards everyone as equally noble and qualified for all posts and offices, whether military, political and civil . . . besides all whites and browns, being equally vassals of his majesty, it is in no way in conformity with Divine Law, Natural Law and the Law of Nations that foreigners be permitted to exclude natives from cultivating the land of their birth, or from the offices and benefits thereof.[60]

In India, as in Brazil, Pombal's imperial policy aimed to harness colonial wealth and rationalize and standardize administration, military organization, and educational training under the purview of the state; where necessary for defense and good government, race and ethnic differences were to be no barrier to office-holding or advancement, and local participation in government was encouraged. The Portuguese language was to be used as a means to integrate indigenous communities, and inter-marriage with Europeans was encouraged in the interests of increasing the population. In these policies the Pombaline government was extremely radical. Yet, high intentions would be modified, molded, and subverted by local circumstances. The barriers of tradition, prejudice, and practicality were formidable everywhere. In imperial and military policy, as with domestic legislation, there is no doubt that when Pombal was able to give problems his complete attention the government performed with efficiency and achieved results. Such oversight, however, was not always possible, especially in Brazil, which remained the central concern. The overseas minister, Martinho de Melo e Castro, put this imperative graphically: "Portugal without Brazil," he said, "is an insignificant power."[61] In fact, more than half of the state's revenues originated directly or indirectly from the overseas empire, especially from Brazil, between 1762 and 1776.[62]

---

[60] These translations and quotations are from Rudy Bauss, "An Overview of Trade and Commercial Policies with Brief Comments on the People and Societies in the Portuguese Eastern Empire, 1750–1850" (unpublished paper). I am most grateful to Dr. Bauss for permission to quote from his excellent work on Portuguese India in the late eighteenth and early nineteenth century.

[61] [Martinho de Melo e Castro] to [Luís de Vasconcellos e Sousa] 1779, *RIHGB* 25 (1862), pp. 479–483.

[62] See the comprehensive analysis of accounts of the Royal Treasury by Fernando Tomaz, "As finanças do estado pombalino 1762–1776," *Estudos e ensaios* (Lisbon, 1990), especially pp. 367 and 371.

7

Public interest and private profit

[Pombal], that great man, known as such by the middle and thinking class
of his nation.

Jacome Ratton, *Recordações* (1810)

Good manners and much money make any kind of knave a gentleman.

Arte e dicionário do comércio e economia portuguesa (1783)

The last decade of Pombal's rule took place within a dramatically changed economic
environment which had significant results for Portugal's political economy. It was a
paradoxical time marked by recession, but also by a formidable concentration of
economic power by Pombal's friends. The 1770s witnessed a major contraction
of gold production in Brazil, and this was the root cause of the changed circumstances
Portugal faced. The exhaustion of the alluvial gold, and the failure to devise improved
techniques within an economy so dependent on the bullion from the Brazilian
interior, had widespread consequences. Above all, the crisis of gold production
produced a prolonged decline in Portugal's capacity to import, especially from
Britain. But these changed circumstances also allowed Portugal to achieve the
objective of Pombal's nationalistic policies; near reciprocity in its dealings with
Britain.

The proceeds from the royal fifth fell sharply. The 100 *arroba* quota on the gold
produced in Minas Gerais had been met and exceeded during the 1750s. But in the
following decade the fifth rendered an average per annum of only 86 *arrobas* of gold,
and between 1774 and 1785 the average had fallen to 68 *arrobas*.[1] The *entradas*, one of
the most sensitive indicators of the volume of commerce between the principal
gold-mining zone and the neighboring captaincies, especially Rio de Janeiro, saw a
sharp contraction in revenues which began during the mid 1760s.[2] A concerned

---

[1] "Rendimento do quinto da capitania de Minas Gerais," 1752–1762, 1763–1773, 1774–1785, AHU,
codex 311, appendices 15, 16, 17.
[2] "Relação dos rendimentos desta capitania de Minas Gerais desde os seus decobrimentos . . . ," Carlos
José da Silva, BNLCP, codex 643, fos. 204–218.

government in Lisbon directed the *junta da fazenda* in Minas Gerais to insist on the immediate imposition of the *derrama* as the 1750 law had envisioned to make up the growing deficit.[3] The French envoy in Lisbon reported during 1772 that "the diminution of the income of Brazil is immense."[4] The amount of gold coin entering into circulation in Portugal declined precipitously by the 1770s, with monetary emission declining by over 50 percent during the period 1771–1782.[5]

Other sectors of the colonial economy were also facing difficulties. Competition from British, French, and Dutch colonial producers had seriously restricted access to traditional markets for Brazilian sugar.[6] The price of Brazilian sugar on the Amsterdam market, 0.33 guldens a pound in 1762, had fallen to 0.23 guldens a pound ten years later and remained at that price until 1776.[7] The recession provoked by declining gold production and loss of markets for Brazilian sugar was felt quickly in the port of Lisbon, where the volume of traffic contracted and customs revenue fell.[8] The London merchant and bullion speculator, William Braund, for example, finding his business at Lisbon had come to an abrupt halt in 1762, withdrew altogether from Portuguese commerce.[9] There were bankruptcies among both large and small entrepreneurs.[10]

The recession, however, did not affect all sectors of Luso-Brazilian commerce. In fact, the major economic supports of the interest groups with whom Pombal had closely linked himself and favored by government policy remained largely untouched. Port wine exports increased.[11] The all-important internal tobacco market remained stable, while the tobacco export trade expanded.[12] And the growing re-export of cotton to Europe, and in particular to France and Great Britain, moreover, provided the same merchant interests with increased profits.[13]

The collapse of the gold sector had dramatic impact, however, on the entrepreneurs whose channel of trade most relied on bullion for its sustenance: the interconnection that linked the British to the gold of Minas Gerais and the gold–silver contraband network in South America. The contraction of British commerce with Portugal, in fact, was little short of catastrophic. The value of British exports to Portugal fell by half

---

[3] [Pombal] to *junta da fazenda*, Minas Gerais, August 2, 1771, June 3, 1772, and September 27, 1773, CCBNRJ, 1-9-23.

[4] Cited by Ignácio José Verissimo, *Pombal, os Jesuítas e o Brasil* (Rio de Janeiro, 1961), p. 296.

[5] "Emissão de moedas de ouro e seu valor parao continente" (Macedo, *A situação económica*, p. 167).

[6] Visconde de Carnaxide, *O Brasil na administração pombalina* (São Paulo, 1940), p. 78; Bourgoing, *Voyage du ci-devant duc du Châtelet en Portugal* I, p. 228.

[7] Magalhães Godinho, *Prix et monnaies*, p. 245.

[8] Borges de Macedo, *A situação económica*, p. 169; Carnaxide, *O Brasil na administração pombalina*, pp. 77–79.

[9] Sutherland, *A London Merchant*, pp. 18, 26, 39.

[10] Borges de Macedo, *Problemas*, p. 188.   [11] Magalhães Godinho, *Prix et monnaies*, p. 253.

[12] "Movimento do mercado do tobaco de época pombalina, volume do comércio do tabaco no reino e fora dele. Rendimento da alfândega do tobaco," doc. 8, in Borges de Macedo, *A situação económica*, pp. 293–294.

[13] For example, see the exports and imports from Portugal to the ports under the direction of Rouen: Pierre Dardel, *Navires et marchandises dans les ports de Rouen et du Havre au XVIIIe siècle* (Paris, 1963), pp. 550–551; Christelow, "Great Britain and the Trades from Cadiz and Lisbon," p. 24.

between 1760 and 1770.[14] The value of British woolen textile exports to Portugal, comprising some 70 percent of total export values, and which had averaged over a million pounds annually in the late 1750s, slumped to £709,000 in the period between 1761 and 1765, and £459,000 between 1766 and 1770.[15] Only Holland and Germany had taken more British goods than did Portugal in 1760; fifteen years later, Holland, Germany, Spain, Italy, and Flanders had relegated Portugal to sixth position among Britain's foreign traders; while Africa, the East Indies, Ireland, and the American colonies far outstripped the Portuguese as buyers of British merchandise.[16]

British exports were also being adversely affected at this time by a loss of markets caused by Hispano-Portuguese rivalry in South America. A high, if unquantifiable, percentage of British exports to Portugal had gone straight to Brazil via Lisbon, and from Brazil to Spanish America as contraband. In 1772 the London *Annual Register* reported:

that the communication between the colony of Santo-Sacramento and Buenos Aires [is] entirely cut off . . . the greater part of the most precious merchandises which arrived from Europe were sent from Rio de Janeiro to that colony, from whence they were smuggled through Buenos Aires to Peru or Chile, and this contraband trade was worth a million and a half piasters of dollars annually to the Portuguese . . . The loss which the almost entire suppression of the contraband trade occasions cannot be calculated.[17]

The disruption of the old contraband networks in the La Plata region had been caused in part by the war against the Jesuit settlements in Paraguay. The more important influence, however, had been the successful struggle against illegal commerce by the revived Spanish administration at Buenos Aires. Collection of revenue in the subtreasury of Buenos Aires more than doubled between 1773 and 1776 and a notable increase in confiscated goods occurred between 1769 and 1775. The creation of the viceroyalty of the Rio de la Plata in 1776 and the comprehensive Spanish trade legislation of 1778 removed the *raison d'être* of contraband by opening direct commerce between the Rio de la Plata and Spain. During the last years of Pombal's regime the Portuguese–Spanish struggle for the control of Colônia, the entrepôt of Plata contraband, further damaged the old clandestine trading networks.[18]

Two factors largely beyond Pombal's control achieved what he had aimed to carry out by policy of government intervention during the 1750s. Britain's vast favorable balance of trade with Portugal was tied to the gold of Minas Gerais and to the silver provided by contraband with Spanish America via Buenos Aires. Both were

---

[14] Schumpeter, *English Overseas Trade Statistics*, p. 17.

[15] H. E. S. Fisher, "Anglo-Portuguese Trade 1700–1770, *EHR*, 2nd series, 16 (1963), p. 229; A. B. Wallis Chapman, "The Commercial Relations of England and Portugal, 1487–1807," *TRHS*, 3rd series, 1, (1907), p. 177. Also Fisher, *The Portugal Trade*, pp. 41–49.

[16] Manchester, *British Preeminence*, p. 46.

[17] *The Annual Register for 1772*, pp. 155–157.

[18] Carneiro de Mendonça, *Pombal e o Brasil*, p. 78; John Lynch, *Spanish Colonial Administration* (London, 1958), p. 37; Alden, in his *Royal Government*, has provided a comprehensive discussion of the complicated events in the south, see especially pp. 59–275.

simultaneously disrupted. The British, who had only recently realized the full intention of Pombal's economic legislation, blamed him for the startling change in their fortunes. Violent anti-Pombal propaganda promoted in London by the British factory's publication of its confidential memoranda to British ministers served to confirm this interpretation of events in the public mind. Yet, in truth, the causes for the reversal in British commercial fortune in Portugal lie elsewhere. Pombal, himself anxious for British support in the late 1760s and fearful of British intentions in South America, vainly sought to explain the changed circumstances to his British critics. In 1767, when the British envoy in Lisbon complained to Pombal and his minister for foreign affairs, Luís da Cunha Manuel (the nephew of Pombal's mentor Dom Luís da Cunha), that "there had been several innovations in the commerce which had affected the trade of British subjects [and] that it was a known certainty that the trade with Portugal was greatly diminished," Luís da Cunha "allowed this to be true," but assigned the reasons for the diminution of the British trade to

the earthquake, the war, the burning of the customs house [1764], but particularly that the trade between Rio de Janeiro and the Nova Colonia [do Sacramento], which was formerly very considerable was now put a stop to by the Spaniards who had blockaded Nova Colônia . . . and therefore the trade was entirely at a stand in the river Plate which occasioned a great diminution in the gold [sic] remittance from Rio de Janeiro and in the consumption of British goods.[19]

In effect, Pombal now confronted a balance of payments problem caused by the fall of gold production in Brazil, aggravated by a fall in Brazilian sugar prices on international markets following the end of the Seven Years War, as well as the competition from the sugar production of both the British and French West Indies.

These new economic conditions, however, produced an economic environment conducive to the growth of manufacturing industries. The research by the Portuguese historian, Jorge Borges de Macedo, has demonstrated that, of the manufacturing establishments set up by the *junta do comércio* during Pombal's regime, 80 percent were authorized after 1770.[20] Pombal's economic measures of the 1750s greatly facilitated the expansion of the new manufactories, to be sure, but the changed economic environment also encouraged their expansion.

Unlike the count of Ericeira at the end of the seventeenth century, who found the competitiveness of his new manufactories undermined by the facility with which Portuguese consumers could import because of the gold boom in Brazil, Pombal found the competitiveness of the products enhanced by the dramatic fall-off in the Portuguese capacity to import. Many of the manufacturing establishments founded after 1770 were involved in the production of luxury goods – silks, hats, chinaware (see fig. 41), tapestry, decorative jewelry, ribbons, and buttons. The Portuguese state

---

[19] "Minutes of a conference with the count de Oeyras and Dom Luís Cunha upon my taking leave of them, Friday 28 August 1767," published by Vera Lee Brown, "The Relations of Spain and Portugal 1763–1777," *Smith College Studies in History* 15 (October 1929–January 1930), pp. 70–71.
[20] Borges de Macedo, *A situação económica*, p. 255.

41 A porcelain figure from the Rato factory, late 1760s (Museu Nacional Machado de Castro, Coimbra)

granted them monopoly privileges, exemption from taxation, and special protection for their supplies of raw materials.[21]

But a very significant new product also enhanced the picture – cotton. The link between the cotton production promoted by the Pombaline monopoly companies in northern and northeastern Brazil and the textile manufacturing industry in Portugal meant that a comparatively large number of cotton textile enterprises were set up, taking advantage of the growing exports of cotton to Portugal from Pernambuco and Maranhão. The textile workshops established with the direct participation of the *junta do comércio* were concentrated in Lisbon and Oporto, close to their seaborne raw materials.[22] Cotton textiles also had another enormous advantage from the Portuguese point of view – they could be protected from British competition. The Methuen Treaty specifically mentioned woolen textiles. By developing a cotton textile sector, Pombal had stumbled onto a brilliant antidote to British commercial penetration of Portugal and the British could find no justification in law to complain about it.

In addition to the reorganization and establishment of royal factories on the model of the Royal Silk Factory agglomeration, the Pombaline state encouraged private manufacturing enterprises with exclusive or monopolistic protection though, given the multiple roles played by Pombal's collaborators, there was also fluidity of funds between royal and private establishments. Joaquim Ignácio da Cruz, for example, used funds from the Royal Silk Factory to encourage his silk stocking and paper box factories in Tomar, as well as the cotton textile workshops there.[23] The violent imposition of a system of apprenticeship served to keep labor costs low at both royal and private manufacturing establishments.[24] A general protective framework for both types of enterprise was provided by a flexible tariff policy of exemptions and prohibitions in favor of Portuguese manufactured products.[25]

---

[21] Ibid., pp. 254–256; Borges de Macedo, *Problemas*, pp. 147, 189–190; Smith, *Pombal* II, p. 146; BNLCP, codex 256, 226. For the more urgent encouragement of silk production during the 1770s see Ratton, *Recordações*, p. 142; *Notizie del Mondo* (February 16, 1773); *Notizie del Mondo* (October 25, 1774).

[22] Luís Fernando de Carvalho Dias, *A relação das fábricas de 1788* (Coimbra, 1955), pp. 21–22.

[23] Carvalho Dias, *A relação*, p. 18: the whole system of guilds and apprenticeships was reformed after 1771. For the collected documents see Franz-Paul Langlans, *As corporações dos ofícios mecánicos: subsídios para a sua história com um estudo do Marcello Caetano*, 2 vols. (Lisbon, 1943).

[24] "Alvará . . . fazer merce a direção da real fábrica das sedas do indulto privativo e privilegio exclusivo do comércio da *goma copal*, produzida nos Dominios da America Portuguesa, prohibida a entrada della nas Alfândagas destes Reinos, que ate agora se introduzido de Paizes Estrangeiros, 10 dezembro, 1770"; "Alvará . . . por bem animar e protegar as fábricas da louca estabelecidas na cidade de Lisboa, e as mais, que se acham de presente, prohibido a entrada de toda a louca fábrica fora della, a exepção da que vier da India, e da China em Navios de Propriedades portuguezes 7 novembro 1770"; "Alvará, porque . . . he servido . . . prohibir a entrada de todos os chapeos fabricados fora destes Reinos, e Dominios em beneficio das fábricas que se acham establecidas nos mesmos Reinos, e das que para o futuro se establecerem, 10 dezembro, 1770," BNLCP, codex 453, fos. 336–339, 393–393, 395–398; "Alvará porque S. M. concedeo a João Baptista Iacatelli privilégio por tempo de dez annos de insenção de todos e qualquer direitos que nos portos do Reino e Dominios Ultramarinos divião pagar os tecidos de Algodão simples, ou com qualquer mistura, extendendese a todos os fabricantes da mesma manufactura, 5 janeiro 1774," BNLCP, codex 455, fos. 349–350.

[25] Borges de Macedo, *Problemas*, pp. 82–95; *A situação económica*, p. 252.

A substantial number of entrepreneurs aided by the *junta* were foreigners. Twenty-seven of fifty-two royal decrees issued for the foundation of new workshops were issued to foreigners, and a third of these to Frenchmen.[26] Typical of the more important recipients was Jacome Ratton. He was born in the province of Dauphiné in 1736, but his parents emigrated to Portugal while he was a child to establish a business in Lisbon. Ratton was one of the first businessmen to develop the re-export trade with France in Brazilian cotton after the Peace of Paris. He engaged in a whole range of manufacturing enterprises, from the production of calico to hats, paper, and cotton textiles.[27] At Marinha Grande, an Englishman, William Stephens, contracted by Pombal personally, and with whom Pombal was to develop a close friendship, set up a glass manufactory with the assistance of the *junta do comércio*, and became a highly successful industrialist.[28]

The Pombaline manufactories were essentially a new industry, fostered by varied techniques within a protective tariff regime, and made possible by the changed economic environment. Despite the traditional bases on which they were constructed, and although surrounded by a system of privileges, monopolies, and apprenticeships, they were innovative in many ways. The intimate relationship between the government's means of encouragement and its recognition of the economic and technical base available to it, both in the resilient household industry of the interior and among the skilled artisans of the coastal cities, contributed to the general success of the establishments created after 1770. Also important was the mobility of funds and of directing personnel between the monopolistic companies, Royal Silk Factory, *junta do comércio*, royal treasury, and the new manufactories. Mining output decline in Brazil had served to create an economic environment in Portugal favorable to the development of import-substituting manufacturing enterprises, but the sector's growth occurred because it was also fostered by the skillful intervention of the Pombaline state.

The special relationship and interconnected interests which had been established during the first decade of Pombal's government – particularly between the Brazil companies and the Royal Silk Factory – had placed Pombal's collaborators in an excellent position to take advantage of the changed economic situation. The 1770s, in

---

[26] Ratton, *Recordações*, pp. 8, 181.

[27] "Cartas originais de G. Stephens dando notícias familiares e de política estrangeira," BNLCP, codex 704, fos. 27–30, 87–89; "Cartas inglezas," BNLCP, codex 691 (this codex is inaccurately stated in the printed catalogue to be codex 690), letters of William Stephens to Marquis of Pombal and translation of the "Letters from Portugal," by Stephens' sister.

[28] "Decreto para Anselmo José da Cruz ficar no contrato do tabaco 7 janeiro 1763"; "Decreto para Anselmo José da Cruz ser Contratador do Sabão," BNLCP, codex 454; "Carta dos Privilégios do Contrato Geral do Tabaco de que sao contratadores, Anselmo José da Cruz, Policarpo José Machado e Companhia etc.," CCBNRJ, 1-1-25; "Contrato . . . do Estanco do sal do Brazil com Joaquim Pedro Quintella, João Ferreira, etc.," CCBNRJ, 1-1-25; "Livro de Receita e Despensa do Thesoureiro Mor do Erário Regio, Joaquim Ignácio da Cruz Sobral," CCBNRJ, 1-1-25; "Livros dos termos de arramatação dos contractos," AHU, codices 298, 299; Myriam Ellis, "A pesca da baleia no Brasil colonial," ACC, 71, 89–90.

fact, found the new merchant oligarchy firmly and powerfully entrenched within the body politic, and a remarkably small, compact, and interrelated group of men in positions of great power and influence. José Francisco da Cruz and his brother Joaquim Ignácio both held the key post of treasurer general of the royal treasury. Anselmo José da Cruz, in association with Policarpo José Machado and Geraldo Wenceslão Braamcamp, held the tobacco contract. Machado, a *provedor* of the *junta do comércio*, was a stockholder in the Lisbon tobacco factory. Anselmo held the royal soap monopoly contract and had an exclusive arrangement to supply soap for industrial uses to the Royal Silk Factory. José Francisco and Joaquim Ignácio da Cruz, the latter heading the administration of the customs house, both held positions in the direction of the commercial companies and the manufacturing enterprises. Bandeira, who had directed the takeover of the Rato factory, was a director of the Pernambuco company and a *provedor* of the *junta do comércio*. António Caetano Ferreira and Luís José de Brito both became officials of the treasury, and the latter a director of the silk factory. Quintella, *provedor* of the *junta do comércio*, was director of both Brazil companies, a stockholder in the Lisbon tobacco factory, and a member of the major company exporting tobacco to Spain. He also held the contract of the *dizimos* of Bahia from 1757 to 1763 and, commencing in 1765, the exclusive rights to whaling along the whole Brazilian littoral. In 1770 he obtained the lucrative salt monopoly contract of the state of Brazil, as well as other Brazilian contracts such as the tax on sweet olive oil imported into the state of Rio de Janeiro, and the right to duties on tobacco and other goods embarked at Bahia.[29] The special protection of Pombal's collaborators continued as before (fig. 42). Quintella's sudden death in 1775 brought a rapid royal enactment to guarantee the orderly succession of his vast business concerns to his nephew Joaquim, who took the name Quintella and continued in all his uncle's capacities. The Quintella company was also granted special tax-collection powers.

The Pombaline state continued to reward with noble titles the heads of the new great Portuguese merchant dynasties it had so carefully stimulated and aided since 1750. The attack on the practice of *Puritanismo*, that is, the caste-like exclusivity of the hereditary aristocracy, was part of the process which had seen the ennoblement of Pombal's collaborators among the businessmen and participants in his state-supported economic enterprises. In 1768, puritanism was formally outlawed by royal decree. Joaquim Ignácio da Cruz obtained the entailed estates and title of Sobral (fig. 43), an ex-Jesuit possession, and the title passed to his brother Anselmo on his death. José Francisco da Cruz obtained the morgado, or entailed estates of Alagoa, a title which became that of his sons, aspiring pupils at the College of Nobles. In 1775 an equestrian statue of Dom José I, the centerpiece of the great new commercial square

---

[29] d'Azevedo, *Estudos*; Ratton, *Recordações*, pp. 184–185; "Sou servido subrogar e substituir seu sobrinho, Joaquim Tiburicio Quintella (tomando o sobrenome do falecido) para a continuação e expediente daquella casa . . . ," November 8, 1775, BNLCP, codex 456, fo. 340; "Registro de ordens para as autoridades de Minas Gerais, 1764–1799," AHU, codex 610, fos. 30–31.

42 Tureen in the form of a goose, bearing the arms of the marquês de Pombal, from the Rato factory, late 1760s

on Lisbon's waterfront, was inaugurated in a lavish ceremony. At the right hand of the beplumed and ceremonious marquês de Pombal stood Anselmo José da Cruz.[30] By 1777 the great merchant houses Pombal had envisioned twenty years before and had sheltered and nurtured with direct and indirect state assistance for two decades had come of age. By state intervention and economic circumstance the Pombalian oligarchy had been created.

The profound changes which affected Portugal and the Luso-Brazilian Atlantic system were not all caused by Pombal, to be sure. They arose from a complicated interplay of social and economic transformation, international politics, and policy decision. The economic changes of the 1770s, in particular, had brought Portugal and its colony in the New World into a new relationship. Since Brazil stood close to the center of Pombal's plans for the regeneration of Portugal, any fractures within the colonial nexus posed a potential hazard to the whole edifice. Pombal's very success in encouraging the emergence of a powerfully entrenched and influential national bourgeoisie in the metropolis held the potential for causing such a fracture. The interests of this new metropolitan merchant-industrial elite were subordinate to a broad imperial scale of priorities under the control of an all-powerful minister. But this might not always be the case, and the metropolitan interest in protected markets in Brazil was likely in time to become increasingly incompatible with the remarkably flexible mercantilism Pombal had so carefully promoted. During Pombal's preeminence, the Lisbon *junta do comércio* directly aided manufacturing and processing enterprises in Brazil. The Company of Grão Pará and Maranhão maintained a cloth manufactory in Pará. Both the monopoly companies and the local colonial administrations used subsidy payments and guaranteed prices to stimulate new export commodities. Moreover, local men, prominent for their opulence and status in society, had been drawn into the new colonial military-administration establishment. None of this was compatible with a strict interpretation of mercantilist maxims.

There was, of course, solid reasoning behind Pombal's cautious policy toward Portuguese America. The heroic tradition of Brazilian opposition to foreign intrusion was never far from his mind. The seventeenth-century struggle of Pernambuco and Bahia against the Dutch, and the early eighteenth-century actions against the French in Rio de Janeiro, were often cited by him in diplomatic, official, and private correspondence. It was just these examples, in fact, which were used by him to justify the wide local base given to the military establishment in the colony by the creation of numerous auxiliary regiments under the control of the local magnates. Pombal even went so far as to bring the historical participation and mobilization of the Brazilians in their self-defense to the attention of the British government, faced with the revolt of their colonists in North America. The tactics of the Anglo-Americans, Pombal observed during November 1775, were identical to those of the "good Portuguese

---

[30] "Parallelo de Augusto Cesar e de Dom José o Magnanimo Rey de Portugal," Lisbon, 1775, BNLCP, codex 456, fo. 44.

43 Tureen and stand with the arms of Inácio da Cruz Sobral (1725–1781), imported from China *c.* 1775

vassals of Pernambuco and Bahia."[31] George III's armies would never defeat the rebels though the loss of British America could be avoided, he believed, if London acted prudently and permitted the colonists their own parliaments, which could always be controlled by royal office holders and by patronage.

The rigidities of the colonial system had already been criticized by the viceroy of Brazil, the marquês de Lavradio. The Brazilian merchants were little more than "simple commissaries," the viceroy complained, a situation that, by reducing the "commerce always to the same articles," prevented their aiding the development of new export commodities from Portuguese America. Lavradio argued, very much with the same logic Pombal had used to help protect and encourage Portuguese merchants against British competition, that only with the emergence of solid entrepreneurs in Brazil, acting on their own account, could this difficulty be overcome.[32]

There were limits, however, to what even the most enlightened governor could

[31] Dauril Alden, "The Marquis of Pombal and the American Revolution," *The Americas* 17, no. 4 (April 1961), pp. 369–376, 377–382.

[32] "Relatório do marquês de Lavradio" (1779), *RIHGB* 4 (2nd edition, 1863), p. 33.

tolerate. The factors which had produced an environment favorable to import substitution in Portugal were also operative in the Americas, especially in the gold–producing interior captaincy of Minas Gerais. There were developments of which neither the viceroy nor the Pombaline government of Minas Gerais approved. The governor of Minas Gerais, António de Noronha, reported in 1775 that numerous manufacturing establishments existed in the captaincy and all of them were in a state of considerable growth. Their development, he observed, threatened to make the inhabitants independent of European goods.[33] The marquês de Lavradio also noted the growth of manufacturing establishments in Brazil: "private individuals have established . . . on their estates workshops and looms," he notified Lisbon, which produced cotton, linen, woolen goods, and tow, so that already "they had become less dependent on those to whom they were debtors." The viceroy believed that the "greater part of the landed proprietors still continued them," despite his representations. He warned that in the case of Minas Gerais, because of the vastness of the region and the rebellious spirit of the population there, such independence was a matter of great moment and might one day produce grave consequences for Portugal.[34] He was right, and indeed, in the late 1780s, it did.

Spanish threats to the southern frontier of the colony had also put the new military framework imposed in Brazil following the Peace of Paris under great strain. The defense of the frontiers had required the dispatch of colonial forces to the south, and together with the ongoing delineation of boundaries, heavy costs were incurred by the viceregal treasury in Rio de Janeiro and that of São Paulo. In both cases expenditures outpaced receipts, with the result that the subsidy for indigo production, for example, lacked prompt payment, and outstanding obligations went into default.[35] Under the system of reciprocal assistance, troops from Minas Gerais were sent both to the south and to Rio de Janeiro during the late 1770s and the military expenditures by the Minas *junta da fazenda* soared to unparalleled heights.[36] The captaincy revenues were hardly sufficient for the regular obligations of the civil, military, and ecclesiastical lists, and the commitments made for food and quartering contracted by the military expeditions of the 1770s remained years in arrears.[37] The startling rise in military expenditures coinciding with rapidly contracting revenue sources placed added strain on the local treasury.

Brazilians were also largely unprepared to implement the whole range of complicated and often far-reaching reforms decreed by Pombal in Lisbon. In its administrative creations on both sides of the Atlantic, the Pombaline state involved

[33] See "Instruções para a visconde de Barbacena" (1786), *AMI* 11 (1953), pp. 117–154.

[34] "Relatório do marquês de Lavradio," *RIHGB* 4 (2nd edition, 1863), p. 453.

[35] Marcelino Pereira Cleto, "Dissertação a respeito da capitania de São Paulo" (1782), *ABNRJ* 21 (1890), p. 196; [Luís de Vasconcellos e Sousa] to [Martinho de Melo e Castro], July 15, 1781, *RIHGB* 51, pt 1 (1886), p. 190.

[36] Manuel Joaquim Pedroso, Vila Rica, January 31, 1782, in AHU, Minas Gerais, doc. case 92.

[37] "Extratto do balança da receita e despeza da tezouraria Gᵃ de Vᵃ Rᵃ," CCBNRJ, 1-10-3; "Balança da receita e despeza dos rendimentos Reaes, Vila Rica (1780)," IHGB, file 8, doc. 4.

local magnates and businessmen in the agencies of government with a deliberation bordering on infatuation. Just as the lack of native entrepreneurs had been a serious obstacle to national economic development in the metropolis, however, the inter-twining of state functions, local business, and landed interests in the colonies worked to the advantage of the Portuguese state only so long as local and imperial interests coincided, and while the constant vigilance of the central government stressed the broader national priorities over the personal and partisan interests of the local oligarchies. Participation by local power groups in the very mechanism of govern-ment, much in the manner that Duke Silva-Tarouca recommended during the early 1750s, did not necessarily result in the strengthening of mutual bonds between metropolis and colony, which had been the duke's objective, and was doubtless, in Pombal's opinion, the implicit corollary of the action. In fact, with divergent economic motivations the very opposite might be the case.

Already during the 1770s as Pombal became more lonely and suspicious, direction slackened as the crushing burdens of the highly centralized government machine he had created produced an immense backlog of administrative business. While in the short run this was of no serious consequence in Portugal, it significantly weakened the rigor of the treasury's surveillance of the colonial *juntas da fazenda*, and the state of affairs had particularly damaging consequences in Minas Gerais, where the regional *junta da fazenda* was partially responsible for the collection of the royal fifth of the captaincy, previously the most important of the Crown's sources of revenue, as well as direct responsibility for the contracting of the substantial farm of the Minas *entradas*, the captaincy *dizimos*, and other revenues. By the late 1770s the stipulations of the 1750 law had been virtually abandoned. In spite of the continuing failure to complete the 100-*arroba* annual gold quota and after several abortive efforts during the early 1770s to raise the treasury revenues, the poll tax or *derrama* intended to make up the amount was never imposed, although required by law.[38]

The local *junta da fazenda* in Minas Gerais had, in fact, argued in 1773 that because of the contraction of the mining sector the retention of the old level of the fifth at the 100 *arroba* per annum level was impossible and the imposition of a *derrama* inadvisable. The failure of the treasury in Lisbon to answer the *junta*'s remonstration of 1773 was conveniently interpreted as concurrence.[39] But avoidance of responsibilities by colonial organs of government was not uncommon and was encouraged by the over-lapping of functions and administrative duties. Responsibility for the collection of the royal fifth, for example, involved not only the *junta da fazenda*, but the intendants of the foundry houses and the municipal councils, not to mention the military and naval officers involved in its safe conveyance to Lisbon. Lack of diligence could be, and was, blamed on others. The overlapping of functions and responsibilities was in some sense intentional in that it facilitated central control over the individual colonial administrative organs, but it was a situation that simultaneously provided built-in

---

[38] "Correspondência da junta da fazenda 1771–1772, 1773," CCBNRJ, 1-9-23.
[39] "Representação da junta da fazenda (1773)," AHU, Minas Gerais, doc. case 92.

excuses for the evasion of responsibilities. These were only a fraction of the complicated and often badly defined jurisdictional overlaps which existed. The viceroy in Rio de Janeiro also retained a vaguely defined oversight jurisdiction over the southern captaincies and Minas Gerais, not to mention the colonial and metropolitan courts and ecclesiastical tribunals, which paralleled, duplicated, multiplied, and superimposed jurisdictions. The *junta da fazenda* of Minas Gerais itself, while directly responsible to the Lisbon treasury, was composed at the local level of civil and judicial officers, such as the governor and magistrates, who fell under the authority of the secretary of state for the overseas dominions. The local governor, meanwhile, was *ex officio* president of the *junta*, which was his own most important organ of local government.

While Pombal remained all-powerful and the president of the royal treasury in Lisbon, close uniformity of policy and agreement existed between the various secretaries of state in Lisbon, and this built-in division of responsibility presented no major problem in terms of overall policy – but such an accord on colonial affairs in Lisbon might not always or necessarily be the case.

Even a clear-cut system of concrete and legally defined responsibilities often failed to restrict fraud, corruption, and evasion of duty. In 1771 the Diamond District was meticulously regulated and made responsible only to the administrators and treasury in Lisbon. But in Brazil implementing the restrictions on diamond production intended to limit the supply of Brazilian diamonds entering the world markets and hence sustaining their price proved difficult. The district, despite the government's best efforts, continued to be a thriving center of contrabandists and diamond smugglers. The intendancy forces were illegally composed of slave soldiers. Their social condition made them totally incapable of upholding the strict restrictive laws of the Diamond District, especially where important local residents deliberately placed slaves in the military guards, doubtless with the protection of their illegal mining and smuggling interests in mind. The strict rules concerning access to the districts were circumvented by the local authorities who granted permits to itinerant traders for the import of *cachaça*, a strong Brazilian sugar-cane brandy. These licenses insured the traders against the attentions of the military patrols, and the imported *cachaça* was a more than acceptable bartering commodity with which to entice stolen diamonds from the district's workers. The Minas Dragoons, the professional corps of Minas Gerais, who shared the charge of guarding the Diamond District against the gangs of unauthorized miners and contrabandists, themselves engaged in lucrative speculations, especially if members of the same family belonged to the officer corps while others were resident within the district itself.[40] The district's fiscal officers might not themselves directly engage in contraband, but members of their families were often among the most notorious embezzlers. Padre José da Silva de Oliveira Rolim, for instance, son of one of the treasurers of the Diamond District, busied himself with a

---

[40] Luís Beltrão de Gouveia de Almeida, *Intendente geral dos diamantes* (1789), BNLCP, codex 697, fos. 142–149, 155–156.

bewildering range of subterfuges, from mining in prohibited areas to the illegal importation of slaves, and as an officially designated administrator of diamond washings, turned in only that portion of the total production he deemed necessary to hide the portion he retained for himself. And despite the strict Pombaline regulations which sought to limit their numbers, a large artisan class, composed of tailors, cobblers, medical men of one type or another, tavern keepers and so on, remained in the Diamond District. Because of their close relations with the intendancy workers these men often acted as agents for contrabandists who supplied them with money for the purchase of stolen precious stones.

Intimate and lucrative interconnections between the abuses of the system and the substantial emoluments that the governor and magistrates gained from the letting out of contracts made chances of reform at the local level unlikely. Shilly-shallying and bribery at the time of the disposal of contracts was perfectly predictable, but the officers of the *junta da fazenda* also received perfectly legally by the system of *propinas* substantial sums from the contracts as contributions to their official salaries. The governor of Minas, for example, obtained from *propinas* on the various Minas contracts a sum amounting to half as much again as his official remuneration, and the same was the case with the magistrates who composed the *junta*.[41]

Contracting of the captaincy revenues from the *entradas* and *dizimos* was, in fact, among the most important of the *junta*'s responsibilities. Yet, the contracting fees were in arrears to a high proportion of their original contract price, often years after the official returns had been due. The contract of *entradas* held by João Rodrigues de Macedo for six years, beginning in 1776, had paid only 298,664$798 *réis* of the contract price of 766,726$612 *réis* by June 1786. Rodrigues de Macedo also held the contract of *dizimos* between 1777 and 1783 for a price of 395,372$957 *réis*. By 1786, he had paid a mere third of this sum. In 1786 in fact, Rodrigues de Macedo, a Portuguese emigrant merchant who had built one of the most imposing town houses of late colonial Brazil in Vila Rica, the capital of the Minas captaincy, was obligated to the Minas *junta da fazenda* at that time for 763,168$019 *réis*, a sum that represented over three times the total official captaincy revenues for 1777, and only slightly less than seventeen times the annual value to the Crown of the salt gabelle of the whole state of Brazil in the year 1776. Rodrigues de Macedo was only one of several substantial businessmen thus indebted to the royal treasury.[42]

Since men like João Rodrigues de Macedo often acted as bankers to Minas governors, and extended credit facilities to magistrates and officers of the captaincy administration, the *propina* system thus provided a semi-legal cover for bribery and corruption. The *junta*'s laxity in collecting its political debts allowed men like

---

[41] "Propinas que vence o governador . . . quando se remitão os contratos" (1780?), AHU, Minas Gerais, doc. case 57.

[42] "Relação dos devedores a Real fazenda," CCBNRJ 1-1-6; "Contos correntes" (1795), CCBNRJ, 1-1-1 (26); "Contrato dos dizimos," IHGB, file 166, doc. 7; "Relações dos contratos" (1786), AHU, Minas Gerais, doc. case 94.

Rodrigues de Macedo to use both the profits made on the contract and the unpaid contract fees due the government for his own private speculations, while the fact that the captaincy customs tariffs were administered by one of the greatest local merchants facilitated manipulation and evasion of these duties to the personal advantage of the contractors' business interests.[43] Despite the clear evidence of greater efficiency when the contracts were not farmed out but directly administered by the *junta*, and several denunciations of the abuse of the system to the secretary of state in Lisbon, maladministration continued, and the arrears were allowed to accumulate. By 1788, on the *entradas* alone, the sum in default had reached the staggering total of 1,554,552$539 *réis*.[44]

The government's authority in its overseas possessions at the local level had always rested on a good deal of mutual tolerance between the local magnates and the royal administration. An eighteenth-century state, while autocratic on paper, possessed in the last resort limited powers for compulsion. The Pombaline system, by the recognition and officialization of this status quo, and lacking efficient and honest bureaucrats, took a considerable risk by intertwining the colonial oligarchies so closely with the administrative structure. Measures which might appear logical in a small country like Portugal, where the authority of the monarch was always close, and the benefits or the displeasure of the central government could more quickly and effectively make themselves felt, could produce totally opposite effects from those intended in the colonial setting. In the vastness of Brazil, power and wealth were untrammeled by the subtler restrictions of a more traditional society. Placing the responsibility for vital tax farms into the hands of a locally constituted body, such as the *junta da fazenda*, responsive to local pressures and influence, was to exaggerate the disadvantages of the contract system, the only justification of which anyway was that it offered the Crown quick returns and spared it administrative expenses. In Minas by no stretch of the imagination was this the result, and the state benefited not at all. Meanwhile the contractors were as ruthless and efficient in the collection of the taxes assigned to them as the *junta da fazenda* was lax in pressing them for the long overdue arrears on the contracting price.[45] The system thus served to place great power into the hands of opulent manipulators like Rodrigues de Macedo, but it also left them dangerously and enormously obligated, in theory at least, to the royal *exchequer*. It was easier to oversee and restrain the activities of the great merchants in Lisbon than control those of the colonial collaborators who had been thrust into the administrative–military framework of Brazil. In Portuguese America the intended agents of royal authority were often indistinguishable from the Brazilian plutocracy. The Portuguese state, far from bending the chosen collaborators to its interests, was

---

[43] Denunciations of Manuel Joaquim Pedroso in AHU, Minas Gerais, doc. case 92.

[44] *Junta da fazenda*, Vila Rica, February 11, 1789, BNLCP, codex 643, fos. 222–224.

[45] The complaint against the harsh methods of collection of the *dízimos* are contained in "consulta" (1789) in "registro de consultas, 1786–1789," AHU, codex 302, fo. 15. Also for responses of the overseas council in "registro das cartas, avisos, ofícios, etc., 1782–1807," AHU, codex 243, fo. 17v.

itself bent to the personal ambitions and greed of the men who composed the new agencies of the government. The practical result of Pombal's fiscal reforms in Brazil, and the appointment of native-born officers, magistrates and fiscal officials to administer them in many instances, encouraged the disputes and vexations that the measures were intended to alleviate.

But it is also important to recognize that many of Pombal's collaborators did labor mightily in the interest of reform, and sometimes at considerable cost to themselves. The marquês de Lavradio complained to Joaquim Inácio da Cruz that, despite the title his office lacked "all means and jurisdiction" to carry out his multiple instructions. And in private correspondence with his brother the Principal de Almeida (warning him in no circumstances to tell Pombal about his predicament) the viceroy observed that

the count of Cunha had sent each year the major part of the revenue of his house [to Brazil], did not give a single public dinner, and [still] owed sixteen thousand *cruzados*, and his [Lavradio's immediate] predecessor . . . was obliged now on his recall [to Lisbon] to sell even the last napkin and [has] just signed a debt obligation of 10.000 *cruzados* in order to have what was needed for his return passage.[46]

Pombal himself fared better than the viceroys. His youth had been impecunious, dependent on his uncle's beneficence; he had complained bitterly when the British failed to pay him the traditional emolument given to departing ambassadors; he grumbled continuously in Vienna about his expenses. But, when he left office, his family fortune was among the three largest of the Portuguese nobility.[47] He and his wife were investors in the Grão Pará company; his own vineyards in Oeiras were included at great profit to his estate's income within the privileged zone for Port wine production despite the fact that Oeiras abutted the Tagus and not the Douro river. The silkworms on his Oeiras mulberry bushes supplied the royal factory. Following the earthquake he accumulated large urban holdings as part of the reallocation of property in Lisbon where his brother Paulo and later his son Henrique served as president of the municipal senate and supervisor of public works. He let out his Lisbon birthplace at an inflated rent to the firm of Purry, Mellish, and Vismes, the principals of which held lucrative monopolies and commissioned the great painting of Pombal by Van Loo.

Pombal claimed his swollen patrimony resulted from the fact that he practiced privately what he recommended publicly: good husbandry, good bookkeeping, and creative capital investment. Jacome Ratton agreed. Pombal, he reported, reserved each Sunday morning for his own business affairs, calling together each week all his managers and overseers, reviewing his double entry accounting books and receiving

---

[46] [Lavradio] to [Principal de Almeida], February 20, 1770; [Lavradio] to [Joaquim Inácio da Cruz] February 20, 1770; and marquês de Lavradio, *Cartas do Rio de Janeiro, 1769–1776* (Rio de Janeiro: Arquivo Nacional, 1975), pp. 106–107 and 174.

[47] Nuno Gonçalo Monteiro, "Poder senhorial, estatuto nobiliárquico e aristocracia," in Mattoso, *História* IV, pp. 333–379 (table of incomes of noble houses, p. 369).

into and paying out from his money chest his earnings and expenses of the previous week. Pombal's "methodical spirit," Ratton wrote in his memoirs, "well demonstrated the old axiom that whoever does not know how to govern his own house, is not worthy of governing the state."[48] This is as may be. But it certainly did no harm that Pombal also exercised the vast powers of an absolutist state, and surrounded himself with a coterie of businessmen on the make who believed, like Pombal, that in their accumulation of wealth, national and personal interests were fused, promoted and justified.

[48] Ratton, *Recordações*, pp. 140–141.

8

The legacy

Your excellency has nothing more to do here.

> Dom João Cosme, Cardinal da Cunha to Pombal following the death of
> Dom José I (1777).

No one can deny him original talents and far-reaching views. By the means of commerce, of agriculture, of population, he has laid the foundations of Portuguese independence, viewed with an envious eye by the greedy rivalry of Great Britain.

> *Gazetta universale* (1777)

Pombal exercised vast powers, but his power had always depended on the king's support. This was both his strength and his weakness in that his position depended entirely on the king's survival. It was the link the conspirators against the king's life had seen in the late 1750s. Dom José I suffered a mild seizure in 1765 but a series of major strokes after 1774 left him partially paralyzed and bed-ridden (fig. 44). Although he attended the inauguration of his equestrian statue in the great new Praça do Comércio (fig. 45) on Lisbon's waterfront a year later, he ceased to receive ambassadors after this date. Luís Pinto de Sousa Coutinho, who had succeeded Martinho de Melo e Castro as Portuguese ambassador in London, advised Pombal confidentially during 1776 that no concrete decisions or aid could be expected from the British government, for it was convinced that Dom José I would not live much longer and with his death the whole orientation of the government in Lisbon would be altered.[1] The clear implication was that Pombal's own future would be in grave question.

The problem with perpetuating the reforms he had initiated was always a central concern to Pombal. Pombal believed, in fact, that the most important change he had initiated was the reform of the University of Coimbra, precisely because he saw the educational reforms as a means of giving continuity to the modernizing impulse by

---

[1] "Carta confidencial," Luís Pinto to Pombal, London, September 10, 1776, BNLCP, codex 695, fos. 11–12.

44 Dom José I

transforming and reforming the mentality of Portuguese public officials. In order to diminish the chances of, and it was strongly suspected to preempt, the succession of the king's pious daughter Dona Maria, Pombal arranged for the marriage of Maria's son, the young prince Dom José, to his aunt, Maria Benedita (a family affair like the marriage of Prince José's mother to her uncle). Maria Benedita was one of Pombal's strongest supporters within the royal circle and Pombal may have been attempting to establish a Salic law whereby the throne would pass directly on the king's death to his grandson, bypassing a female succession.[2] The curious fall from grace of one of Pombal's close collaborators, José Seabra da Silva, who was banished to Angola, seems to have been related to his betrayal of the plan to Dona Maria. This marriage did take

---

[2] See discussion by Montalvão Machado, *Quem livrou Pombal*, pp. 164–165.

45 The Praça do Comércio, from a photograph of 1872 with the statue of Dom José I by Joaquim Machado de Castro in the foreground (Arquivo Nacional de Fotografia)

place as the king lay dying. The young Prince José had been carefully educated under Frei Cenáculo's direction and was a fervent admirer of Joseph II of Austria. He was, however, never to succeed to the Portuguese throne. He succumbed in 1788 to smallpox against which his mother had not permitted him to receive the recently discovered inoculation (fig. 33).[3]

The king, Dom José I, died in 1777, and Pombal's position, as had been predicted in London, became at once untenable. The new queen, Dona Maria I, the first female monarch in Portugal's history, had been for long the focus of hope of Pombal's enemies, and her husband and consort, who became Dom Pedro III, had been close to the Jesuits. The pent-up frustrations of those interests long repressed by the

---

[3] Opposition to the inoculation was not confined to the most traditional. Van Swieten had prevented any of the Austrian imperial family from being inoculated against smallpox, believing the treatment harmful. But after 1767 Maria Theresa arranged for her children and her officers to be inoculated by John Ingenhousz sent out from England at the recommendation of George IV. See Beales, *Joseph II* I, p. 158.

Pombal regime – the merchants who did not benefit from the special privileges and protections of Pombal's collaborators, the ultramontane clergy, the aristocrats who had not compromised with the regime, and the British – all found receptive audiences for their complaints in the changed political environment.

Pombal, who had sought to resign his office, found himself immediately barred from the new royal circle, and former allies like Cardinal da Cunha seeking to ingratiate themselves with the new monarch quickly turned away from him.[4] Amid wide rejoicing and disorder in the streets, Pombal's removal from office was decreed in the queen's name and under the signature of Pombal's old colleague, the secretary of state for the overseas dominions, Martinho de Melo e Castro.[5] The new monarch counted among her principal advisers well-known Pombal enemies, including the marquês de Marialva, the marquês d'Angeja, and the viscount of Vila Nova de Cerveira. Angeja had been one of King Dom José I's lords of the bedchamber, but he had throughout Pombal's preeminence "conducted himself so dexterously," the British minister in Lisbon, Robert Walpole, reported to London, "that Pombal has at times confessed that of all the noblemen he was the only one he could not penetrate." The marquês d'Angeja was in his late sixties, and not, Walpole thought, capable of much "laborious business." The viscount of Vila Nova de Cerveira was the son of one of Pombal's victims, his father having died in prison. Ribeiro dos Santos, in private correspondence, observed that the viscount wished to rule Portugal by means of "the system of the four I's: inquisition, infidelity, ignorance, and indigence."[6]

Martinho de Melo e Castro, one of the few members of the new administration held over from Pombal's cabinet, was a younger son of the noble house of Galveias. He had, according to the British minister, "always been careful to pay great court to the marquis d'Angeja," and he had remained neutral during Pombal's clashes with the clergy. Melo e Castro's recall from London had been at the king's personal initiative, not Pombal's, and the relationship between Melo e Castro and Pombal during the final years of Pombal's preeminence had not been cordial. Melo e Castro was regarded by the British, and by Jacome Ratton, as being favorable to British interests.[7] Pina Manique, who had carried out some of the most repressive measures of the Pombaline period (including the burning of the fishing village of Trafaria on the southern bank of the Tagus in January 1777 which the government claimed was a hotbed of deserters and vagrants), retained his police role in the Lisbon area, and was in 1780 promoted to the powerful position of intendant general of police for the capital and kingdom.[8]

Many, though not all, of Pombal's closest associates were removed from office following his fall from power. Frei Cenáculo was ordered to resign as the prince's

[4] Cited by Montalvão Machado, *Quem livrou Pombal*, p. 191.
[5] March 4, 1777, BNLCP, codex 695, fo. 36.
[6] Cited by José Estêves Pereira in *O pensamento político em Portugal no século XVIII: António Ribeiro dos Santos*, p. 122.
[7] Robert Walpole to Foreign Office, Lisbon, April 4, 1795, PRO, FO, 63/20.
[8] Ratton, *Recordações*, p. 245. F. A. Oliveira Martins, *Pina Manique* (Lisbon, 1948), pp. 10, 19, 25.

tutor, and required to take up residence at his bishopric of Beja. The reformer of the University of Coimbra, Francisco de Lemos, was dismissed and Pombal's sister, the abbess of the convent of Santa Juana, was deposed. The Jesuits incarcerated since 1760 were released, as was the former bishop of Coimbra who had opposed the regalist writers. The surviving aristocratic conspirators were also released. In all, some 800 political prisoners were set free under Queen Maria's clemency decisions.[9]

Pombal's fall from grace was rapid. The situation became sufficiently threatening in Lisbon for him to withdraw first to Oeiras and then to move north to his properties near Pombal. He was forced to travel incognito, but his empty coach was stoned. Troops were called out to prevent his Lisbon house from being burned and the crowd had to be satisfied with burning his effigy instead. There was an explosion of denunciation and satires. Abandoned by many of his allies (though not all, by any means) Pombal prepared to face his enemies both in the juridical proceedings instituted and through the systematic written defense of his policies and actions.[10]

The fall of Pombal from office, and the removal of his old antagonist Grimaldi in Madrid opened the way for a settlement of the South American border war. At San Ildefonso in 1778 Spain and Portugal agreed to a new line of demarcation; Portugal lost Colônia, but retained Rio Grande. The ban on North American shipping which Pombal had imposed in the hope of encouraging Britain to support Portuguese pretensions in South America was lifted and Portugal assumed a neutral position towards the dispute between Britain and her former colonies.[11] The new regime was also faced immediately with the need for a decision over the future of one of the most notorious of Pombal's creations, the Company of Grão Pará and Maranhão, and the question of the prorogation of the monopoly soon became the subject of a heated propaganda battle. It was one of the paradoxes of Pombal's image that, although the catastrophic decline in British commerce with Portugal had been caused by a profound change in the economic system following the decline of gold production in Brazil, the memory of the bitter disputes of the 1750s associated and credited Pombal's measures during that period with the consequent achievement of a more balanced trade with Britain. The creation of the monopoly Brazilian companies thus became one of the central policies for which his regime was at the same time praised or condemned, depending on the personal interest or nationality of the observer. Defense of the measures of the 1750s in fact became tantamount to a defense of Pombal himself. On one side stood the company's directors, and on the other those interests suppressed since the late 1750s and now vociferous in their hostility to all things Pombaline. They were backed by some of the company's debtors in Brazil who saw in the change of regime an opportunity to escape their obligations. Strong

[9] Veríssimo Serrão, *Pombal*, pp. 168–169; the marquês de Alorna and the three brothers of the marquês de Távora refused to leave prison unless their innocence was recognized. The queen agreed to a revision commission in 1780.
[10] *Apologias*, BNLCP, codex 695, fos. 19–31, 194–201, 230–231, 233–246, 306–308; also see discussion by Veríssimo Serrão, in *Pombal*, pp. 173–184.
[11] Scott, *British Foreign Policy*, pp. 222, 224.

pressure was brought to bear on the new ministry to extinguish the monopoly and open the trade of Pará and Maranhão to all.[12]

In their written memoranda to the queen, the company's directors stressed the national objectives behind the company's establishment and their success in reducing Portugal's dependency on Great Britain. The capital invested in Brazil, they asserted, had introduced and stimulated the now thriving cotton and rice production and commerce. The directors of the Pernambuco company, which was also faced with the threat of extinction, pointed to the regulatory functions their company had performed, and the capital employed to reestablish sugar and tobacco production in northeastern Brazil.[13]

The company's investment in Brazil, however, was precisely what had led to the huge debts of the colonists, and the regulation of the supply of metropolitan merchandise to colonial production was blamed by the colonists for having produced high prices and shortages in the Brazilian monopoly regions. The Pernambucan planters and sugar mill owners, acting through the municipal councils of Olinda and Recife, expressed their opposition to the company's privileges in no uncertain terms. They reminded the new queen that they were "the descendants of those ancient Pernambucans who at the cost of their property, blood, and lives, took this great part of America from the hands of enemies and restored the crown."[14] Queen Maria's Council of State voted in favor of the abolition of the Company of Grão Pará and Maranhão. The decision was six to three, with two votes for the compromise solution, and the failure to prorogue the Pernambuco company's monopoly was a logical consequence.[15] The new era, claimed one of the anti-monopoly memorialists, would bring the "liberty of commerce and the competition of businessmen," and mark the end to "private privileges, half understood taxes, and a thousand vexations."[16]

The decision not to renew the companies' privileges was a visible triumph for the freetraders and the old system, as well as for the companies' debtors in Brazil.[17] Yet the achievement was more apparent than real. The situation of 1777 was not that of the 1750s, despite the reappearance of the old debate. During the intervening years the economic circumstances in Portugal and in the South Atlantic Luso-Brazilian commercial system had been transformed. Despite the popular hysteria that

[12] "Correspondência official do governador do Grão Pará, 1752–1777," IHGB/AUC, 1-1-3, fo. 378; "Súplica a rainha," IHGB/AUC, 1-1-8, fo. 62. Also Artur Cezar Ferreira Reis, "Negadores e entusiastas da companhia do comércio," *ACC* I, 11–18.

[13] "Apontamentos vários sobre a Companhia do Grão Pará e Maranhão," IHGB/AUC, 1-1-8, fo. 16.

[14] "Representação que a Sua Magestade Fizerão as câmaras da cidade de Olinda, Villa do Recife, e moradores de Pernambuco," 1780, IHGB/AUC, 1-1-8, fos. 1–8.

[15] For the voting on this issue see IHGB/AUC, 1-1-8, fo. 133.

[16] "Vasta exposição de mótivos a Rainha a favor da extinção das companhias de comércio exclusivas . . . por José Vasque da Cunha," IHGB/AUC, 1-1-8, p. 133.

[17] For extinction of companies, Manuel Nunes Dias, "A junta liquidatária dos fundos das Companhias do Grão-Pará e Maranhão, Pernambuco e Paraíba (1778–1837)," *Revista Portuguesa de História* 10 (1962), pp. 156–161. Also Ribeiro Júnior, *Colonização*, pp. 171–208.

accompanied the change of regime, Pombal's collaborators were far too deeply embedded in the social structure, and too closely associated with the collection of revenue and fiscal agencies of government, to disappear by the mere abolition of the monopoly privileges of the Brazil companies. The deeper socio-economic factors which underlay their position in society made the attack on the monopoly companies, in so far as it was an attack on them as a privileged group, at best a matter of form.

The close interconnection between the Company of Grão Pará and Maranhão and the local fiscal and administrative structure, the investment in Brazil, particularly in cotton, could not be obliterated by the stroke of a pen in Lisbon. In fact the "extinct company" remained a very real force, retaining administrators in Brazil, and actually continued trading during the 1780s. The removal of a central and unchallenged focus within the government was by no means a disadvantage to the interest of the opulent merchant houses that had arisen during the Pombaline era.

The marquês d'Angeja, who lacked administrative experience and was uninformed on economic matters, became the president of the royal treasury – the linchpin of the Pombaline administration and fiscal apparatus – and the most immediate consequence of Pombal's fall was that the vital directing influence of the centralized administrative structure, already overburdened and backlogged, faltered. Under Angeja's dilatory care the role of the treasury was weakened, the administrative machinery of the treasury less closely supervised and infinitely more susceptible to corruption.[18] The debilitation of this vital central government agency, together with the lack of a clear-cut focus of power within the new regime, created a situation where the privileged interests which for so long had been encouraged, protected, and used by the state to further its nationalistic and imperial pretensions, found themselves in a position to manipulate the state for their own advantage. The contract holders and opulent merchants, because of their key role in the royal treasury and the customs administration, their directing influence in the royal manufactories, and their personal wealth and influence, were in an unassailable position which the weakness of the state served to exaggerate. Thus, while Pombal's enemies tilted at the windmills of the privileged companies, his collaborators increased and strengthened their wealth and influence.

The other great administrative agent of Pombaline government was also weakened. Membership in the *junta do comércio* was reduced to three, Francisco José Lopes, Jacinto Fernandes Bandeira, and the secretary, Teotónio Gomes de Carvalho, because of the queen's failure to reappoint deputies.[19] In 1788 the administration of the manufactories was placed under the care of a new body, the *junta da administração das fábricas do Reino e aguas livres*, composed of an inspector and four deputies.[20] As the title implied, the new *junta das fábricas* was concerned exclusively with metropolitan establishments and the activities of the old Pombaline *junta do comércio* in encouraging colonial manufacturing enterprise were not repeated. The new regime also witnessed

[18] Ratton, *Recordações*, p. 121.
[19] Ibid., p. 202.
[20] Borges de Macedo, *Problemas*, p. 224.

the state's retreat from direct administration of the royal manufacturing enterprises established or reorganized during the previous reign. Again "liberalization" was claimed to be the objective, but this did not mean the removal of privileges, the special protection of raw materials, or easy access to colonial markets. The royal manufactories were alienated into the hands of the very private capitalists who had been closely involved in their establishment. The royal factories of Covilhã and Fundão with all their privileges, including the monopoly of the military and royal household contracts, were transferred to João Ferreira, Joaquim Ignácio Quintella, Jacinto Bandeira, and Joaquim Machado. Later, the Porto Alegre factory was taken over by Anselmo José da Cruz and Geraldo Braamcamp and then passed into the control of the Ferreira–Quintella–Bandeira group.[21] Meanwhile the expansion of the manufacturing industry continued with added momentum, 263 new workshops were established between 1777 and 1778. By way of comparison the previous reign had seen a mere 96.[22] The new *junta das fábricas*, in fact, provided a focus for metropolitan manufacturing interests.

Thus, while the reputation of Pombal, "that great man, known as such to the middle and thinking class of his nation," as Ratton wrote much later, went into eclipse, the group he had favored remained and prospered.[23] The fall of Pombal, far from undermining their power and influence, served to provide a cover for the manipulation of the state in their own interests, and their takeover of most of the enterprises the state had established. The merchant–industrial oligarchy retained the lucrative soap and tobacco monopolies from which, as the contract prices were rarely reassessed, they acquired gigantic profits. Ratton calculated that the contractor of the tobacco monopoly gained in one year more than the treasury had received from the contract's disposal in forty years.[24] Extension of contract periods at set annual prices also advantaged the contractors to the detriment of royal revenues. The Quintella group, for example, was granted the salt gabelle contract for the state of Brazil for 48,000 *milréis* per annum for thirteen years commencing in 1788.[25] The opulence of these Portuguese noble businessmen of the last quarter of the eighteenth century was praised by poets and pamphleteers and impressed visiting literati. "The large and magnificent houses" of the Quintellas, Braamcamps, and Bandeiras were noted by the English poet Robert Southey at the turn of the century (fig. 46). And the ever-caustic William Beckford noted their "glaring display of false taste and ill-judged magnificence."[26] "Is there any one who does not do business?" asked Bernardo

[21] Ratton, *Recordações*, p. 202; Luís F. de Carvalho Dias, *A relação das fábricas de 1788* (Coimbra, 1955), pp. 20, 25, 63, 73.

[22] Luís F. de Carvalho Dias, *A relação das fábricas de 1788*, p. 95.

[23] Jacome Ratton, *Recordações*, p. 152.

[24] See Ratton's calculations in this respect, *Recordações*, pp. 112–202.

[25] "Livros dos termos de arrematação dos contratos reaes da América," AHU, codices 297, 298, 299, 306.

[26] Robert Southey, *Journal of a Residence in Portugal 1800–1801*, ed. A. Cabral (Oxford, 1900), pp. 137–139; and William Beckford, *The Journal of William Beckford in Portugal and Spain 1787–1788*, ed. Boyde Alexander (London, 1954), pp. 257–258.

46 The Lisbon town house of a merchant businessman of the late eighteenth century, the "Palácio Ludovice"

de Jesus Maria in his *Arte e dicionário do comércio e economia portuguesa*, published in Lisbon in 1783. "Good customs and much money" ran the contemporary jingle, "make any kind of knave a gentleman."[27]

Almost a year and a half after his removal from office, the complaints against Pombal led to a famous judicial case. Pombal was subjected to grave accusations of abuse of power, corruption, and other types of fraud. The marquês employed all his remaining energy to combat these attacks and organized his defense in a very audacious manner, claiming (in a way which will be more familiar to the twentieth century than the eighteenth) he had never acted without the king's authority. From October 1779 to January 1780 Pombal was interrogated. He was almost 80 years of age at the time, but he always maintained his attitude that the king was responsible for the actions of his administration, and that he was merely following orders from his master "of sacred memory," as he put it. A committee of five judges examined the evidence but was divided on how to proceed. Dona Maria I cut the process short in 1781 by issuing an edict declaring Pombal deserving of "exemplary punishment" but instituting no proceedings against his person because of "his age and feeble

[27] Cited by Borges de Macedo in *Problemas*, p. 216.

condition."[28] These extraordinary proceedings fascinated Europe. Extracts from Pombal's writings and commentary about his activities were, by the mid 1780s, circulating in multiple editions in several languages.

Pombal died in 1782, five years after his fall from power, a forlorn, very sick, but still defiant old man. Dom Francisco de Lemos did not abandon his old mentor and friend, performing his funeral rites and paying personally for the expenses of the ceremony. The Papal Nuncio in Lisbon from 1794 to 1802, Bartolomeu Cardinal Pacca, was outraged by how much of the Pombaline legacy remained. He compared the Portuguese relationship to the papacy as not much short of Anglicanism. He claimed Pombal had turned the University of Coimbra into a "true seat of pestilence" and he singled out for particular blame the Portuguese bishops and Dom Francisco de Lemos, whom he held directly responsible for the "propagation in Portugal of the Febonian and Jansenist maxims."[29]

For his children and posterity Pombal composed a series of *apologias* – each explaining his principal activities in government and attacking what he regarded as the calumnies against his reputation. His immediate successors judged him harshly, but by the turn of the century many of his acolytes returned to positions of power. Portuguese historians, like Pombal's contemporaries, remain divided as to his merits and the importance of his reforms. It was a century and a half before he received national recognition in the form of a great statue which now dominates Lisbon at the end of the Avenida da Liberdade.

But how should we judge Pombal today? The key to understanding Pombal in eighteenth-century Portugal lies, in part, in the coincidence of enlightenment with the struggle of an old power to be great again, by adopting and adapting self-consciously the techniques its rulers believed their competitors had used to surpass them. The role of intellectual construction is, therefore, something we are obliged to take into account if we are to understand Pombal and eighteenth-century Portugal. Many years ago Fritz Hartung distinguished clearly between absolutism – that is, a form of government which is not hampered by parliamentary institutions, but which voluntarily submits to laws and acknowledges the rights of subjects – and despotism, which is equivalent to unchecked tyranny. Pombal's Portugal was in a way a hybrid, part-absolutist, part-despotic. The endeavor to intensify the state's power by increasing the efficiency of the administration and the army, by stimulating the national economy, that is, by a policy of mercantilism, was not uniquely or especially a characteristic of enlightened absolutism – certainly Pombal did all these things. Yet Pombal also acquired and established for the Portuguese state four key monopolies of power – over coercion, over taxation, over administration and over law-making, which was indeed the enlightened absolutist's task and aim.[30]

---

[28] The European reaction to Pombal's fall from power has been extensively analyzed by Franco Venturi in *The End of the Old Regime in Europe 1776–1789*, translated by R. Burr Litchfield (Princeton, 1991), pp. 200–236.

[29] *Mémoires historiques du cardinal Pacca, traduites de l'italien* (Paris, 1844), pp. 269–274.

[30] See discussion by Isser Woloch, *Eighteenth Century Europe: Tradition and Progress, 1715–1789* (New York, 1982), pp. 4–26.

The particular combination of methods Pombal used, however, reflected the peculiarities of Portugal's position. There was, of course, a counterpoint between opportunity and necessity in all Pombal's activities. Many of his most important interventions were both reactive and creative at the same time. The reconstruction of Lisbon, perhaps Pombal's most visible and lasting achievement, was made possible by the catastrophe of the 1755 earthquake. The reform of the military followed the Spanish invasion of 1762. His reform of the educational system was the inevitable result of the expulsion of the Jesuits. The break with the papacy forced a reevaluation of state–church relations. The increased emphasis on manufacturers followed the creation of an economic environment favorable to import substitution. But simply to enumerate opportunities does not imply they are inevitably taken advantage of.

Often opportunities are wasted, lost, or unseen. In fact, it in no way diminishes Pombal, in my view, to see the intimate relation between opportunity and response. Indeed, it was his skillful manipulation of circumstances which guaranteed the measure of success he enjoyed in the economic and social sphere. Essentially, the all-powerful minister placed the power of the state decisively on one side of the conflict that had developed among Portuguese entrepreneurs as a consequence of the gold boom. He chose the large established merchants over their smaller competitors because he saw the small merchants as mere creatures or commission agents of the foreigners whom he hoped the large Portuguese merchants with the state's assistance would be able to challenge. Likewise, in the north of Portugal Pombal threw the state's support behind the large producers of the upper Douro, protecting them from competition and, in the process, stabilizing prices and quality. He also gave the Douro company a retail monopoly alienating the independent tavern keepers as well as the small producers. When they revolted, he crushed them ruthlessly. Likewise, in the long struggle over pedagogy and education, by adopting the recommendations of the Oratorians and of Vernei, he chose one side in a preexisting quarrel. The dispute with the papacy was part and parcel of the reform movement in Catholic Europe which sought to diminish ultramontane pretensions and in effect nationalize the church. The reformation and codification of laws served to impose duties and obligations on subjects, not to grant citizens individual rights.

Pombal was a pragmatic and subtle adaptor, one who almost always pressed against the limits of what was possible within the constraints with which he had to work – those of the long Portuguese eighteenth century and the Atlantic system. Within these parameters Pombal could draw on the considerable body of past Portuguese thinking as well as his own observations in London and Vienna. Above all, he did not hesitate to act. Indeed, in his action is his monument – for better or for worse. And whether it was better or worse depended mainly on who you were. To the great merchant houses he helped create, he was a hero. To the small traders he suppressed, he was a tyrant. To the Port wine growers he protected, he was a patron, to the vineyard owners whose vines he ordered pulled up, he was a scourge. Unlike most rulers of the Enlightenment, more concerned with theory than with practice, he by and large achieved his objectives. His educational reform opened the doors to a late eighteenth-century flowering of Portuguese science and philosophy. The merchants he favored became the basis of a rich and opulent bourgeoisie. In both cases the role of the state as patron, partner, and protector was critical. As Dom Luís da Cunha had recommended in his political testament, the liberty of the many was restricted to the benefit of the few. Thus, in eighteenth-century Portugal it was the state that created the bourgeoisie, not, as in Anglo-America, the bourgeoisie which restrained the state.

Pombal's economic policy was a logical one in view of Portugal's position in the eighteenth-century international trading system. It relied on a renewed state intervention within the entrepreneurial structure as well as in domestic and colonial markets, commerce, and production. The policy protected mutually beneficial trade – the Port wine trade, for instance – but it also sought to develop a powerful national class of businessmen with the capital resources and the business skills needed to challenge their foreign competitors. Far from being an imported policy it was one which grew out of a long tradition of Portuguese experimentation and debate dating back to the 1660s. It was based on a sophisticated assessment of the balance of social forces in Portuguese society. This nationalistic policy, imposed by the implacable power of the state, produced reactions inside Portugal precisely because it intersected with other conflicts in Portuguese society – between old nobility and upstart businessmen, between modernizers of the educational system and defenders of tradition, and between small and large entrepreneurs. Pombal dealt with the opposition ruthlessly. His reforms and his despotism are, therefore, inseparable. They were two sides of the same coin.

Hence, the Enlightenment, rationality, and progress have a very different meaning in this context from that to which we have grown accustomed. It is fundamentally the enhancement of state power we are speaking about, not the extension of individual freedoms. Pombal's actions were needed, his apologists argued, to achieve progress. Yet the problem with the idea of progress, especially for those deemed not to have progressed, was that it implied the stigma of backwardness, providing thereby a justification for actions, which tradition, law or ethics had previously restrained. The interplay of these two notions – progress and backwardness – within the social, political, and economic realities of eighteenth-century Portugal is inextricably woven, consciously or not, into any interpretation of the age. Bolstered by rationalistic ideology which provided a convenient excuse for despotism, the contradictory images of eighteenth-century Portugal are, in this perspective, to a large degree dissolved. In a very real sense both images are accurate, because the other side of the coin of backwardness can be order, and the other side of progress can be tyranny. In neither was there much room for the rights of the individual. That space had been decisively preempted by the state.

The great conflict between tradition and innovation was, therefore, unresolved and the inherent incompatibilities between parts of Pombal's reform program became more obvious once the dominating and integrating presence of the all-powerful minister was gone. And his own collaborators soon faced the need to confront intellectually the dilemma of despotism and enlightenment. No one was more aware of the conflict at the core of Pombaline absolutism than António Ribeiro dos Santos. Writing privately several years after Pombal's death, he observed:

the principal and most important obligation of a minister who the prince places at the head of his government is to maintain the first and fundamental constitutional law of all civil societies, which is the real and personal security of the citizens which was and is the reason that men came together in society and for which they sacrifice a great part of their liberties and natural rights . . . The marquis of Pombal continually violated this law throughout the whole period of his government. This sacrosanct law was trodden under the infamous feet of the tyrant.[31]

These were not issues on which all the Pombaline apologists, among whom Ribeiro dos Santos had been one of the most prominent in the 1770s, agreed. His old colleague in the reform of the University of Coimbra, Pascoal José de Melo Freire, later denounced him to the queen in 1789 as a "propagandist of populist and republican doctrines."[32] This he was not. In fact, he was the author of several books attacking non-Christian interpretations of the Enlightenment. But this bitter disagreement among old colleagues in the Pombaline regime – one, Ribeiro, who had begun to espouse a more constitutionalist interpretation of the state and the role of civil society, the other who clung to the absolutist vision – was a precursor of the debate to come as the eighteenth-century crisis over government and representation entered its most acute and violent stages and it would tear Portugal itself apart for the first thirty years of the nineteenth century.

The story of Pombal's administration is, therefore, an important antidote to the overly linear and progressive view of the role of the eighteenth-century Enlightenment in Europe and the relationship between the Enlightenment and the exercise of state power. The Anglo-American historical tradition still tends to assume that the Enlightenment is synonymous with liberty, especially those liberties enshrined in the United States Constitution and Bill of Rights – rights which have as their fundamental objective the protection of the individual from the state. In France the Enlightenment is still seen as a forerunner, or at the very best, a conditioning agent for the revolution of 1789. We also very often assume when discussing the eighteenth century that liberty is the handmaiden of progress. But this view is not always sustained by an examination of the European periphery. Here, as the positivists later summarized the matter, the more common union was of "Order and Progress," not the happy union of "Order and Freedom" that Macaulay and the Whig tradition claimed as the great attribute of eighteenth-century England. We are beginning to learn again, in fact, in central, eastern, and southern Europe, that the Enlightenment was more often married to absolutism than to constitutionalism. Here the eighteenth century is less characterized by the individual seeking protection from the state than by the state seeking protection from over-powerful individuals. Marc Raeff has gone

---

[31] Lisbon, codex 4712, fols. 200–201, cited by José Estêves Pereira in *O pensamento político em Portugal no século XVIII*, p. 248, n. 1.

[32] Ibid.; also, L. F. de Carvalho Dias, "Algumas cartas do doutor António Ribeiro dos Santos," *Revista Portuguesa de História* 14 (1974), pp. 415–519.

so far as to characterize the legal formulations of eighteenth-century reformism in the German territories and Russia as being aimed at the creation of "a well ordered police state."[33] This is perhaps the extreme view, yet in many of its facets the Pombaline experience is close to that of the Raeff model and a revisionist body of historical literature is beginning to accumulate which is rethinking the whole context of enlightened despotism and its meaning.

Portugal is rarely considered in these debates, though it offers a fascinating example of Enlightenment absolutism in its most statist form. To be sure, Pombal's regime represents a complicated and contradictory case. Portugal is a small country when compared to the multinational empires other European rulers had to contend with. It is also one of Europe's oldest nation states and remarkably homogeneous in terms of its population and culture compared to its neighbors. Yet the eighteenth century, it should not be forgotten, was also one of Portugal's great imperial periods, comparable in some respects to the sixteenth century. And it was Portugal's overseas projection that made its reformist policies broader in scope than might appear at first sight, a factor not lost on Pombal's friend in Vienna, Duke Silva-Tarouca, for instance. As this book has tried to demonstrate, some of Portugal's peculiarities are well worth considering in a comparative context. And the story of the paradoxes of Pombal's rule has the merit of helping to unravel some of the wider paradoxes that lie behind the coexistence of the reformist and authoritarian traditions in southern as well as eastern Europe.

Yet in the end the dilemmas which marked the Portuguese eighteenth century were never fully resolved by Pombal's rule. The most fundamental rested in the dependency of Portugal on Brazil, since it was the South Atlantic dimension of the long Portuguese eighteenth century that set the chronological framework for the whole epoch. For historical reasons initially and then for reasons related to the growing imbalance between Brazil and Portugal, the relationship between Portugal and Brazil throughout this whole period was never merely that of a colonial servant and European master. The historical reasons went back to the period between 1580 and 1640 when Portugal had fallen under the rule of the Spanish Habsburg monarchy and a substantial section of Brazil's most prosperous northeastern sugar producing region had been seized by the Dutch. As the Brazilians never forgot and continually reminded Lisbon in case the central government should have a lapse of memory, the struggle to reestablish Portuguese sovereignty in Brazil had been largely a Brazilian affair. The more astute Portuguese leaders throughout the period from the late seventeenth century until the early nineteenth century were always aware that the Brazilians had contributed mightily to the restoration of Portuguese sovereignty in South America and had mobilized against other foreign threats when they had presented themselves, particularly against the French in the early years of the

---

[33] Marc Raeff, "The Well-ordered Police State and the Development of Modernity in Seventeenth and Eighteenth Century Europe: An Attempt at a Comparative Approach," *AHR* 80, no. 5, (December 1975), pp. 1221–1243.

eighteenth century and against the Spaniards over the whole period. As a consequence, they were careful to treat the Brazilians with suitable respect and caution.
Pombal, in particular, while ferocious in his defense of royal privilege and authority
in Portugal itself, sought to coopt and integrate Brazilians into the mechanisms of
government both in Brazil and in Portugal. Yet Portugal was in the final analysis a
small country with a large empire, and the notion that Brazil would eventually surpass
Portugal in population and wealth led several leading figures, Dom Luís da Cunha
among them, to foresee the eventual move of the seat of government across the
Atlantic.

The role of the Cortes had been important in the days of penury and weakness
following the restoration of independence in 1640. The Bragança claim to the throne,
moreover, had emerged after all out of an act of rebellion and from among the upper
reaches of the Portuguese aristocracy. The relationship of the Braganças to the
upper nobility was thus a complicated one and the Portuguese monarchy had as a
consequence often drawn its most intimate advisers from other sources. The Jesuits
from the time of Vieira until the 1750s played a key role as confessors, and as special
advisers and agents for the Crown. Colonials had performed a similar role during the
reign of Dom João V in the person of his influential Brazilian-born private secretary,
Alexandre de Gusmão. Later on, Francisco de Lemos, another Brazilian, worked
intimately with Pombal, and was the reforming rector of the university at Coimbra.
Pombal himself was from the minor gentry and his family had long served in positions
of dependency on the Crown. But it was, above all, Brazilian gold that provided the
means to consolidate the Portuguese absolutist state and emancipate the Bragança
monarchy from both aristocratic competition and the Cortes.[34]

A fundamental objective of Pombal's education reforms, his creation of a College
of Nobles, and the provision of the education of the provincial nobility at Coimbra,
was intended precisely to create a service nobility, free, as the statutes of the College
of Nobles put it, "from the pernicious notion that they could live free of virtue." But
here the dilemmas facing such social engineering in eighteenth-century Portugal
were profound. The traditional nobility was small, intermarried, and intensely
traditionalist. The Inquisition and its obsession with purity of blood, with ferreting out
subversion, with Judaism and heresy, was a powerful bastion against reform. Yet the
Inquisition was also a powerful arm in the defense of the state, and the Bragança
monarchs were faced here with their own ambiguities. Dom João V was proud of his
title of "Most Faithful" (Fidelíssimo), with his plans for the Patriarchate of Lisbon,
with his expensive promotion of religious ceremonial, and not least his project at
Mafra. Yet the Braganças had also permitted, or had been forced to permit because of
the need for defensive alliances with the Protestant maritime powers, the practice
of the Protestant religion within their own capital. And their more thoughtful royal
advisers, from the Jesuit António Vieira to Dom Luís da Cunha to Pombal, had all

---

[34] See Kenneth Maxwell, "The Atlantic in the Eighteenth Century: A Southern Perspective on the
Need to Return to the 'Big Picture,'" *TRHS*, 6th series, 3 (1993), pp. 209–236.

believed that Portugal needed to recuperate the "New Christian" and Jewish wealth and business expertise lost to Portugal because of the Inquisition's depredations.

There was, of course, an element of paranoia to these views since they were sometimes a mirror image in their expectation of Jewish and "New Christian" entrepreneurial perspicacity, and of the Inquisition's fear of it. But these tentative steps in the direction of social reform and toleration were part of a wider clash between the traditional values of the Counter Reformation and a reform program that aimed at reestablishing national control over the economy, at shoring up the power of the state, and at the education of a new generation of skillful businessmen and enlightened aristocrats. And here the ambiguity of the Crown's own response to these conflicting tendencies was most acute. Dom João V wanted initiative and orthodoxy to flourish at the same time, and they could not. Pombal, by contrast, had thrown the state's support wholeheartedly behind reform but with a ferocity and despotism which left his measures dangerously dependent in the end on his personal power and left them vulnerable, therefore, to reversal and rejection after his fall. And he had in a curious way so fused authoritarianism to reform that the succeeding reign of the ultra-pious Dona Maria I recalled at times the confusion of her extravagant grandfather. So that as the queen retreated into the pastoral fantasies of her palace at Queluz and set out to build the great basilica at Estrela (fig. 47), both in inspiration and style as far removed from the utilitarian neoclassicism of the new Pombaline Lisbon or the designs of Colonel William Elsden for the new laboratories and observatories of Coimbra as could be imagined, she also permitted the new Royal Academy of Sciences to be inaugurated, and encouraged the great "philosophical" expeditions of Alexandre Rodrigues Ferreira and his colleagues who set out to record the natural history of the Amazon, Angola, and Mozambique.[35] Once the regency was formally declared in 1799 many of Pombal's acolytes returned to office, including Francisco de Lemos, who returned to Coimbra to continue his interrupted work.

The second great dilemma of the long Portuguese eighteenth century involved the apparently conflicting interests of trade and industry. When the gold began to flow from Brazil, it became cheaper to import finished goods than to manufacture them at home. Thus the gold of Brazil helped kill off the infant industries the count of Ericeira had tried to develop in the late seventeenth century. Conversely, when gold remittances declined, the changed economic environment helped to stimulate the

---

[35] See the excellent book by William Joel Simon, *Scientific Expeditions in the Portuguese Overseas Territories (1783–1808) and the Role of Lisbon in the Intellectual Scientific Community of the Late Eighteenth Century* (Lisbon, 1983). There is some disagreement among Portuguese and Brazilian historians on the relative importance of economic and geopolitical factors in the demise of Portugal's late eighteenth-century industrial boom. Vitorino Magalhães Godinho tends to support the view that the impact of cheaper British textiles had directly affected Portuguese production by the turn of the century (Magalhães Godinho, *Prix et monnaies*); whereas Jorge Borges de Macedo (*Problemas*) sees the Napoleonic invasion as decisive. Recent work by José Jacobson de Andrade Arruda, *O Brasil no comércio colonial* (São Paulo, 1980) and David Justino (see review in *RHES*, Lisbon, 11 [January–June 1983], pp. 126–130) tends to support Magalhães Godinho's interpretation. Queen Maria I was declared mentally incompetent in 1799, when her second son João became prince regent. The queen died in Rio de Janeiro in 1816.

47 The Estrela church, Lisbon, built by Dona Maria I, from a photograph of 1872 (Arquivo Nacional de Fotografia)

new manufactories set up by the Pombaline regime by removing the means of payment for foreign imports. So subtle had been Pombal's approach and so powerful were the incentives to Portuguese manufacturing that by the end of the century Portugal was benefiting both from its own manufactured products, which came to comprise a significant portion of Portuguese exports to Brazil, as well as from a surge in colonial re-exports, some traditional like sugar, but others new like cotton, which together brought a true reciprocity to its commercial dealings with the rest of Europe, and with Britain in particular, something that had been the aim of all good mercantilists in Portugal since the restoration of Portuguese independence in the mid-seventeenth century.

Thus, protectionist manufacturing interests within Portugal could with full justice claim to be heirs to the Pombaline tradition, as could those in the colonies who sought more scope for colonial enterprise, and here again the classic constraint of the long eighteenth century came into play. The age of mercantilism was passing. In England the industrial revolution was beginning. The freetraders were pushing for a removal of barriers and special relationships. Adam Smith in fact made the Anglo-Portuguese commercial relationship in general, and the Methuen Treaty in particular, the classic example of restraint on trade. The Lancashire cotton textile producers and exporters were pushing the government in London for a direct relationship with the lucrative markets of the Americas. Thus ironically, just as the mercantilist dream had been achieved, the context within which mercantilism worked as far as the Portuguese were concerned was about to be overthrown and the ferment of innovation within Brazil was already raising wider questions which could only point to the pertinence of the example of the thirteen colonies. It was a portentous combination of circumstances that the growing conflict of interest within the Luso-Atlantic imperial framework coincided with the shattering of the mercantilist system of the most powerful European colonial power and Portugal's old ally.

This denouement came about of course as a result of the third dilemma of the long Portuguese eighteenth century: the invidious role of Portugal within the struggle for hegemony in the Atlantic between France and Britain. In the climactic moments of that long struggle, the revolutionary and Napoleonic wars, the final break occurred, though it was France and not Britain that provoked the rupture when Napoleon decided that Portuguese neutrality could not be tolerated and that the port of Lisbon provided too serious a breach in his Continental system. But Napoleon had miscalculated the degree to which the Portuguese monarchy had prepared for the move to Brazil or the willingness of the British to facilitate this historic transfer of the seat of government from metropolis to colony in their own self-interest.

The fundamental problem for Portugal in the end arose from the logic of the Brazil-based eighteenth-century Atlantic system. In the final analysis, Brazil would inevitably become the dominant partner within the Portuguese-speaking empire. If the political constraints, which had governed the whole period from the 1660s to the end of the eighteenth century, also changed, that is if, for example, Great Britain no longer saw it in its own interest to protect Portugal from her Continental neighbors, then the British might opt for a direct relationship with the colony rather than with the mother country. Since the whole basis of Portugal's prosperity had been built on the manipulation of colonial monopolies, cash-crop exports, colonial markets, and colonial gold, such a rupture would bring fundamental change and would close an epoch. Thus, the French seizure of Lisbon in 1807 collapsed the structure of the Luso-Atlantic system as it had existed since the 1660s, and direct access between Europe and the Brazilian ports destroyed Lisbon's role as a required intermediary. The year 1807 brought the long Portuguese eighteenth century to an end. Left unresolved, despite Pombal's efforts, was the old conflict between innovation and tradition. As the nineteenth century opened without the benefit that the wealth of Brazil provided, this struggle became bitter indeed.

Bibliographical essay

Despite the importance attributed to Pombal by historians, many aspects of his rule remain surprisingly understudied. The principal biographies dating from the nineteenth century are more doctrinal tracts in the ongoing battle between liberals and traditionalists than the products of serious archival research. The body of this literature – both for Pombal and against him – is immense. The National Library of Lisbon published a bibliography of over 3,000 items on the bicentenary of Pombal's death in 1982 (*Marquês de Pombal: catálogo bibliográfico e iconográfico*, ed. António Barreto [Lisbon, 1982]). Curiously, one of the best accounts in English is still that of John Smith published in the 1840s. It is highly favorable to Pombal and its accuracy in places was questioned by Camilo Castelo Branco in his *Perfil do marquês de Pombal* (facsimile based on 19th edition, Oporto, 1982, pp. 161–172). A more recent popular biography was written by a British diplomat, Sir Marcus Cheke, in the 1930s (Marcus Cheke, *Dictator of Portugal: Life of the Marquis of Pombal* [London, 1938]). The 1982 bicentenary of Pombal's death provoked a series of publications (and republications) of mixed value. The Jesuits produced a special edition of the magazine *Brotéria*, 2 vols. (London, 1982) and the Masons, *Pombal revisitado*, ed. by Maria Helena Carvalho dos Santos, 2 vols. (Lisbon, 1982). The most useful collection, however, is that published as a special two-volume issue of the journal *Revista de História das Ideias: O marquês de Pombal e o seu tempo*, ed. Luís Reis Torgal and Isabel Vasques, 2 vols. (Lisbon, 1982), which contains many important contributions including a valuable review of the historiography by Luís Reis Torgal in his introduction. There was also an excellent catalogue, *Exposição, Lisboa e o marquês de Pombal*, 3 vols. (Lisbon: Museu da Cidade, 1982), which is lavishly illustrated.

The best general introduction to Pombal in Portuguese remains José Lúcio d'Azevedo, *O marquês de Pombal e a sua época*, 2nd edition (Lisbon, 1922), though the volume by Veríssimo Serrão, *O marquês de Pombal: O homem, o diplomata, e o estadista* (Lisbon, 1982), is helpful. The most comprehensive overview of the theoretical background to Pombal's legislation is provided by the Brazilian historian, Francisco José Calazans Falcon, *A época pombalina: política, econômica e monarquia ilustrada* (São Paulo, 1982), supplemented now by a series of three substantive articles by J. S. da Silva Dias in *Cultura* (Lisbon, 1981, 1982, 1983). An excellent example of the growing professionalism of the younger generation of Portuguese historians is José Barreto's edition of Sebastião José de Carvalho e Melo, *Escritos econômicos de Londres (1741–1742)* (Lisbon, 1986). Barreto's notes and commentary are exemplary and do away with many a confusion and inaccuracy in the general literature.

Brazilian historians have made a substantial contribution to our knowledge of the imperial dimensions of Pombal's concerns which help clarify many elements of his actions. The eighteenth century was, after all, one of Portugal's great and most creative colonial ages, and it deserves its just place alongside the history of the adventures and misadventures of the Portuguese experience overseas in Asia during the Renaissance and in Africa in more recent times. The European dimension, both diplomatic and economic, has also received some attention, especially the latter, as has the history of ideas and role of the Enlightenment in Portugal.

Portuguese historians have been, on the whole, unconcerned with Pombal's place among the reformers of his age. The most recent contributions to Pombaline scholarship in fact go so far as to deny Pombal any originality at all, something even his contemporaries recognized. This national self-effacement may be in the nature of Portuguese historiography which is more concerned with what might be called the vertical rather than the horizontal dimension – that is, Pombal is almost always seen in terms of the projection of his activities into the disputes of the nineteenth century rather than his projection within the world of the eighteenth century. Pombal, however, remains, in my view, one of the more interesting rulers of the period. The body of his own writing is surprisingly rich, which means the historian can discover more about his thoughts and motivations than is the case with many of his contemporaries. Among the major contributions to Pombaline studies are those of Jorge Borges de Macedo (*A situação económica no tempo de Pombal* [Oporto, 1951]) and Vitorino Magalhães Godinho (*Prix et monnaies au Portugal* [Paris, 1955]), who have transformed our view of the economic context – the conjuncture – within which Pombal acted. There are still very few analyses of economic and social structures of Portugal in this period; Albert Silbert, *Le Portugal méditerranéen à la fin de l'ancien régime: XVIII–début du XIX siècle*, 2 vols. (Paris, 1966), is useful, but concentrates mainly on the nineteenth century and is concerned only with central and southern Portugal. For an indication of the richness of the archive sources on fiscal matters, see Alzira Teixeira Leite Moreira, *Inventário do fundo geral do erário régio* (Lisbon, 1977) and the analysis by Fernando Tomaz, "As finanças do estado pombalino, 1762–1776," in *Estudos e ensaios* (Lisbon, 1990), pp. 255–388.

The Anglo-Portuguese commercial and diplomatic connections, by way of contrast, are well covered in H. E. S. Fisher, *The Portugal Trade* (1971), and David Francis, *Portugal 1715–1808* (London, 1985). Virgílio Noya Pinto, *O ouro brasileiro e o comércio anglo-português* (São Paulo, 1979) has provided important data on colonial economic history, especially the eighteenth-century Brazilian gold boom and its impact on Atlantic commerce. José-Augusto França has delineated the social and cultural dimensions of one of the most lasting of Pombal's inspirations, the reconstruction of Lisbon, in *Une ville des Lumières: la Lisbonne de Pombal* (Paris, 1965). Rómulo de Carvalho, António Alberto Banha de Andrade, and J. S. da Silva Dias have helped reshape views of the intellectual environment of the period. Especially useful are the collected essays of Banha de Andrade, *Contributos para a história da mentalidade pedagógica portuguesa* (Lisbon, 1982), and Rómulo de Carvalho, *História da fundação do Colégio Real dos Nobres de Lisboa (1761–1772)* (Coimbra, 1959).

Also useful are the three substantial articles by J. S. da Silva Dias in *Cultura* 1 ([1982], pp. 45–114; 2 [1983], pp. 185–318; and 3 [1984], pp. 27–151). José Estêves Pereira provides an excellent analysis of the writing of António Ribeiro dos Santos, a key figure in the reform of the teaching of canon law at Coimbra and theoretician of regalism in church questions: *O pensamento político em Portugal no século XVIII: António Ribeiro dos Santos* (Lisbon, 1983). For some indication of the extraordinary richness of the archival materials concerning the activities of Frei Manuel do Cenáculo Vilas Boas, one of Pombal's most influential collaborators in the educational area, see "Excertos do 'diário' de Dom Frei Manuel do Cenáculo Vilas Boas, notas de João Palma-Ferreira," in *Revista da Biblioteca Nacional de Lisboa* 2, 1 (1982). For the reform of the Inquisition, see Francisco José Calazans Falcon, "Inquisição e poder: o regimento do santo oficio da Inquisição no contexto das reformas pombalinas (1774)," in *Inquisição: ensaios sobre mentalidade, heresias e arte*, organized by Anita Novinski and Maria Luiza Tucci Carneiro (São Paulo, 1993), pp. 116–139. For the military reform there is good coverage in Christa Banaschik-Ehl and Scharnhorsts Lehrer, *Graf Wilhelm von Schaumburg Lippe in Portugal die Heeresreform 1761–1777: 3 Studien zur Militargeschichte, Militarwissenschaft und Konfliktsforschung* (Osnabruck, 1974). The Brazilian industrialist and Pombal *aficionado*, Marcos Carneiro de Mendonça, produced a series of fundamental documentary collections, including the important correspondence between Pombal and his brother, *A Amazônia na era pombalina*, 3 vols. (Rio de Janeiro, 1963). Susan Schneider provided a fascinating analysis of the Douro during Pombal's rule in her *O marquês de Pombal e o vinho do Porto* (Lisbon, 1980). In the case of the administrative reforms overseas, Dauril Alden wrote an account of the viceroyalty of the marquês de Lavradio, one of Pombal's more impressive collaborators (*Royal Government in Colonial Brazil* [Berkeley and Los Angeles: University of California Press, 1969]) and Heloísa Liberalli Bellotto has provided an excellent complement to this with her study of the activities of the morgado de Mateus as governor of the captaincy of São Paulo in Brazil, *Autoridade e conflito no Brasil colonial: o govêrno do morgado de Mateus em São Paulo* (São Paulo, 1979). The monopoly companies have been investigated by several historians, among them José Ribeiro Junior on the Pernambuco company, *Colonização e monopólio no nordeste Brasileiro: a Companhia Geral de Pernambuco e Paraíba 1759–1780* (São Paulo, 1976), and Manuel Nunes Dias on the Company of Grão Pará and Maranhão, *A Companhia Geral do Grão Pará e Maranhão 1755–1778*, 2 vols. (Pará, 1970). On the role of the church we now have the excellent monograph by Samuel J. Miller, *Portugal and Rome c. 1748–1830: An Aspect of the Catholic Enlightenment* (Rome, 1978). For the Italian context for some of these reforms as well as reactions to Pombal's measures, see Franco Venturi, *Settecento riformatore*, 5 vols. (Turin, 1969) II, pp. 3–29. The nineteenth-century historiographical tradition, of course, makes anticlericalism an important element, but one result of this position was to obscure the very important role of the clergy in Pombal's reform program, the strength of the regalist arguments emanating from the Portuguese church and the vital ideological component this formed in the whole Pombaline enterprise. See the persuasive concluding comments by Cândido dos Santos, "António Pereira de Figueiredo, Pombal e a *Aufklärung*," in *RHDI/M de P* I, pp. 167–203. I have also drawn here extensively on my own previous work, especially "Pombal and the Nationalization of the Luso-Brazilian Economy," in *HAHR* (November 1968) and *Conflicts and Conspiracies: Brazil and Portugal 1750–1808* (Cambridge, 1973) where the focus of the latter is mainly on colonial policy. Also see "Pombal: The Paradox of Enlightenment and Despotism," in *Enlightened Absolutism: Reform and Reformers in Later Eighteenth Century Europe*, ed. H. M. Scott (London, 1990); "State and Individual in Eighteenth Century Portugal: The Pombaline Inheritance," *Portuguese Studies Review* 2, 2 (1993), pp. 30–50, and "Eighteenth-Century Portugal: Faith and Reason, Tradition and Innovation during a Golden Age," in Jay Levinson, ed., *The Age of the Baroque in Portugal* (Washington, DC; New Haven, CT, 1993).

There are useful documents on both Brazil and Portugal in *Quadro elementar das relações politicas e diplomaticas de Portugal com as diversas potencias do mundo: desde o principio do XVI seculo da monarchie Portuguesa até aos nossos dias*, ed. Visconde de Santarém, 18 vols. (Lisbon, 1843–1860). Also interesting for Brazil is "Correspondência do bispo do Rio de Janeiro com o govêrno metropolitano nos anos de 1754 a 1800," *RIHGB* 63 (1901/1902), pp. 39–92. Of prime importance for the economic history of Bahia, and with detailed statistics of sugar exports, commercial conditions, the Africa trade, is "Discurso preliminar, historico, introductivo com natureza de descripção economica da comarca e cidade do Salvador," *ABNRJ* 27. For a most important source on the origins of Pombal's commercial companies as well as of his long term strategical aims in the north see Marcos Carneiro de Mendonça, *A Amazônia na era pombalina: correspondência inédita do governador e capitão-general do estado do Grão Pará e Maranhão, Francisco Xavier de Mendonça Furtado, 1751–1759* (Rio de Janeiro: IHGB, 1963). Carneiro de Mendonça has also published an important collection of Pombal's instructions to his viceroys under the title *O marquês de Pombal e o Brasil* (São Paulo, 1960). The preoccupations of Pombal for the security of Portuguese America and the connections between the English and the Jesuits in the south of Brazil are clearly seen in "Correspondência official da corte de Portugal com os vice-reis do estado do Brasil: conde da Cunha, Ayres de Sá e Mello, e o conde de Azambuya nos annos 1766, 1767, 1768," *RIHGB* 33, 1 (1870).

An excellent source for pithy comments on Pombal's personality and policies and for the English factory at Lisbon is *The Private Correspondence of Sir Benjamin Keene, K.B.*, ed. Sir Richard Lodge (Cambridge, 1933). There are valuable insights into the economic logic of Portugal *vis-à-vis* Great Britain in *Punch's Politiks: In Several Dialogues Between Him and His Acquaintance* (London, 1762). In this work Punch poses the flight of the king of Portugal to Brazil as a likely and sensible outcome of an invasion of the kingdom by France and Spain. For two discussions on the Methuen Treaty, one favorable and one critical, see Charles King, *The British Merchant* III (London, 1748), and Adam Smith, *An Inquiry into the Nature and Causes of the Wealth of Nations* II, 4 (London, 1796), p. 323.

Two contrasting works of prime importance are the *Recordações de Jacome Ratton: sobre ocorrências do seu tempo em Portugal de maio de 1747 a setembro de 1810*, ed. J. M. Teixeira de Carvalho, 2nd edition (Coimbra, 1920) and *Adventures of Alonso: Containing Some Striking Anecdotes of the Present Prime Minister of Portugal* – in facsimile, anonymously published in London in 1755 and now attributed to Thomas Atwood Digges (1741–1821) of Warburton Manor, Maryland, ed. Thomas J. McMahon (New York, 1948). Ratton was one of the émigré entrepreneurs encouraged by Pombal to set up factories in Portugal. His autobiography is a unique and detailed account of the history of late eighteenth-century Portugal with inside information on economic policy decisions, the personality of ministers, etc. Digges, who was a merchant engaged in trade with Portugal, gives an interesting account of the reactions of the "free-trade" interlopers who were removed from the Brazil commerce by Pombal's regulatory measures.

Portuguese colonial policy under Martinho de Melo e Castro became more explicitly "colonialist" than it had been with Pombal. The administrations which followed Pombal were not, however, by any means marked by blind reaction. Melo e Castro's desire was to exploit the colony more fully and more efficiently. This is clearly seen in his "Instrucções de Martinho de Mello e Castro a Luís de Vasconcellos e Sousa, acerca do governo do Brasil, 27 jan. 1779," *RIHGB* 25 (1862), pp. 479–483. Detailed values of exports from Rio de Janeiro in 1779 and other important data can be found in "Memórias políticas e económicas da cidade de São-Sebastião de Rio de Janeiro, para uso do vice-rei Luís de Vasconcellos, 1779–1789," *RIHGB* 47, 1 (1884), pp. 25–52. Also valuable is "Mappa de moeda circulante, mappa de toda a qualidada de modas que girão n'esta capitania na real caza da moeda do Rio de Janeiro do anno 1768 até 1796," *RIHGB*, 46, 1 (1883), pp. 189–193. Further and more detailed statistics are available in "Productos exportados da cidade de Rio de Janeiro no anno de 1796," *RIHGB*,

46, 1 (1883), pp. 195–205 and in "Memória histórica da cidade de Cabo Frio, anno de 1797," *RIHGB*, 46, 1 (1883), pp. 205–236.

A copy of the *alvará* ordering the closing of all factories in Brazil except those manufacturing coarse cloth for slaves is published with other correspondence as "Vice-reinado de Luís de Vasconcellos: correspondência com a corte, anno de 1788," *RIHGB* 36, 1 (1873), pp. 135–156. Also indicative of the encouragement given by viceroys to primary production in Brazil see "Correspondência da corte de Portugal com o Brasil, 1790–1794," *RIHGB* 37, 1 (1874), pp. 5–31, particularly "Carta escripta ao conde de Rezende em 1793 sobre as uteis especulados que por meio da provadas experiencias havia feito João Manso Pereira, e das quaes hao resultar conhecidos vantagens ao progresso das artes e manufacturas; como ao commercio nacional," pp. 27–28. There are odd pieces of economic intelligence in *Diario de viagem do Dr. Francisco José de Lacerda e Almeida pelas capitanias do Pará, Rio Negro, e São Paulo, nos annos de 1780–1790* (São Paulo, 1841). There is an interesting letter to Melo e Castro from Fernando José de Portugal in 1794 published as "Carta do governador da Bahia D. Fernando José de Portugal, de 18 de junho de 1794, sobre opiniao de um frade capuchinho relativamente a escravidao no Brasil," *RIHGB*, 60 (1897), pp. 155–157. The governor laments the pernicious emancipation ideas the Italian monk has been spreading and tells how he has had him removed from Brazil where his theories threatened "deadly consequences for the preservation and subsistence of this colony."

An October 1799 decree on the "Distinction Between European and American Vassals" declared that "all my vassals are Portuguese, and all are equally eligible for any employment in any part of my dominions," see *RIHGB* 46, 1 (1883), pp. 237–238.

For background to the financial and banking activities, see "Fundaçao da casa da moeda, 1799, José Venancio de Seixas a D.R. de S.C.," Sept. 30, 1799, *RIHGB* 33, 1 (1870), pp. 123–134, and the various memoirs published by Pinto de Aguiar under the title, *Bancos no Brasil colonial* (Bahia, 1960). For the clearest statement of late eighteenth-century overall Brazilian policy, in all its aspects, see *Discurso* of 1798. This is published as document no. 4 (i) by M. Carneiro de Mendonça, *O intendente Câmara* (São Paulo, 1958). There are many other important documents published here as well.

A more general picture of the economy at the end of the century can be gained from Frei José Mariano de Conceição Velloso's *Discurso sobre o melhoramento da economia rustica do Brazil* (Lisbon, 1799), Lúis dos Santos Vilhena, *Notícias soteropolitanas e brasílicas*, ed. Brás do Amaral (Bahia, 1921), *Cartas económico-politicas sobre a agricultura e comércio da Bahia pelo recembargador João Rodrigues de Brito* (Lisbon, 1821), and D. José Joaquim da Cunha de Azeredo Coutinho, *Ensaio económico sobre o commércio de Portugal e suas colonias offerecido ao serenissimo principe de Beira, D. Pedro e publicado de ordem da Academia Real das Ciências*, 2nd edition (Lisbon, 1816). Azeredo Coutinho was an authentic mercantilist, believing that the metropolis "because it is the mother and grants to the colonies, her daughters, all the good offices and necessary aids for defense . . . these benefits demanded equal recompenses." This meant effectively no factories in the colonies and no possibility of trade except with Portugal. Among Azeredo Coutinho's other works is *Discurso sobre o estado actual das minas do Brazil* (Lisbon, 1804) and his *Memória sobre o preço do açúcar* (this is bound with the *Ensaio económico* in the edition at the Biblioteca Nacional, Rio de Janeiro). For some commentary on this letter there is Sergio Buarque de Holanda, "Introduccão a memória sobre o preco do açúcar de D. José Joaquim de Azeredo Coutinho," *Brasil Açucareiro* (December 1944–January 1945). Also, Myriam Ellis' interesting article, "Um documento anônomio do seculo XVIII sobre relações comerciais entre o Brasil e o Portugal," *RHSP* 38.

The "Epitome da vantagems que Portugal pode tirar das suas colonials do Brasil pelo liberdade do comércio do sal n'aguelle continente" Ellis attributes in this article to Azeredo Coutinho. This seems very likely for it has marked similarities with sections of the *Ensaio económico*. Also included in Myriam Ellis' discussion is an extremely valuable list of Azeredo Coutinho's writings.

Travel literature on Portugal and Brazil is remarkably rich and varied. Before the opening of the ports in 1808 the accounts are mainly confined to descriptive passages on the Bay of Guanabara. All testify to the secrecy with which the Portuguese officials shrouded all knowledge of Brazil. Occasionally an unfortunate individual might fall foul of the Portuguese authorities and, confined to Brazil awaiting judgment, have the opportunity to present a fuller and more detailed picture of the country. Much of the literature of the early period is about the metropolis and only indirectly deals with Brazil. It is nonetheless valuable, if only occasionally.

After the opening of the ports a whole army of eager travelers descended on Brazil, some naturalists and scientists, others merchants and adventurers. Many of them (particularly the Germans) had been inspired by Baron von Humboldt. Together they present a picture of practically the whole of Brazil – backlands and urban centers – during the first two decades of the nineteenth century.

Travel literature has its dangers, however. The foreigner does not always see all. Neither is he (or she) accurate in observation. It is unfortunate that too much of the history of Brazil (and of Portugal) has been written from the observations of foreigners. These travel accounts, therefore, are valuable, but they must be used carefully and critically.

An early and surprisingly detailed account of Bahia and the trade of the port is contained in the Instituto Ibero-Americano of Göteborg's (Sweden) publication "De passagem pelo Brasil e Portugal em 1756 por Johan Brelim," translated by C. P. de Almeida (Lisbon, 1955). Important information on Rio de Janeiro and the intercoastal trade to the south appears in Lewis de Bougainville, *A Voyage Round the World: Performed by Order of His Most Christian Majesty in the Years 1766, 1767, 1768, 1769, by Lewis de Bougainville*, translated from the French by John Reinhold Forster (London, 1772). The use of Rio as a port of call for India-bound vessels is described by James Forbes, *Oriental Memoirs Selected and Abridged from a Series of Letters Written During Seventeen Years Residence There, Including Observations on Parts of Africa and South America and a Narrative of Occurrences in Four India Voyages*, 4 vols. (London, 1813). Forbes bears witness to just how difficult it was for a foreigner in this period to get any information at all about the interior.

There is important information on intercolonial trade as well as Portugal's more general commercial relations in Jean François Bourgoing, *Voyage du ci-devant duc du Châtelet, en Portugal où se trouvent des détails intéressants sur les colonies sur M. de Pombal et la Court*, 2 vols. (Paris, 1798–1808). A source of the first order is the letters of Arthur William Costigan, *Sketches of Society and Manners in Portugal* (London, 1787). Costigan was a member of the Irish Brigade and saw service in Spain. Another military writer, Major William Dalrymple, *Travels Through Spain and Portugal in 1774* (London, 1777) contains useful asides. Also useful are James Murphy, *Travels in Portugal* (London, 1795); Janet Schaw, *Journal of a Lady of Quality: Being a Narrative of a Journey from Scotland to the West Indies, North Carolina, and Portugal in the Years 1774 to 1776*, ed. E. W. Andrews (New Haven, 1934); Richard Twiss, *Travels Through Portugal and Spain in 1772 and 1773* (London, 1775). Three fascinating and beautifully written accounts of the period after the fall of Pombal are William Beckford, *The Journal of William Beckford in Portugal and Spain, 1787–1788*, ed. Boyde Alexander (London, 1954); Henry Fielding, *The Journal of a Voyage to*

Lisbon, ed. Austin Dobson (Oxford, 1907); and Robert Southey, *Letters Written During a Short Residence in Spain and Portugal*, 2nd edition (Bristol, 1799). This latter work contains an interesting paper "written by a Portuguese Secretary of State" on the setting up of a Free Port at Lisbon. Fielding's *Journal* was his last work for he died in Lisbon during October 1754 and was buried in the British cemetery there. For Spanish visitors to Portugal in this period there is *Viajentes espanhoes em Portugal: textos do século XVIII publicados e prefáciados por Fidelino de Figueiredo* (São Paulo, 1947).

An extremely rare and valuable picture of Brazil with comments of importance on free-masonry, law processes, colonial society, is contained in the observant and intelligent writing of Thomas Lindley, *Narrative of a Voyage to Brazil Terminating in the Seizure of a British Vessel and the Imprisonment of the Author and the Ship's Crew by the Portuguese with General Sketches of the Country, its Natural Productions, Colonial Inhabitants, etc. and a Description of the City and Provinces of St. Salvador and Porto Seguro* (London, 1805).

Great lacunae remain concerning Pombal. We still know very little about the man himself, his family, and even less about the Court and the enigmatic Dom José I, without whose acquiescence (or passivity) Pombal would have achieved nothing. We need to know more about Portuguese actions in Africa and Asia in this period despite the work of Fritz Hoppe, *A África oriental portuguesa no tempo do marquês de Pombal 1750–1777* (Lisbon, 1970) and António Carreira, *As companhias pombalinas* (Lisbon, 1983) though Joseph Miller's monumental study *Way of Death: Merchant Capitalism and the Angolan Slave Trade 1730–1830* (Madison, WI, 1988) has opened important new vistas in the area of Portuguese activities in Africa. There is a paucity of serious studies of the international influences or connections during the Pombaline period, especially in so far as these had a direct role in Pombal's measures. These were, however, surprisingly extensive and a potential topic for some interesting comparative work. Some preliminary indications of these interactions can be seen in *Pombal revisitado* I (Lisbon, 1982), pp. 287–306 and in Rómulo de Carvalho's remarkable *História do gabinete de física da Universidade de Coimbra* (Coimbra, 1978). The reform of the University of Coimbra was of particular interest to Spanish reformers, as can be seen in the correspondence between Cenáculo and the count of Aguilar in Sevilla and Campomanes in Madrid. António Mestre, *Ilustración y reforma de la Iglesia: pensamiento político religioso de Don Gregorio Mayans y Siscar (1699–1781)* (Valencia, 1968), appendix documental no. 9, pp. 495–497. Also, Claude-Henri Frèches, *Voltaire, Malagrida et Pombal* (Paris, 1969). For an excellent account of Ribeiro Sanches' career, see "António Ribeiro Sanches, élève de Boerhaave, et son importance pour la Russie," by David Willemse is to be found in *Janus: Revue internationale de l'histoire des sciences, et de la médecine, de la pharmacie et de la technique*, VI, supplements (Leiden, 1966). We have little available on the bureaucracy and the state apparatus, however, despite the fact that Pombal's action was to make the state all-encompassing and monopolistic in its power. The vast body of Pombaline legislation is rarely examined for what it says about the motivations and justification for the reforms codified. The most comprehensive attempt to look at the ideological context of Pombaline legislation and action is that of Francisco José Calazans Falcon in his *A época pombalina: política econômica e monarquia ilustrada* (São Paulo, 1982), especially his final chapter, "A prática do pombalismo," pp. 369–445. Calazans Falcon's analysis of the legislation of the Pombaline epoch is based on the collection at the Academy of Sciences in Lisbon organized by Francisco Trigoso de Arajão Morato.

We know little in detail about the households of the aristocracy. However, the work in progress by Nuno Gonçalo Monteiro will soon remedy this deficiency (Nuno Gonçalo

Monteiro, "Notas sobre nobreza, fidalguia e titulares nos finais do Antigo Regime," *Ler História* 10 (1987), and "O poder senhorial," in José Mattoso, *História de Portugal*, 8 vols. [Lisbon, 1994], IV, pp. 333–379). It is also clear that we need a new look at literary production during this period, both high and low, though here a new generation of Portuguese historians is beginning to delve into the enormously rich archival material of the Pombaline regime with obsessive categorization and inventories providing what must be one of Europe's richest bodies of material on libraries, books, censorship decisions, and socio-economic data, most of it still awaiting modern analysis. The whole propaganda effort of the Portuguese in this period, for instance, cries out for attention. Some indication of the importance of this propaganda effort can be seen in the activity of Niccolò Pagliarini, a Roman printer who secretly published anti-Jesuit materials for Ambassador Almada and later escaped from Rome to Portugal via Naples with the assistance of the Neapolitan chief minister Tanucci, to become official printer to the king and Pombal in Lisbon (Samuel Miller, *Portugal and Rome*, pp. 117–119, 122–125); the work of the anti-Jesuit pamphleteer, the Abbé Platel (also known as P. Parisot or Père Norbert), described in Miller, *Portugal and Rome*, pp. 73, 111–113, 117, 122, and Claude Michaud, "Un anti-Jésuite au service de Pombal," *Pombal revisitado* 1, pp. 389–401; and the publications of the University Press of Coimbra founded by Pombal in 1772 (José Antunes, "Notas sobre o sentido ideológico da reforma pombalina: a propósito de alguns documentos da imprensa da Universidade de Coimbra," *RHDI/M de P* 2, pp. 143–197.

Bibliography

ARCHIVAL SOURCES

AHN, Madrid, state file 4536 (2)

AHU, Lisbon, codex 311, appendices 15, 16, 17

codices 297, 298, 299, 306

codex 610, fos. 30–31

ANRJ, files 86/3, 94/2, 99/3

ANTT, Lisbon, Min Jus M22, vol. 417

BNL, fundo geral, codex 875

BNLCP, Lisbon, codex 51, fo. 178v

codex 94, fos. 24, 24v, 25v, 46v

codices 165, 167, 342, 343

codex 453, fos. 47–50v, 96–112, 275–290, 291–294, 328–333, 336–339, 391–393, 395–398

codices 444, 446, 454

codex 454

codex 455, fos. 27, 69, 349–350

codex 456, fos. 44, 138, 340

codex 458, fos. 147–148

codex 611, fos. 262–266, 383

codex 612, fos. 61, 62–64

codex 638, fo. 210

codex 640, fos. 20–23

codex 643, fos. 204–218

codex 691, fo. 2

codex 695, fos. 11–12, 36

codex 704, fos. 27–30, 87–89

BNRJ/C dos C, 1-1-25

IHGB, file 8, doc. 26

file 71, doc. 17

IHGB/AUC, 1-1-8, fos. 18, 43, 290–309

1-2-11, fos. 31, 47

1-2-39, fo. 69

PRO/FO, 63/20

PRO/SP, 89/47, fo. 109

89/47, fo. 145

PRINTED PRIMARY SOURCES

Accioli de Cerqueira e Silva, Coronel Ignácio, *Memórias históricas e políticas da província da Bahia*, ed. Bahia: Brás do Amaral. 6 vols., 1919–1940.

Annual Register for 1758 (London)

Annual Register for 1770 (London)

Avila, Affonso, ed., *Resíduos seiscentistas em Minas (textos do século do ouro e as projeções do mundo barroco)*. 2 vols. Belo Horizonte: 1967.

Azeredo Coutinho, J. J. da Cunha de, *Obras económicas*, ed. Sergio Buarque de Holanda. São Paulo: 1966.

Azevedo, Pedro de, ed., *O processo dos Távoras*. Lisbon: Biblioteca Nacional, 1921.

Balbi, Adrien, *Essai statistique sur le royaume de Portugal et d'Algarve*. 2 vols. Paris: 1822.

Variétés politico-statistiques sur la monarchie portugaise. Paris: 1822.

Barreiros, José Baptista, *Correspondência inédita entre o conde da Barca e José Egídio Alvares de Almeida, secretário particular de El Rei D. João VI.* Lisbon: 1962.

Barrow, John, *Life and Correspondence of Sir William Sidney Smith.* 2 vols. London: 1848.

Beckford, William, *The Journal of William Beckford in Portugal and Spain 1787–1788*, ed. Boyde Alexander. London: 1954.

Betencourt, José de Sá, *Memória sobre a plantação dos Algodoes.* Lisbon: 1798.

Biefeld, le Baron de, *Institutions politiques.* 2 vols. Leiden: 1767.

Bourgoing, Jean François, *Voyage du ci-devant duc du Châtelet en Portugal . . .* 2 vols. Paris: 1798–1808.

Brelim, Johan, *De passagem pelo Brasil e Portugal em 1756*, translation from Swedish by Carlos Perição de Almeida. Lisbon: 1955.

Byron, John, *A Voyage Round the World in His Majesty's Ship "Delphin" Commanded by the Honurable Commodore Byron*, 2nd edition. London: 1767.

Caeiro, Francisco da Gama, *D. Frei Manuel do Cenáculo: aspectos da sua actuação filosófica.* Lisbon: 1559.

Caeiro, José, s.j., *História da expulsão da Companhia de Jesus da província de Portugal (século XVIII)* vol. 1. Lisbon: 1991.
Primeira publicação após 160 anos do manuscrito inédito de José Caeiro sobre os Jesuítas do Brasil e da India na perseguição do marquês de Pombal. Bahia: 1936.

Caldas, José António, *Noticia geral de toda esta capitania da Bahia desde o seu descobrimiento até o presente anno de 1759.* Facsimile. Bahia: 1949.

Carneiro de Mendonça, Marcos, *A Amazônia na era pombalina: correspondência inédita do governador e capitão-general do estado do Grão Pará e Maranhão, Francisco Xavier de Mendonça Furtado, 1751–1759.* 3 vols. Rio de Janeiro: 1963.
Aula do comércio, documentos do arquivo do Cosme Velho. Rio de Janeiro: 1982.
O marquês de Pombal e o Brasil. São Paulo: 1960.

Collecção dos negocios de Roma no reino de El-Rei Dom José 1755–1759, 1760–1769, 1769–1774, 1774–1776 (3 parts and addendum). Lisbon: 1874, 1875.

Cortesão, Jaime, ed., *Alexandre de Gusmão e o Tratado de Madrid.* 9 vols. Rio de Janeiro: 1950–1963.

Costigan, Arthur William, *Sketches of Society and Manners in Portugal* 2 vols. London: 1787.

Croft, John, *A Treatise on the Wines of Portugal.* Oporto: Instituto do Vinho do Porto, 1940 (facsimile of 1788 edition).

Dalrymple, Major William, *Travels Through Spain and Portugal in 1774.* London: 1777.

Daupias d'Alcochete, Nuno, *Humanismo e diplomacia: correspondência literária (1789–1804) de Francisco José Maria de Brito com Dom Frei Manuel do Cenáculo.* Paris: 1976.

Descriptive List of the State Papers of Portugal 1661–1780. 3 vols. Lisbon: 1979.

Digges, Thomas Atwood, *Adventures of Alonso Containing Some Striking Anecdotes of the Present Prime Minister of Portugal.* 2 vols. London: 1775. Facsimile by United States Catholic Historical Society, monograph series 18, New York: 1943.

Eckart, Anselmo, *Memórias de um Jesuíta, prisioneiro de Pombal.* Lisbon: 1987.

Fielding, Henry, *The Journal of a Voyage to Lisbon*, ed. Austin Dobson. Oxford: 1907.

Gonzaga, Thomas António, *Obras completas*, ed. M. Rodrigues Lapa. 2 vols. Rio de Janeiro: 1957.

Gorani, José, *Portugal, a corte e o país nos anos de 1765 a 1767.* Lisbon: 1944.

Goudar, Ange, *Relations historiques du tremblement de terre . . .* The Hague: 1756.

Guerra, Luís de Bivar, *Inventário e sequestro da casa de Aveiro em 1759*. Lisbon: 1952.

Hansard, T. C., *The Parliamentary History of England from the Earliest Period to the Year 1803*, XV. London: 1818.

História dos establecimientos scientificos, literarios, e artisticos de Portugal nos successivos reinados da monarchia I. Lisbon: 1871.

Instrucções inéditas de D. Luís da Cunha a Marco António de Azevedo Coutinho, ed. Pedro de Azevedo with a preface by António Baião. Coimbra: 1929.

Keene, Sir Benjamin, *The Private Correspondence of Sir Benjamin Keene*, ed. Sir Richard Lodge. Cambridge: 1933.

King, Charles, *The British Merchant*, 3rd edition. 3 vols. London: 1748.

Koster, Henry, *Travels in Brazil*, 2nd edition. 2 vols. London: 1817.

Lindley, Thomas, *Authentic Narrative of a Voyage from the Cape of Good Hope to the Brazils . . . in 1802, 1803 . . .* 2nd edition. London: 1808.

Lingham, Edward James. "Vindicae Lusitanae, or An Answer to a Pamphlet Entitled The Causes and Consequences of the Late Emigration to the Brazils." Pamphlet. London: 1808.

Luz Soriano, José da, *História do reinado de El Rei D. José I e da administração do marquês de Pombal*. 2 vols. Lisbon: 1867.

Mably, Abbé de, *De la legislation ou principes des loix*. Amsterdam: 1786.

Remarks Concerning the Government and Laws of the United States of America. London: 1795.

Marcadé, J., *Frei Manuel do Cenáculo Vilas Boas de Beja. Archevêque d'Evora*. Paris: 1978.

Monteiro de Campos, Roberto, ed., *Sistema, ou collecção dos regimentos reaes, contem os regimentos pertencentes a fazenda real, justiças, e militares . . .*, IV. Lisbon: 1783.

Murphy, James, *Travels in Portugal*. London: 1767.

Observations on a Pamphlet Lately Published, Entitled the Genuine and Legal Sentence Pronounced by the High Court of Judicature of Portugal upon the Conspirators against the Life of His Most Faithful Majesty . . . by William Shirley Late of Lisbon, Merchant. London: 1759.

Occasional Thoughts on the Portuguese Trade and the Inexpediency of Supporting the House of Braganza on the Throne of Portugal. London: 1767.

Pombal, marquês de, *Catálogo bibliográfico e iconográfico*, ed. António Barreto. Lisbon: 1982.

Punch, *Punch's Politiks*. London: 1762.

Ratton, Jacome, *Recordações . . . sobre ocorrências do seu tempo em Portugal . . . 1747 . . . [até] 1810*, 2nd edition, ed. J. M. Teixeira de Carvalho. Coimbra: 1920.

Raynal, Abbé. *Histoire philosophique et politique des establissements et du commerce des Européens dans les deux Indes*. 4 vols. Amsterdam: 1770.

The Revolution of America. London: 1781.

Riscos das obras da universidade de Coimbra [by William Elsden]. Coimbra: 1983.

Rebelo da Costa, Agostinho, *Descripção topográfica e história da cidade do Porto*. Oporto: 1787.

Relação geral do estado da universidade, 1777. Coimbra: 1983.

Robertson, William, *The History of America*, 12th edition. 4 vols. London: 1812.

Rodrigues de Brito, João, *Memórias políticas sobre as verdadeiras bases da grandeza das nações e principalmente Portugal*. Lisbon: 1821.

Rodrigues de Brito, João et al., *Cartas económico-políticas sobre a agricultura e comércio da Bahia*. Lisbon: 1821.

Rodrigues Lapa, M., *Vida e obra de Alvarenga Peixoto*. Rio de Janeiro: 1960.

Say, Jean-Baptiste, *A Treatise on Political Economy or the Production, Distribution, and Consumption of Wealth*, trans. C. R. Prinsep, 4th edition. Philadelphia: 1830.

Schaw, Janet, *Journal of a Lady of Quality . . . 1774 to 1776*. New Haven: 1934.

Silva Lisboa, Balthezar de, *Discurso histórico, político, e económico dos progressos e estado actual de filosofia natural português . . .* Lisbon: 1786.

Smith, Adam, *An Inquiry into the Nature and Causes of the Wealth of Nations*. 3 vols. Edinburgh: 1811.

Sousa, Manoel de Barros, and L. A. Rebello da Silva, eds., *Quadro elementar das relações políticas e diplomáticas de Portugal com as diversas potencias do mundo*, XVIII. Lisbon and Paris: 1860.

Southey, Robert, *Journal of a Residence in Portugal 1800–1801*, ed. A. Cabral. Oxford: 1900.

 Letters Written During a Short Residence in Spain and Portugal, 2nd edition. Bristol: 1799.

Staunton, George, *An Authentic Account of an Embassy from the King of Great Britain to the Emperor of China*, 2nd edition. 3 vols. London: 1798.

Twiss, Richard, *Travels through Portugal and Spain, 1772, 1773*. London: 1775.

Vilhena, Luís dos Santos, *Recopilação de notícias soteropolitanas e brasílicas (1802) contidas em XX cartas*, ed. Brás do Amaral. 3 vols. Bahia: 1922–1935.

A Voyage Round the World: Performed by the Order of His Most Christian Majesty in the Years 1766, 1767, 1768, 1769, by Lewis de Bougainville, translated from the French by John Reinhold Forster. London: 1772.

SECONDARY SOURCES

Books

Aguiar, Pinto de, *Bancos no Brasil colonial*. Bahia: 1960.

Alden, Dauril, *Royal Government in Colonial Brazil*. Berkeley and Los Angeles: 1968.

 (ed.) *The Colonial Roots of Modern Brazil*. Berkeley and Los Angeles: 1973.

Almeida, Fortunato de, *História da igreja em Portugal*. 3 vols. Coimbra: 1922.

Almeida, José d', *Vice-reinado de D. Luís d'Almeida Portugal, marquês de Lavradio*. São Paulo: 1941.

Amzalak, Moses Bensabat, *Do estudo e da evolução das doutrinas económicas em Portugal*. Lisbon: 1928.

Antunes, Manuel, *et al.*, *Como interpretar Pombal*. 2 vols. Lisbon: 1982.

Antunes de Moura, Américo Brasiliense, *Govêrno do morgado de Mateus no vice-reinado do conde da Cunha: São Paulo restaurado*. São Paulo: 1938.

Arruda, José Jacobson de Andrade, *O Brasil no comércio colonial 1796–1808*. São Paulo: 1972.

Azevedo, J. Lúcio d', *Estudos de história paraense*. Pará: 1893.

 Os Jesuítas no Grão Pará, suas missões e a colonização. Lisbon: 1901.

 O marquês de Pombal e a sua época, 2nd edition. Lisbon: 1922.

Azevedo, Thales de, *Povoamento da cidade do Salvador*, 2nd edition. São Paulo: 1955.

Bandeira, Manuel, *Guia de Ouro Prêto*. Rio de Janeiro: 1938.

Banha de Andrade, António Alberto, *Vernei e a cultura do seu tempo*. Coimbra: 1966.

 A reforma pombalina dos estudos secundários no Brasil. São Paulo: 1978.

 Vernei e a projecção da sua obra. Lisbon: 1980.

 Contributos para a história da mentalidade pedagógica portuguesa. Lisbon: 1982.

Barros, Carlos Vitorino de Silva, *Real fábrica de vidros da Marinha Grande*. Lisbon: 1969.

Bazin, Germain, *L'Architecture religieuse baroque au Brésil*. 2 vols. Paris: 1956.

Beales, Derek, *Joseph II*, II: *In the Shadow of Maria Theresa 1741–1780*. Cambridge: 1987.

Beirão, Caetano, *D. Maria I, 1772–1792*, 3rd edition. Lisbon: 1944.

Bellotto, Heloísa Liberalli, *Autoridade e conflito no Brasil colonial: o governo do morgado de Mateus em São Paulo*. São Paulo: 1979.

Birmingham, David, *A Concise History of Portugal*. Cambridge: 1993.

Blanning, T. C. W., *Joseph II and Enlightened Despotism*. London: 1970.

Borges de Macedo, Jorge, *A situação económica no tempo de Pombal*. Oporto: 1951.

    Problemas de história da indústria portuguesa no século XVIII. Lisbon: 1963.

Boxer, C. R., *Some Contemporary Reactions to the Lisbon Earthquake of 1755*. Lisbon: 1956.

    Salvador de Sá and the Struggle for Brazil and Angola. Oxford: 1960.

    The Golden Age of Brazil 1695–1750. Berkeley and Los Angeles: 1962.

    The Portuguese Seaborne Empire, 1415–1825. Oxford: 1963.

    Race Relations in the Portuguese Colonial Empire, 1415–1825. Oxford: 1963.

Braga, Joaquim Theophilo Fernandes, *História da universidade de Coimbra*. III. Lisbon: 1898.

Brotéria, no bicentenário do marquês de Pombal. 2 vols. Lisbon: 1982.

Calazans Falcon, Francisco José, *A época pombalina: política, econômica e monarquia ilustrada*. São Paulo: 1982.

Calogeras, João Padia, *As minas do Brasil e sua legislação*. 3 vols. Rio de Janeiro: 1904–1905.

Câmara Municipal de Cascais, *A real fábrica de lanifícios de Cascais*. Cascais: 1964.

Capistrano de Abreu, *Capítulos de história colonial, 1500–1800*, 4th edition. Rio de Janeiro: 1954.

Carnaxide, Visconde de, *O Brasil na administração pombalina*. São Paulo: 1940.

Carneiro de Mendonça, Marcos, *O intendente Câmara, Manuel Ferreira da Câmara Bethencourt e Sá, intendente geral das Minas e diamantes 1764–1835*. São Paulo: 1958.

Carrato, José Ferreira, *As Minas Gerais e os primórdios do Carraca*. São Paulo: 1963.

    Igreja, iluminismo, e escolas mineiras coloniais. São Paulo: 1968.

Carreira, António, *As companhias pombalinas de Grão-Pará e Maranhão e Pernambuco e Paraíba*. Lisbon: 1983.

Carvalho, Rómulo de, *História da fundação do Colégio Real dos Nobres de Lisboa 1761–1772*. Coimbra: 1959.

    Relações entre Portugal e Rússia no século XVII. Lisbon: 1979.

    A física experimental em Portugal no século XVIII. Lisbon: 1982.

Carvalho Dias, Luís Fernando de, *A relação das fábricas de 1788*. Coimbra: 1955.

Cheke, Marcus, *Dictator of Portugal: A Life of the Marquis of Pombal 1699–1782*. London: 1938.

Conde de Carnota (John A. Smith), *Marquis of Pombal*, 2nd edition. 2 vols. London: 1871.

Costa Filho, Miguel, *A cana de açúcar em Minas Gerais*. Rio de Janeiro: 1963.

Dardel, Pierre, *Navires et marchandises dans les ports de Rouen et du Havre au XVIIIe siècle*. Paris: 1963.

Daupias d'Alcochete, Nuno, *Bourgeoisie pombaline et noblesse libérale au Portugal*. Paris: 1969.

Delaforce, John, *The Factory House*. London: 1983

Dornas, Filho, João, *O ouro das Gerais e a civilização da capitania*. São Paulo: 1957.

Dourado, Meunas, *Hipólito da Costa e o correio brasiliense*. 2 vols. Rio de Janeiro: 1957.

Duarte, A. de Calazans, *Os Stephens na indústria vidreira nacional*. Figueira da Foz: 1937.

    A indústria vidreira na marinha grande. Lisbon: 1942.

Edwards, Michael M., *The Growth of the British Cotton Trade 1631–1801*. Manchester: 1967.

Ellis, Myriam, *O abastecimento da capitania das Minas Gerais no século XVIII*. São Paulo: 1951.
  O monopólio do sal no Estado de Brasil, 1631–1801. São Paulo: 1955.
  Aspectos da pesca da baleia no Brasil colonial. São Paulo: 1959.
Felicio dos Santos, Joaquim, *Memórias do distrito diamantino da comarca do Serro Frio*, 3rd edition. Rio de Janeiro: 1956.
Fernandez, António Paulo Cyraro, *Missionários jesuítas no Brasil no tempo de Pombal*. Porto Alegre: 1936.
Ferrand d'Almeida, Luís, *A propósito do testamento político de D. Luís da Cunha*. Coimbra: 1948.
Ferreira Reis, Arthur Cezar, *A Amazônia que os Portugueses revelaram*. Rio de Janeiro: 1956.
Fisher, H. E .S., *The Portugal Trade*. London: 1971.
Fortunato Queirós, Francisco, *A real fábrica de lanifícios de Portalegre em 1781*. Portalegre: 1981.
França, José-Augusto, *Une ville des Lumières: la Lisbonne de Pombal*. Paris: 1965.
  A reconstrução de Lisboa e a arquitectura pombalina. Lisbon: 1981.
Francis, A. David, *The Methuens and Portugal, 1691–1708*. London: 1966.
  Portugal, 1715–1808: Joanine, Pombaline, and Rococo Portugal as seen by British Diplomats and Traders. London: 1985.
Frieiro, Eduardo, *O diabo na livraria do cônego*. Belo Horizonte: 1957.
Freitas, Caio de, *George Canning e o Brasil*. 2 vols. São Paulo: 1958.
Hamilton, Earl J., *War and Prices in Spain, 1651–1800*. Cambridge, MA: 1947.
Hansen, Carl A., *Economy and Society in Baroque Portugal 1668–1703*. Minneapolis: 1981.
Harlow, Vincent T., *The Founding of the Second British Empire 1763–1793*. 2 vols. London: 1952, 1964.
Hoppe, Fritz, *A África oriental portuguesa no tempo do marquês de Pombal (1750–1777)*. Lisbon: 1960.
Kendrick, T. D., *The Lisbon Earthquake of 1755*. London: 1956.
Koebner, Richard, *Empire*, 2nd edition. New York: 1961.
Kubler, George and Martin Soria, *Art and Architecture in Spain and Portugal and their American Dominions 1500–1800*. Harmondsworth: 1959.
Langlans, Franz-Paul, *As corporações dos ofícios mecânicos: subsídios para a sua história com um estudo do Marcello Caetano*. 2 vols. Lisbon: 1943.
Leite, Serafim, *História da companhia de Jesus no Brasil*. 10 vols. Lisbon and Rio de Janeiro: 1938–1950.
Lima Junior, Augusto de, *A capitania das Minas Gerais, origens e formação*, 3rd edition. Belo Horizonte: 1965.
Livermore, Harold, ed., *Portugal and Brazil: An Introduction*. Oxford: 1963.
  A Short History of Portugal, 2nd edition. Cambridge: 1975.
Luz Soriano, Simão José da, *História da guerra civil*. Rio de Janeiro: 1938.
Lynch, John, *Spanish Colonial Administration*. London: 1958.
Machado Filho, Aires da Mota, *O negro e o garimpo em Minas Gerais*, 2nd edition. Rio de Janeiro: 1964.
Magalhães Godinho, Vitorino, *Prix et Monnaies au Portugal 1750–1850*. Paris: 1955.
Manchester, Alan K., *British Preëminence in Brazil*. Chapel Hill: 1933.
Mattoso, José, ed., *História de Portugal*. 8 vols. Lisbon: 1994.
Mauro, Frédéric, *Le Portugal et l'Atlantique au XVIIe siècle 1570–1670*. Paris: 1960.
Maxwell, Kenneth, *Conflicts and Conspiracies: Brazil and Portugal, 1750–1808*. Cambridge: 1973.

Miller, Joseph C., *Way of Death: Merchant Capitalism and the Angolan Slave Trade, 1730–1830*. Madison, WI: 1988.

Miller, Samuel J., *Portugal and Rome c. 1748–1830: An Aspect of the Catholic Enlightenment*. Rome: 1978.

Morineau, Michel, *Incroyables gazettes et fabuleux métaux*. Cambridge/Paris: 1985.

Mörner, Magnus, *The Expulsion of the Jesuits from Latin America*. New York: 1965.

Mota, Carlos Guilherme, *Brasil em perspectiva*. São Paulo: 1968.

Atitudes de inovação no Brasil, 1789–1801. Lisbon: n.d.

Novais, Fernando A., *Portugal e Brasil na crise do antigo sistema colonial (1770–1808)*. São Paulo: 1978.

Nóvoa, António, *Le Temps des professeurs, analyse socio-historique de la profession enseignante au Portugal (XVIII–XX siècle)*. 2 vols. Lisbon: 1987.

Noya Pinto, Virgílio, *O ouro brasileiro e o comércio anglo-português*, 2nd edition. São Paulo: 1979.

Nunes Dias, Manuel, *A Companhia Geral do Grão Pará e Maranhão (1755–1778)*. 2 vols. Pará: 1970.

Oliveira, Fernando de, *O motim popular de 1757: uma página na história da epoca pombalina*. Oporto: 1930.

Palmer, R. R., *The Age of Democratic Revolution*. 2 vols. Princeton: 1959, 1964.

Pares, Richard, *War and Trade in the West Indies 1739–1763*. London: 1936.

Pereira, Angelo, *D. João VI, príncipe e rei: a retirada da família real para o Brasil*. Lisbon: 1953.

Pinto, Ercília, *O marquês de Pombal, lavrador e autodidacta em Souré*. Coimbra: 1967.

Porto, Aurélio, *História das missões orientais do Uruguai*. Rio de Janeiro: 1943.

Jesuítas no sul do Brasil. Porto Alegre: 1954.

Prado Junior, Caio, *A formação do Brasil contemporâneo*, 7th edition. São Paulo: 1963.

Ramos de Carvalho, Laerte, *As reformas pombalinas de instrução pública*. São Paulo: 1978.

Redford, Arthur, *Manchester Merchants and Foreign Trade, 1794–1858*. Manchester: 1934.

Ribeiro Júnior, José, *Colonização e monopólio no nordeste Brasileiro: a Companhia Geral do Pernambuco e Paraíba (1759–1780)*. São Paulo: 1976.

Rizzini, Carlos, *Hypólito da Costa e o correio brasiliense*. São Paulo: 1957.

Russell-Wood, A. J. R., *Fidalgos and Philanthropists: The Santa Casa da Misericórdia of Bahia, 1650–1755*. Berkeley and Los Angeles: 1968.

Ruy, Affonso, *A primeira revolução social brasileira*. São Paulo: 1942.

Santos Filho, Lycurgo, *Uma comunidade rural do Brasil antigo, aspectos da vida patriarcal no sertão da Bahia nos séculos XVIII e XIX*. São Paulo: 1956.

Saraiva, António José, *Inquisição a Cristãos-Novos*, 4th edition. Oporto: 1969.

Saraiva, José Mendes da Cunha, *Companhia Geral de Pernambuco e Paraíba*. Lisbon: 1940.

Schneider, Susan, *O marquês de Pombal e o vinho do Porto; dependência e subdesenvolvimento em Portugal no século XVIII*. Lisbon: 1980.

Schumpeter, Elizabeth Boody, *English Overseas Statistics*. Oxford: 1960.

Schuyler, R. L., *The Fall of the Old Colonial System*. New York: 1945.

Scott, H. M., *British Foreign Policy in the Age of the American Revolution*. Oxford: 1990.

ed., *Enlightened Absolutism: Reform and Reformers in the Later Eighteenth Century*. London: 1990.

Serrão, Joel, ed., *Dicionário de história de Portugal*. 7 vols. Lisbon: 1965.

Sideri, Sandro, *Trade and Power: Informal Colonialism in Anglo-Portuguese Relations*. Rotterdam: 1970.

Silbert, Albert, *Do Portugal de antigo regime ao Portugal oitocentista*. Lisbon: 1977.

Simonsen, Roberto C., *História econômica do Brasil 1500–1820*, 5th edition. São Paulo: 1967.

Smith, John Athelstone, *The Marquis of Pombal*. 2 vols. London: 1843.

Sombra, Severino, *História monetária do Brasil colonial*. Rio de Janeiro: 1938.

Sousa, Octavio Tarquinio de, *História dos fundadores do império do Brasil*, 1. Rio de Janeiro: 1960.

Sutherland, Lucy S., *A London Merchant 1695–1774*. Oxford: 1933.

Teixeira de Salles, Fritz, *Associações religiosas no ciclo do ouro*. Belo Horizonte: 1963.

Torres, João Camillo de Oliveira, *História de Minas Gerais*. 5 vols. Belo Horizonte: 1962.

Trinidade, Cônego Raimundo, *São Francisco de Assis de Ouro Prêto*. Rio de Janeiro: 1951.

Vasconcellos, Sylvio de, *Vila rica, formação e desenvolvimento, residências*. Rio de Janeiro: 1956.

Verger, Pierre, *Bahia and the Western African Trade*. Ibadan: 1964.
  Flux et reflux de la traite des nègres entre le golfe de Bénin et Bahia de Todos os Santos du dix-septième au dix-neuvième siècle. Paris: 1966.

Veríssimo, Ignácio José, *Pombal, os Jesuítas e o Brasil*. Rio de Janeiro: 1961.

Veríssimo Serrão, Joaquim, *O marquês de Pombal: o homem, o diplomata, e o estadista*. Lisbon: 1982.

Viveiros, Jeronimo de, *História do comércio do Maranhão, 1612–1898*. 2 vols. São Luís: 1964.

Walford, A. R., *The British Factory*. Lisbon: 1940.

Zemella, Mafalda, *O abastecimento da capitania das Minas Gerais no século XVIII*. São Paulo: 1951.

Articles

Alden, Dauril, "Manuel Luís Vieira: an Entrepreneur in Rio de Janeiro during Brazil's Agricultural Renaissance." *HAHR* 39 (November 1959): 521–537.
  "The Population of Brazil in the Late Eighteenth Century." *HAHR* 43 (1963): 173–205.
  "Yankee Sperm Whales in Brazilian Waters and the Decline of the Portuguese Whale Fisher, 1773–1801." *The Americas* 20 (1964): 267–288.
  "The Growth and Decline of Indigo Production in Colonial Brazil: A Study in Comparative Economic History." *Journal of Economic History* 25 (1965): 35–60.
  "Economic Aspects of the Expulsion of the Jesuits from Brazil: A Preliminary Report." In *Conflict and Continuity in Brazilian History*, ed. Henry H. Keith and S. F. Edwards, 25–65. Columbia, SC: 1969.
  "The Significance of Cacao Production in the Amazon Region During the Late Colonial Period: An Essay in Comparative Economic History." *Proceedings of the American Philosophical Society* 12, 2 (April 1976): 103–128.

Antunes de Moura, Américo Brasiliense, "Govêrno do morgado de Mateus no vicereinado do conde da Cunha: S. Paulo restaurado." *Revista do Arquivo Municipal* 52 (1938): 9–155.

Borges de Macedo, Jorge, "Portugal e a economia 'pombalina': temas e hipóteses." *RHSP* 19 (July–September 1954).

Bourdon, Léon, "Trois Lusitaniens à Paris au début de la révolution française." *BEP* (July 1790–April 1791): 107–160.

Boxer, C. R., "Brazilian Gold and British Traders in the First Half of the Eighteenth Century." *HAHR* 49, 3 (August 1969): 455–472.

Braga Santos, Piedade, "Actividade da real mesa censória: uma sondagem." *Cultura, História, e Filosofia* 2 (1983): 377–440.

Brasio, D. António, "Os projectos para a navigabilidade do Tejo." *Ciências* 24, 2 (1959).

Brown, Vera Lee, "The Relations of Spain and Portugal 1763–1777." *Smith College Studies in History* 15 (October 1929–January 1930): 70–71.

Bulção Sobrinho, António de Araujo de Aragão, "O patriarcha da liberdade Bahiana, Joaquim Inácio de Sequeira Bulção." *RIHGB* 217 (1952): 167–185.

Burns, E. Bradford, "The Enlightenment in Two Colonial Libraries." *Journal of the History of Ideas* 25 (1964): 430–438.

"The Role of Azeredo Coutinho in the Enlightenment of Brazil." *HAHR* 44 (May 1964): 145–160.

Cabral de Moncada, L., "O século XVIII na legislação de Pombal." *Estudos de História do Direito* (1948).

Calazans Falcon, Francisco J. [and Fernando A. Novais], "A extinção da escravatura africana em Portugal no quadro da política económica pombalina." *Anais do VI simpósio nacional dos professôres universitários de história*, 405–431. São Paulo: 1973.

Cardoso, Manoel, "The Brazilian Gold Rush." *The Americas* 3, 2 (1946): 137–160.

"Another Document on the Inconfidência Mineira." *HAHR* 32 (1952): 540–551.

"Tithes in Colonial Minas Gerais." *Catholic Historical Review* 38 (1952): 175–182.

"Azeredo Coutinho and the Intellectual Ferment of His Times." In *Conflict and Continuity in Brazilian History*, ed. Henry H. Keith and S. F. Edwards, 148–183. Columbia, SC: 1969.

Chapman, A. B. Wallis, "The Commercial Relations of England and Portugal 1487–1807." *TRHS* 3rd series, 1 (1907): 157–179.

Christelow, Allan, "Economic Background to the Anglo-Spanish War of 1762." *Journal of Modern History* 18 (1946): 22–36.

"Great Britain and the Trades from Cadiz and Lisbon to Spanish America and Brazil 1759–1782." *HAHR* 27 (February 1947): 2–29.

Daupias d'Alcochete, Nuno, "Lettres familières de Jacques Ratton 1792–1807." *BEP* 23 (1961): 118–251.

"Lettres de Jacques Ratton à António de Araujo de Azevedo, Comte de Barca 1812–1817." *BEP* 25 (1964): 137–256.

Davidson, David M., "How the Brazilian West Was Won: Freelance and State on the Mato Grosso Frontier, ca. 1737–1752." In *The Colonial Roots of Modern Brazil*, ed. Dauril Alden, 61–106. Berkeley and Los Angeles: 1973.

Delson, Roberta M., "Planners and Reformers: Urban Architects of Late Eighteenth Century Brazil." *Eighteenth Century Studies* 10, 1 (Fall 1976): 40–51.

Ellis, Myriam, "A pesca da baleia no Brasil colonial." *Anais do Congresso Comemorativo do Bicentenário da Transferência da Sede do Governo do Brasil da Cidade do Salvador para o Rio de Janeiro* 71 (1959): 89–90.

Ferrand d'Almeida, Luís, "A fábrica de vidros de Marinha Grande em 1774." *Revista Portuguesa da História* 18 (1980).

"Problemas do comércio luso-espanhol nos meados do século XVIII." *RHES* 8 (July–December 1981): 95–131.

Ferrão, António, "O marquês de Pombal e os meninos de Palhavã." *Academia das Ciências de Lisboa, Estudos Pombalinos* 1 (1923).

Ferreira da Rocha, José Alvaro and Manuela F. Marques Rocha, "A Companhia do Grão-Pará e Maranhão." *História e Sociedade* 10 (1982): 43–72.

Fisher, H. E. S., "Anglo-Portuguese Trade 1700–1770." *EcHR* 2nd series, 16 (1963).

Graham, Richard, "Slave Families on a Rural Estate in Colonial Brazil." *JSH* 9, 3 (Spring 1976): 382–402.

Hansen, Carol A., "D. Luís da Cunha and Portuguese Mercantilist Thought." *JAPS* 15 (1981).

Lamego, Alberto, "Os sete povos das missões." *Revista do Património Histórico e Artístico Nacional* (1940): 55–81.

Lodge, Richard, "The English Factory at Lisbon." *TRHS* 4th series, 16 (1933): 220–226.

Lugar, Catherine, "The Portuguese Tobacco Trade and Tobacco Growers of Bahia in the Late Colonial Period." In *Essays Concerning the Socio-economic History of Brazil and Portuguese India*, ed. Dauril Alden and Warren Dean. Gainesville: 1977.

Magalhães Godinho, Vitorino, "Le Portugal, les flottes du sucre et les flottes de l'or 1670–1770." *Annales-Economies-Sociétés-Civilisations* 5, 2 (April–June, 1950).

Maxwell, Kenneth, "Pombal and the Nationalization of the Luso-Brazilian Economy." *HAHR* 47 (1968): 608–631.

Mota, Carlos Guilherme, "Mentalidade ilustrada na colonização portuguesa: Luís dos Santos Vilhena." *RHSP* 72 (1967): 405–416.

Novais, Fernando A., "A proibição das manufacturas no Brasil e a política econômica Portuguesa do fim do século XVIII." *RHSP* 67 (1967): 145–166.

"O Brasil nos quadros do antigo sistema colonial." In *Brasil em perspectiva*, ed. Carlos Guilherme Mota, 53–71. São Paulo: 1968.

"Considerações sobre o sentido da colonização." *Revista do Instituto de Estudos Brasileiros* 6 (1969): 55–65.

"Sistema colonial, industrialização e etapas do desenvolvimento." In *Comunicação ao encontro sobre história e desenvolvimento*, 55–65. São Paulo: 1969.

"Notas para o estudo do Brasil no comércio internacional do fim do século XVIII e início do século XIX (1796–1808)." In *Colóquio internacional de história quantitativa do Brasil*. Paris: 1971.

"As dimensões da independência." In *1822: Dimensões*, ed. Carlos Guilherme Mota, 15–26. São Paulo: 1972.

"Colonização e sistema colonial: discussão de conceitos e perspectiva histórica." In *Anais do IV simpósio nacional dos professôres universitários de história*, 243–268. São Paulo: 1973.

Nunes Dias, Manuel, "A junta liquidatária dos fundos das Companhias do Grão-Pará e Maranhão, Pernambuco e Paraíba (1778–1837)." *Revista Portuguesa da História* 10 (1962): 156–161.

"As frotas do cacao da amazônia 1756–1773: subsídios para o estudo do fomento ultramarino português no século XVIII." *RHSP* (April/June 1963): 363–377.

"A tonelagem da frota da Companhia Geral do Grão-Pará e Maranhão." *RHSP* (January/March 1964).

"Fomento e mercantilismo: política econômica portuguesa na baixada Maranhense, 1755–1778." *V. colóquio internacional de estudos luso-brasileiros, Actas* II, 17–99. Coimbra: 1965.

"Fomento ultramarino e mercantilismo: a Companhia Geral do Grão Pará e Maranhão 1755–1778." *RHSP* 66 (April–June 1966).

"Política pombalina na colonização da Amazônia, 1755–1778." *Studia* 23 (April 1968).

Oliveira, Aurélio de, "A renda agrícola em Portugal durante o antigo regime." *RHES*
(July–December 1980): 1–56.

Pantaleão, Olga, "A penetração comercial da Inglaterra na América espanhola, 1715–1783."
Boletín LXII da Faculdade de Filosofia, Ciências e Letras da Universidade de São Paulo. São
Paulo: 1946.

"Aspectos do comércio dos domínios portugueses no período de 1808 a 1821." *RHSP* 41
(March 1960): 91–104.

Pedrosa, Manoel Xavier de Vasconcellos, "Estudantes brasileiros na faculdade de medicina de
Montpellier no fim do século XVIII." *RIHGB* 243 (1959): 35–71.

Queirós Mattoso, Katia M., "Epidemias e flutuações na Bahia no século XIX." In *Colóquio
internacional de história quantitativa do Brasil.* Paris: 1971.

"Os preços na Bahia de 1750 a 1930." In *Colóquio internacional de história quantitativa do
Brasil.* Paris: 1971.

Rodrigues, Manuel Augusto, "A Faculdade de Teologia da Universidade de Coimbra e a
reforma pombalina," *Brotéria* 114 (5–6) (May/June 1982): 553–571.

Silva Dias, José Sebastião da, "Portugal e a cultura européia sec. XVI a XVIII." *Biblio* 28
(1953).

"Pombalismo e teoria política." *Cultura, História, e Filosofia* 1 (1982): 45–114; 2 (1983):
134–185; 3 (1984): 22–151.

Silva Dias, Maria Odila da, "Aspectos da ilustração no Brasil." *RIHGB* 278 (1968): 105–170.

Smith, Robert C., "The Colonial Architecture of Minas Gerais." *The Art Bulletin* 21 (1939).

Vicente, António Pedro Pires, "Memórias políticas, geográficas, e militares de Portugal,
1762–1796." *Boletim do Arquivo Histórico Militar* 41 (1971).

Wheeler, G. G., "The Political Discourse Attributed to Pombal." *EHR* 19 (1904).

Willemse, David, "António Ribeiro Sanches, élève de Boerhaave, et son importance pour la
Russie." *Janus: Revue internationale de l'histoire des sciences, de la médecine, de la pharmacie, et
de la technique* VI. Leiden: 1966.

Unpublished theses

Beal, Tarcísio, "Os jesuítas, a Universidade de Coimbra e a igreja brasileira: subsídios para a
história do regalismo em Portugal e no Brasil, 1750–1850." Ph.D. dissertation, The
Catholic University of America: 1969.

Davidson, David M., "Rivers and Empire: The Madeira Route and the Incorporation of
the Brazilian Far West 1737–1808." Ph.D. dissertation, Yale University: 1970.

Glossary

aldeia	mission village: usually, in the context of this book, an Amerindian mission settlement supervised by the Jesuits
alfândega	customs house
alqueire	a measure of capacity, equivalent to 36.27 litres in Rio while it equalled 13.80 in Lisbon
alvará	royal decree
arroba	a measure of weight equal to 32 lb. or 14.75 kg.
cachaça	sugar-cane brandy
caixa	(i) treasurer; (ii) box
capitão-mor	in this period most often the commandant of a company of second-line militia
capitania	captaincy, territory, an administrative unit
casa de fundição	smeltery, foundry-house
casa de inspeção	inspection board to oversee production and export of colonial staples, especially sugar and tobacco
Casa de Suplicação	Supreme Court of Appeals
comarca	administrative unit, county
comissários volantes	itinerant traders
cruzado	Portuguese coin, worth 400 *réis*
data	mining claim, allotment
décima	general 10 percent tax on property without exemptions, originally raised by the Cortes in response to the emergency of the restoration of Portuguese independence from Spain; reimposed by Pombal following Portugal's involvement in Seven Years War
desembargador	judge, senior crown magistrate
derrama	poll tax
devassa	judicial inquiry
dízimos	church tithes
entradas	customs duties on merchandise, slaves, and livestock entering Minas Gerais
fazenda	(i) landed estate; (ii) treasury

garimpeiro	prospector for precious metal, usually, in the context of this book, a freelance diamond prospector
junta da fazenda	captaincy exchequer board
junta do comércio	board of trade, Lisbon
maço	bundle
mestre do campo	colonel of infantry regiment
Minas Gerais	the General Mines, region of Brazil
mineiro	(i) miner; (ii) an inhabitant of Minas Gerais
Misericórdia, Santa Casa da	Holy House of Mercy, charitable lay brotherhood
morgado	entailed estate; heir to an entailed estate
ouvidor	crown judge, circuit judge, superior crown magistrate of a *comarca* (an administrative district)
pacote	package
pardo	colored man, most often mulatto
Paulista	an inhabitant of São Paulo
procurador	person with power of attorney
provedor	comptroller, superintendent of bureaucratic office
propinas	perquisites, emoluments
quinto	royal fifth
regimento	standing orders, instructions, rules and regulations
réis	money of account
relação	high court of appeals
sargento-mor	commissioned military officer
sesmaria	concession of land
senado da câmara	municipal council
senhor de engenho	owner of a sugar mill
várzea	floodplain of a river
vereador	municipal councillor
vizinho	resident householder in a community

Index